T0266452

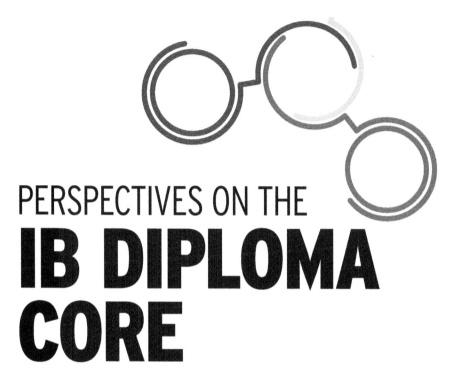

PERSPECTIVES ON THE
IB DIPLOMA CORE

EDITED BY

JUDITH FABIAN, MARY HAYDEN
AND JEFF THOMPSON

First Published 2019

by John Catt Educational Ltd,
15 Riduna Park, Station Road,
Melton, Woodbridge IP12 1QT

Tel: +44 (0) 1394 389850
Email: enquiries@johncatt.com
Website: www.johncatt.com

ISBN: 978 1 912 906 61 1

Set and designed by John Catt Educational Limited

Contents

Editorial preface

We were delighted to be invited to edit yet another book in the Taking Forward series published by John Catt Educational, not least because we have been privileged to have worked with so many experienced and talented authors, and because we have received such positive feedback from the many readers within the IB community (and beyond), together with the appreciation of the International Baccalaureate itself for the part that the books, and their authors, have played during periods of programme revision within the IB organisation. In a similar way this book is offered as a contribution to the ongoing review of the IB Diploma Programme (DP), concentrating on the conceptualisation, representation, function and realisation of a core and its separate elements within that programme. We are particularly grateful to Jenny Gillett, who currently holds the post of Senior Curriculum Manager, working in the IB's learning and teaching division, for providing a *Foreword* which sets the scene and identifies the issues which surround the DP core, and which are explored in the chapters to follow.

Origins of the core

Many readers may be surprised to learn that the notion of a 'core' was not part of the original conception of the DP and only came into being, as part of a curriculum model, some 15 years after the DP was created. Up to that point the DP 'core' was the name given to the combination of the three elements, Theory of Knowledge (TOK), Extended Essay and CAS (Creativity, Action, Service) on the basis that they were the compulsory and common elements in the programme; in fact, at the outset only the TOK and 'Service' were defined as essential aspects: the Extended Essay was a later compulsory feature for all students.

The origin of the core as a feature of the combination of TOK, Extended Essay and CAS, lies in the first attempt at the conceptualisation of the DP as a curriculum model. The former Deputy Director General of the IB, Dr Ian Hill, recorded the event in the April 2007 edition of the *International Schools Journal* (Hill, 2007). The relevant extract reads as follows:

> The Diploma Programme was first depicted as a hexagon by Professor Jeff Thompson, at the time chief examiner for chemistry and the physical sciences (*sic*). It occurred during a conference of the Fondazione Cine in Venice, 9-11 December 1983 where he spoke about the IB Diploma Programme and presented it on an overhead project transparency (Renaud 2001b). Jeff is well known for his propensity to visualise ideas. His geometrical shape corresponded to the six groups of subjects with the extended essay, theory of knowledge and CASS (creative and aesthetic activity, and social service), as it was at the time, in the middle. CASS became CAS (creativity, action, service) in 1989.

Renaud had been present at the meeting in Venice and liked the visual representation. In a paper on the Theory of Knowledge, Renaud (1986) refers to the way in which Thompson's schema showed the coherence of the IB programme through the hexagonal structure. Renaud saw the Theory of Knowledge as the centre piece. He then went on to say how better it would be if the figure became three-dimensional with the hexagon at the base of a pyramid and the Theory of Knowledge at the peak. The base and sides give volume to the pyramid in the same way that, from the disciplines at the base, the pyramid draws its volume culminating in the Theory of Knowledge at the summit. This interesting idea was never implemented.

Thompson used the hexagon again at a major IB conference at the University of London in 1988 (Hayden *et al*, 1995, pp 131-2). However, it was not until 1993 that the hexagonal representation of the Diploma Programme first appeared officially in IBO documents, notably in a number of subject guides printed that year.

Further exploration of the notion of a 'curriculum core' took place in the context of the research conducted in relation to the creation of a structural typology for baccalaureate–style curricula, developed as part of the establishment of a Welsh Baccalaureate. The analysis of the characteristics of baccalaureate curricula, arising from a wide range of systems, identified a 'core' to be "a compulsory element offering learners a common experience, in addition to optional or elective elements" (Thompson, Hayden and Cambridge, 2003). The model, depicted in Figure A, was adopted and used by the IB as its curriculum model, for over 25 years.

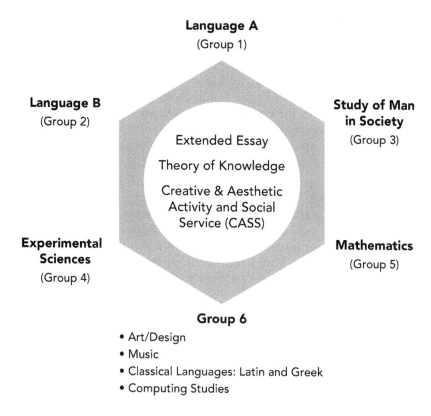

Language A
(Group 1)

Language B
(Group 2)

**Study of Man
in Society**
(Group 3)

Extended Essay

Theory of Knowledge

Creative & Aesthetic
Activity and Social
Service (CASS)

**Experimental
Sciences**
(Group 4)

Mathematics
(Group 5)

Group 6
- Art/Design
- Music
- Classical Languages: Latin and Greek
- Computing Studies

Figure A: The hexagon model of the IB Diploma curriculum (after Thompson, 1983)

The organisation of the book

In discussion with experienced colleagues familiar with the IBDP, as potential contributors to this book, it became clear that major interests in the topic of the core fell broadly into two areas. The first of these concerned the *nature of the core*, both as devised originally and as perceived as a result of reflection and evaluation of the core in relation to ideas and theories produced in the broad educational sphere, during which the DP has itself developed as a response to demand and diversity of opinion. Thus in Part A: The Nature of the Core, the authors raise issues relating to the nature of truth and scepticism, the links between philosophy and TOK, experiential learning and CAS, and the challenges in assessing the learning that is intended through TOK. Wider issues are explored including the potential cohesive power of the core within the curriculum overall, the role of the core in contributing to a more peaceful world, and suggestions are also included for the ways in which the IB itself can move forward in developing the core to meet future needs and challenges.

In Part B: The Core in Practice, aspects relating directly to the teaching and learning within TOK, Extended Essay and CAS, are addressed. They include the promotion of lifelong learning and an alternative approach to independent learning, both in TOK, the ways in which the Extended Essay could be further extended and the role of the school librarian in supporting it, the choice of a CAS project and the process of reflection upon the outcomes, and connecting the CAS experience with the six DP subjects. Questions concerning the core as a whole – developing students as internationally minded thinkers, bringing coherence to the core and developing an holistic approach to the curriculum through team work – round off this part of the book.

We wish to express our thanks to all those who have been involved in the production of this book. To those who have written chapters, thereby sharing the academic and professional knowledge arising from their experience, we offer our gratitude. We are certain that their contributions will be appreciated by those teachers, coordinators and researchers involved in the DP core. To our colleagues in John Catt Educational we extend our thanks for their support throughout yet another publication in which we, as Editors, are pleased to have been involved.

Judith Fabian

Mary Hayden

Jeff Thompson

References

Thompson J J, Hayden M C and Cambridge J (2003) 'Towards a Structural Typology for Baccalaureate-style Curricula in Post-16 Education Systems', in *The Baccalaureate: A Model for Curriculum Reform*, Phillips G and Pound T (eds), Kogan Page, London.

Hill I (2007) 'Early Stirrings in International Education Part XII: Marketing the IB Diploma Programme to Ministries of Education', *International Schools Journal*, 26 (2), 76-85.

About the contributors

Edward Allanson studied at the Universities of Oxford, St Andrews, and Birmingham. He is currently Head of Faculty of Humanities and Religious Studies, and TOK Coordinator, at Stonyhurst College in Lancashire, UK. He started his career working in various educational charities, after which he took his first teaching post in 2007. He lives in the beautiful Ribble Valley in the UK, with his wife, Mags, and their two children, Sophie and Benjamin.

Tom Brodie has been an international educator for 16 years. He has taught in schools throughout Europe in Switzerland, Norway, Czechia and the UK. His roles have included IBDP Coordinator, Head of Department and CAS Coordinator – but always classroom teacher. He is a member of the IB Educator Network involved in running and developing workshops, promoting good practice. He is currently Head of Humanities at St. George's International School, Montreux, Switzerland. When he is not teaching he can be found climbing mountains or spending time with his family or both!

John Cannings started his teaching career in Australia and then moved to the UK, teaching in national schools before engaging with IB programmes in Switzerland. He worked at the Inter-Community School in Zurich and Institut Montana as a Geography and TOK teacher, and served as Diploma, CAS, TOK and Extended Essay coordinator. Since 2001 he has been for the IB an examiner, and workshop leader (online and face to face) for CAS, Development of the Core and Geography. He also served on curriculum reviews for CAS and co-authored books on CAS and Geography, as well as having articles and blogs published on a number of topics.

Christian Chiarenza was born in Vancouver, Canada; he has been an IB educator since 1999, working in IB World Schools on four continents. Following his studies in Philosophy at the University of British Columbia and York University, he has focused on understanding how best to use the DP core to improve student performance. Christian has worked for the IB as workshop leader in programme coordination, TOK, and Approaches to Teaching and Learning, and contributed to curriculum development in TOK. Through consultancy and workshops Christian now works with IB schools to strengthen their programmes. He is currently working in Barcelona, Spain.

Mary Donnellan is the IB Diploma Coordinator at Copenhagen International School, having previously worked in schools in the Seychelles, the UK, Poland and Denmark. She has experience in leading workshops on DP Coordination and on the Extended Essay; she is also an IB school visitor and consultant, and is a member of the current IB Diploma Extended Essay curriculum review team.

Judith Fabian taught English and Drama in secondary schools in London for 10 years, followed by 15 years as department head and principal in international schools in Jordan, Tanzania and Germany. She joined the IB in 2004 and was appointed Chief Academic Officer in 2007, leading the development of IB curriculum for students aged 3 to 19 years. Judith left the IB in 2014 to work as an educational consultant, editor and author, and is currently a non-executive director for Estyn, the inspectorate for schools in Wales, and a lay member of the Council of Cardiff University.

Jenny Gillett has worked for the IB at their global centre in The Hague for the past eight years, where she currently holds the post of Senior Curriculum Manager. Working in the IB's learning and teaching division, she oversees the development of the DP Theory of Knowledge and Philosophy courses, and leads on elements such as approaches to teaching and learning in the DP. Before joining the IB, Jenny worked as a teacher for seven years at schools in the UK. She has a degree in philosophy and theology from Oxford University and a PhD in philosophy.

Mary Hayden is Professor of International Education at the University of Bath. Her research interests relate to international schools and international education, areas in which she has published widely in research journals and books as well as supervising Masters and Doctoral students and leading a number of major research projects. She is Editor-in-Chief of the Journal of Research in International Education, a founding Trustee of the Alliance for International Education and a member of the advisory boards for a number of international education projects.

Robin Julian is IB curriculum manager for the DP Extended Essay and school-based syllabuses. He came to the IB with considerable experience at school level, having been an IB Coordinator, and he also coordinated the Extended Essay, TOK and CAS. As a DP teacher, he taught TOK and Social and Cultural Anthropology, being a member of that subject's IB curriculum review team. He has been an IB examiner and a content developer for face-to-face and online professional development. He has masters' degrees in Applied Anthropology and Asian Studies, and a degree in education.

Julian Kitching has more than 30 years of experience in IB schools as a teacher and member of senior management. He is currently Director of Studies at the SOS-Hermann Gmeiner International College in Ghana. He has taught the Theory of Knowledge course since 1990, and has been an examiner since 1996, holding the position of TOK Chief Assessor from 2010 to 2018. These commitments have been augmented through involvement in the last four IB curriculum reviews of the TOK course and by experiences as a TOK workshop leader.

Justin Laleh completed his studies (BA, MA, PhD) in Continental Philosophy at the University of Warwick, studying for a year in Freiburg as a DAAD Junior Scholar award holder. He is currently Head of Academic Extension and Departmental Head of Politics and Sociology at Ardingly College, UK where he teaches Philosophy and Politics as well as running the TOK and EE programmes.

Ann Lautrette has taught in IB schools since 2005 and was DP Coordinator at The British School Jakarta before moving to Switzerland to become DP Coordinator at Inter-Community School Zurich. Her IB roles include being a face-to-face regional and in-school workshop leader for DP English A and TOK, a DP consultant and school visits team leader. She is an examiner for English A Language and Literature.

James MacDonald is a long time IB educator, and has held various positions throughout his career, including Head of School at two different IB World schools in Asia: Yokohama International School and NIST International School, Bangkok. James is also the former chair of the IB Regional Council for Asia Pacific and more recently the Senior Vice President of Education for GEMS Education, overseeing multiple schools. He has a Master of Arts degree from the University of Bath and a Master of Business Administration from the University of British Columbia.

Shona McIntosh is a Lecturer in International Education at the University of Bath with research interests in the problems and potential of experience-based education, particularly within the context of the IB DP. She has been an educator for 25 years, in the UK and in Spain, teaching secondary school English and Drama and examining A-level in both subjects. Her interest in the learning process has been applied to research in a variety of contexts, including adult professional development and adolescents both in and out of classrooms.

Heather Michael is a teacher, DP Coordinator, researcher and IB Educator Network workshop leader from Citadel High School in Halifax, Nova Scotia, Canada. Her teaching and research interests include stories across spaces, meaningful reflection, student DP experiences, and equitable access to an IB education. Her doctorate, from Teachers College Columbia University, focused on the spatial lives and stories that adolescents tell and how they connect to school. In 2016, she received the IB Jeff Thompson Research Award and recently completed a two-year study on how DP students in North America made sense of the DP core.

Paul Regan was founding Headteacher of two IB schools in Bosnia (United World College, Mostar) and India (Oaktree International School, Kolkata), and has also worked as a Headteacher in the UK, Kenya, and the Ukraine. His primary expertise and interest lies in the application of the IB programme, in particular, and international education in general, to building peace and reconciliation in conflict and post-conflict regions and communities. After graduating in Russian, he taught Modern Languages and History, and later TOK. More recently, his interest in TOK has led him into research into the philosophical traditions of scepticism and epistemology.

John Royce started out as a teacher, but in his first school was pushed (extremely reluctantly!) into taking on the school library. He has never regretted that enforced change of career direction, and has gone on to obtain library qualifications. As a school librarian, he regards himself as a teacher – a teacher without a timetable. He has taught in Zambia, England, Malawi, Germany and Turkey, and has 16 years' experience in IB schools. Since 2004 he has led IB workshops, face-to-face and online, on the Extended Essay, academic writing, academic honesty and workshops for librarians, as well as developing and writing.

John Sprague is TOK Coordinator at Tanglin Trust School Singapore, where he also teaches philosophy. He is on the IB Theory of Knowledge Senior Examining team, and is the author of *TOK: Skills for Success* published by Hodder Education. He began teaching TOK and IB Philosophy in 2000 at King's College School, Wimbledon, UK, and subsequently became Director of IB at Sevenoaks School, UK. He was Lead Editor of IB Review, an IB Student magazine.

Jeff Thompson is Emeritus Professor of Education at the University of Bath, with particular teaching and research interests in the fields of international education and international schools; he teaches and supervises postgraduate students at Masters and Doctoral levels and has led many research projects. He has been involved with the IB since its earliest foundations in a number of senior roles, and continues to be a member of a wide range of advisory boards and governance bodies; he has published many articles and books arising from his extensive experience in the field.

George Walker studied Chemistry at Oxford University and Music at the University of Cape Town. The first part of his career was devoted to science education; the middle part to the leadership of state secondary schools in the UK; and the final part to international education when he became Director General of the International School of Geneva and subsequently of the IB. He was Visiting Professor at the University of Bath, which awarded him the honorary degree of Doctor of Education. He has written extensively on international education and lectured in most parts of the globe.

Glossary of terms

Advanced Placement (AP) – a programme in the US created by the College Board which offers college-level curricula and examinations to high school students.

A Levels – taken in England, Wales and Northern Ireland, and also worldwide, the Advanced Level is a qualification in a specific subject, typically taken by school students aged 16–18, at a level above GCSE. A Levels can lead to university, further study, training, or work.

Areas of Knowledge (AOKs) – the different academic disciplines in which knowledge is constructed in a variety of ways. The Theory of Knowledge course distinguishes between eight AOKs: Mathematics; Natural Sciences; Human Sciences; History; The Arts; Ethics; Religious Knowledge Systems; Indigenous Knowledge Systems.

CE and BCE – Common Era or Current Era (CE) is one of the notation systems for the world's most widely used calendar era. BCE (Before the Common Era or Before the Current Era) is the era before CE. BCE and CE are alternatives to the Dionysian BC and AD system respectively.

Creativity, Activity, Service (CAS) – one of three components of the IB Diploma Programme core. Studied throughout the Diploma Programme, CAS involves students in a range of activities alongside their academic studies. CAS is mandatory for all DP students; it is not formally assessed.

Extended Essay – one of three components of the IB Diploma Programme core. An independent, self-directed piece of research, finishing with a 4,000-word paper. The Extended Essay is mandatory for all DP students.

GCSE – General Certificate of Secondary Education, a standard qualification in England, Wales and Northern Ireland, in a specific subject, typically taken by school students aged 14–16, at a level below A Level.

Higher Level and Standard Level (HL and SL) Diploma Programme courses – two different levels of courses taken in the IB's Diploma Programme. To achieve the Diploma, students must take typically three subjects at Higher Level, and three subjects at Standard Level. The levels are differentiated by the level of content in the courses.

IGCSE – International General Certificate of Secondary Education, a British qualification offered to schools globally in a specific subject, typically taken by school students aged 14–16, at a level below A Level.

IB Diploma Programme Core (DP Core) – The International Baccalaureate Diploma Programme (DP) is a two-year educational programme primarily aimed at 16 to 19 year olds. DP students complete assessments in six subjects, one from each subject group, and three core requirements – Theory of Knowledge (TOK), the Extended Essay, and Creativity, Activity, Service (CAS).

IB Diploma or Diploma – the terms sometimes used to describe the IB Diploma Programme as a whole, as in 'students' experience of the Diploma may vary' or '…once they achieve their Diploma'.

IB Educators' Network (IBEN) – IBEN brings together IB trained educators who implement the IB's professional development and school services. It consists of a diverse and active community of educators to ensure high quality in IB World Schools.

IB Examination Sessions (May and November) – a major part of the assessment system for the IB Diploma Programme are examinations marked by the IB. These examinations are held annually in two sessions: typically in May for Northern hemisphere schools, and in November for Southern hemisphere schools.

IB Heads' Council – this council is part of the governance structure of the IB and serves as an advisory group to the Director General. It assists with issues that affect IB World Schools. It consists of 12 members elected by IB World School heads, with four members from each IB global region.

IB Learner Profile – a list of ten attributes of lifelong learners: inquiring, knowledgeable, thinkers, communicators, principled, open-minded, caring, risk-takers, balanced and reflective. It embodies the IB's mission statement and is at the heart of all IB programmes.

IB Programme Resource Centre – an IB managed online resource centre for schools and teachers, for the search and navigation for IB programme materials.

IB World School – the title given to a school that is officially authorised by the IB to offer at least one IB programme.

Knowledge Framework – in the Theory of Knowledge course, a knowledge framework is a way of analysing the Areas of Knowledge and provides a vocabulary for comparing AOKs.

Knowledge Questions – in the Theory of Knowledge course knowledge questions are questions about knowledge. Instead of focusing on specific content, they focus on how knowledge is constructed and evaluated. Knowledge questions are open in the sense that there are a number of plausible answers to them.

Theory of Knowledge (TOK) – one of three components of the IB Diploma Programme core. It asks students to reflect on the nature of knowledge, and on how we know what we claim to know. TOK is mandatory for all students and is assessed through an oral presentation and a 1,600 word essay.

UNESCO – The United Nations Educational, Scientific and Cultural Organisation is a specialised agency of the United Nations based in Paris. Its declared purpose is to contribute to peace and security by promoting international collaboration through educational, scientific, and cultural reforms in order to increase universal respect for justice, the rule of law and human rights, along with the fundamental freedoms proclaimed in the United Nations Charter.

United World Colleges (UWC) – a global educational movement with the mission to "make education a force to unite people, nations and cultures for peace and a sustainable future". UWC consists of 18 schools and colleges on four continents.

Ways of Knowing (WOKs) – the Theory of Knowledge course identifies eight specific ways of knowing: language; sense perception; emotion; reason; imagination; faith; intuition; memory.

Foreword

Jenny Gillett

"It is a sin of the soul to force young people into opinions ... but it is culpable neglect not to impel young people into experiences."

(Kurt Hahn)

The IB has an explicitly and unashamedly values-driven mission to create a better and more peaceful world through education. While the terminology and emphasis used to articulate and discuss this mission may have changed over the last 50 years, the underlying commitment at its heart has not.

The power and distinctiveness of an IB education is often seen particularly clearly when talking to IB Diploma Programme (DP) students, alumni, and educators about their experiences with the three elements of the DP core: the Extended Essay (EE), Creativity, Activity, Service (CAS), and Theory of Knowledge (TOK). For many students, the core is a source of experiences and encounters that shape them and stay with them long beyond their graduation from the programme. For many educators, the core stands out as one of the most special and unique aspects of the DP, and is one of the key features they identify as helping to ensure that the DP is a holistic programme rather than simply a collection of elements.

The transformative potential of the DP core lies in the opportunities it creates for stimulating experiences and thoughtful self-reflection. Clearly the core does not have a monopoly on these kinds of opportunities. But the three core elements do provide a hugely rich ground for this kind of exploration and self-discovery. For example, the intention is that students will develop a richer and more nuanced understanding of themselves as knowers and thinkers through their TOK discussions, of themselves as researchers through their Extended Essays, and of the role they can play in their communities through CAS. In this way, the core makes a special contribution to the wider aim that "at the end of the IB experience, students should know themselves better than when they started" (Peel, 1988).

The development of the DP core

Each of the three elements of the DP core has its own interesting origin and history. The core elements also follow the same thorough and collaborative process of curriculum review as all other DP subjects, meaning that they continue to evolve and develop.

The Extended Essay

In the early days of the IB, the EE took the form of 'extended work', before becoming the Extended Essay. This extended, independent, research-based work began as a requirement within the literature course, was expanded to being a requirement for each of the student's three Higher Level (HL) subjects, and then in 1974 this requirement was reduced to just one single EE. This change was due in part to a recognition of the heavy workload that having three EEs was placing on students. It also reflected the fact that the primary aim of the task was to develop research skills and independent thought, which could be developed in any of the subjects.

The EE has remained a key feature of the DP experience ever since, with this focus on the value of the process becoming increasingly prominent. In 1991 a dedicated guide to the EE was created (previously advice had been given only within individual subject guides), which gave additional advice to coordinators and supervisors on how to support students through this experience. The task gives students an opportunity to experience the kind of independent, extended research and writing likely to be expected in post-secondary education, but with the added support and guidance of a dedicated supervisor. Providing additional guidance on the role of supervisor has been a key focus of recent curriculum review cycles, and reflects an increased emphasis on process as well as product. This can also be seen in the increased prominence of student reflection within the task, with the current iteration of the EE strongly recommending the use of a "researcher's reflection space" as a way to help students better articulate and understand their research and writing process.

In addition to the increased focus on process, the nature of the EE task itself has also continued to evolve. In 2005 the option to complete a World Studies Extended Essay was introduced as a pilot option, providing students with an opportunity to undertake an interdisciplinary essay focused on a global issue. This variation on the EE began as a proposal from the UWC (United World College) Mahindra College, India, and was then developed in close collaboration with the Harvard Graduate School of Education. It recognises the power of interdisciplinary thinking in helping to explore complex contemporary global issues such as migration, terrorism and climate change.

Creativity, Action, Service

One of the figures who most influenced the origins of CAS, particularly in terms of the commitment to community service, was the German educator Kurt Hahn. Hahn was one of 15 heads of school who attended a UNESCO organised meeting in 1949 for schools interested in developing their international outlook (Hill, 2010: 20). Having met Hahn at a conference, Alec Peterson worked with Atlantic College on its curriculum in the early 1960s, and then creative, physical and social service activities were included in the early DP curriculum guides from 1970. The inclusion of the service and physical activity elements in particular was strongly influenced by Hahn's thinking. Hahn (1965) was highly critical of the rise in what he called 'spectatoritis', and he believed that service and outdoor exploration could play a crucial role in deepening students' curiosity, compassion, and resilience.

The early variation 'CASS' (Creative and Aesthetic activity and Social Service) evolved into 'CAS' in 1989. In 2015 the name evolved again, from 'Creativity, Action, Service' to 'Creativity, Activity, Service'. This shift from action to activity was mainly made to address an inconsistency in how the term 'action' was being used across the IB, with action being seen as an integral part of all subjects and programmes rather than just a part of CAS. It was also intended as a nod to the earlier more prominent emphasis given to creative and physical activity as it was felt that, in some cases at least, service was becoming such a strong focus of many CAS programmes that the creativity and activity elements were being given relatively less value.

One particularly important development within CAS has been the increased emphasis placed on encouraging students to consider more carefully the ethical implications of their choices and actions. This focus on responsible and principled action is something that is being given greater prominence in all three elements of the DP core. It links particularly strongly with the descriptor of the attribute 'Principled' in the IB Learner Profile (IB, 2013), which refers to students developing a "strong sense of fairness, justice and respect for the dignity and the rights of people everywhere". Along with issues of power, ethics has been a dominant topic of discussion in the current curriculum reviews for both CAS and TOK.

Theory of Knowledge

TOK is intended to underpin and unite the subjects that students encounter in the rest of their DP studies. The course provides an opportunity for explicit and deliberate reflection on how knowledge is arrived at in different disciplines, what the disciplines have in common and the differences between them. Students are encouraged to become more aware of their own perspectives, to critically evaluate beliefs, and to question the evidence for claims.

The proposal for an early version of the TOK course was accepted in 1967, with the first full syllabus appearing in the 1970 IB general guide. The development of the TOK course reflects the bringing together of two interesting but slightly different original priorities. During the initial conversations about the development of the DP there had been a push to have some element of philosophy be made compulsory, as it was, for example, in the French system. At the same time, Alec Peterson was deeply influenced by debates in education about the role of "forms of knowledge" (Hirst, 2012) and "realms of meaning" (Phenix, 1964) as a foundation for curriculum, and strongly believed that having students reflect on topics such as the nature and methods of different disciplines would help them to make greater sense of their overall educational experience. Which of these factors was most influential in the original inclusion of the TOK course is not completely clear from the early IB documentation. However, the influence of both on the nature of the TOK course is clear to see.

The TOK course has evolved through different iterations, each with different curriculum emphases and assessment formats (including non-assessed TOK work, a TOK examination, portfolios, essays, and oral presentations). Through these different iterations and evolutions, the key focus of the course has continued to be on exploring the question of how we know, and on encouraging students to see why it is valuable to ask that question. It provides an opportunity for students to step back and reflect on their knowledge and experiences gained both inside and outside of the classroom, and to consider the nature, scope and limitations of human knowledge and the process of knowing. In feedback on the course materials, TOK was recently described by an external academic consultant as "a brilliant initiative with unparalleled potential". However, throughout the curriculum reviews for the different iterations of the course, a key tension has been how to help ensure that this rich potential is realised in practice.

The coherence of the core

In addition to the development of each of the three individual elements of the DP core, there has also been increasing emphasis placed on the relationship between the three elements. This discussion is not new; for example, in 1991 a committee of IB staff and chief examiners considered a proposal to combine the three elements of the core into a more coherent, single, overall assessed component. However, the coherence of the core became a particular focus from 2008-2012 as it was prioritised by the then Head of Curriculum Development for the DP core, Chris Mannix. He firmly believed that the IB's commitment to the principle of developing the whole person would be best supported if the three elements of the core worked together more explicitly.

This work on articulating the aims and value of the core as a whole, as opposed to the individual elements of the core, did not focus on trying to identify similarities between the three core elements or on trying to remove any of the unique features of each element. Instead, it focused on identifying and articulating common aims that underpin all three elements. This led to the development of text on the coherence of the core in 2012 that was then used in all three core subject guides. This text articulated the different elements of the core which are grounded in three common aims:

1. to support, and be supported by, the academic disciplines,

2. to foster international mindedness, and

3. to develop self-awareness and a sense of identity.

Challenges and opportunities

All three elements of the DP core are currently under review, with the new iteration of the TOK course due to launch in 2020 and the new iterations of CAS and the EE due to launch in 2023. The curriculum review discussions frequently highlight the potential of the core and the special regard in which it is held by so many. However, they also highlight some significant challenges, particularly relating to the practical implementation of the core elements.

In the chapters of this book, many different opportunities and challenges for the DP core are explored and discussed. However, at this point I would like to share four provocations for the reader to consider.

1. Many DP students today do not complete the whole Diploma, but instead opt to complete just a small number of individual DP courses. This means that a significant number of students taking DP courses do not engage with the core at all. How should the changing percentage of full Diploma candidates impact on the future development of the DP core?

2. The question of 'points'. An ongoing area of discussion and divergence within the DP community relates to the points allocated to the core elements. Currently a student's grades for their EE and TOK are combined together in a matrix that generates a maximum of 3 points towards the 45-point maximum for the Diploma. Some would like to see the value given to the core reflected in increased points; for example, suggesting that the core elements should be worth the same as a Standard Level (SL) or Higher Level (HL) subject. However, there are also those who believe that the core should not be about points at all, and who would like to see the core not count towards the points total for the Diploma. Is part of the purpose of the core to highlight that not everything is about points?

3. The implementation of the three elements of the DP Core in schools highlights huge variation in the levels of engagement and enthusiasm from students, parents and teachers. In some cases the core is seen as peripheral or as an unnecessary additional burden on busy DP students, as opposed to being seen as the heart of the programme. How can the value of the core be more clearly and convincingly articulated to students, parents and educators?

4. Service learning. In recent iterations of the CAS guide there has been a move towards a more explicit emphasis on service learning and on students building on their prior knowledge and experiences to help them make links between their academic disciplines and their student experiences. While many DP educators have welcomed this shift, others see it as part of an 'over-intellectualisation' of CAS that contributes to a loss of some of the joy and freedom of the core. What should be the role and status of service learning in future iterations of the DP?

Conclusion

In conversations about the DP core, teachers and alumni frequently make reference to the 'spirit' of the core. By this, they are often referring to the more intangible, dispositional aspects of the core such as the way that it can help foster curiosity and open-mindedness, or the impact on students of collaborative shared experiences. These conversations highlight that the core is most powerful when it moves away from a focus on tasks and requirements. When CAS experiences turn into hours to be completed, or TOK discussions focus solely on preparing for the assessment tasks, some of the most special and valuable aspects of the core are lost. It is understandable that within the busy and demanding schedules of DP students and teachers the focus can shift to these practical concerns. But the more inspirational dimension of the core does not have to be in conflict with the practicalities of its implementation. Shifting from a language of tasks and requirements to a language of aspirations and impact can help enthuse and excite students about the opportunities that the core presents them. In words attributed to Antoine de St. Exupery (1948), "If you want to build a ship, don't drum up the men to gather wood, divide the work and give orders. Instead, teach them to yearn for the vast and endless sea."

References

Hahn K (1965) *Outward Bound*. Address at the Outward Bound Conference in Harrogate, 9th May 1965.

Hill I (2010) *The International Baccalaureate: pioneering in education*. Woodbridge: John Catt Educational.

Hirst P [1974] (2012) *Knowledge and the Curriculum*. London: Routledge.

International Baccalaureate (1970) *General Guide to the International Baccalaureate*. Geneva: International Baccalaureate.

International Baccalaureate (2013) *IB Learner Profile*. The Hague: International Baccalaureate.

Peel R (1988) *Report of the Director General*, Roger Peel, to the IB Council of Foundation.

Phenix P (1964) *Realms of Meaning*. New York: McGraw Hill.

St Exupery A (1948) www.quotationspage.com/quotes/Antoine_de_Saint-Exupery

Part A

The Nature of the Core

Chapter 1

TOK, Scepticism, and the Free Speech Deficit

Paul Regan

Introduction

In October 2018 a woman was released in Pakistan after eight years on Death Row. Her alleged crime was not, as might be expected, murder, treason or arson, but blasphemy against the Prophet Mohammed. In Pakistan it is still a capital offence to defame the Prophet and this harsh law not only has wide mass support, but is unlikely to be repealed anytime soon. It is noteworthy that the accused was cleared by the Court, not because the punishment was deemed wrong, but because of insufficient evidence to convict.

It is useful for those of us fortunate not to be living under such repressive laws, to recollect that in many places in Europe, it was equally likely up until the eighteenth century CE for a blasphemer – or heretic likewise – to be execcuted or punished severely. To give just two examples: the Spanish Inquisition was not abolished until 1834 in the reign of Isabella II (1834–1868); and during the reign of Elizabeth I of England (1558–1603), to be a practising Catholic was to be a traitor and would have carried the death penalty. The gulf separating that time from our own period seems huge, but it is worthwhile to reflect how much intellectual courage and clarity were expended by outstanding individuals, such as the 'Father of Liberalism', John Locke, in England (1632–1704) and Voltaire in France (1694–1778). They asserted fresh ideas in relation to free speech, freedom of worship and separation of Church and State, which eventually helped to overturn the centuries of religious repression.

Does TOK live up to its expectations?

What connection has any of the above to the teaching of the IB TOK (Theory of Knowledge) course? Quite a lot, in fact. The core objectives of the TOK *inter alia*, relate specifically to the idea that there are 'many different ways of thinking, and perspectives and assumptions we have because of our cultural and individual positions may obscure the way we see the world' (Theory of Knowledge, 2018). This objective is not, as it first seems, a relativist perspective. Rather, it implies that by being aware of our own limitations, we can thereby broaden our intellectual horizon and bravely defend it. Simultaneously, we can subject other beliefs and opinions to a positive but critical analysis and challenge them, not in order to score points, but to seek new knowledge and, where possible, agreement and compromise.

The epistemological and ethical bases of TOK can be traced in a line directly back to those philosophers of classical Greece, most notably Socrates (470–399 BCE), Plato (427–348 BCE), and Aristotle (384–322 BCE) who most famously posed questions about the limits of knowledge and truth, human freedom and our relationship to the State and to the Divine. Submerged for almost 2000 years, those same questions were asked again by philosophers such as Voltaire and Locke, *inter alios*, and their persistent scepticism helped over time to transform our socio-political landscape. But is that landscape about to change again, and are we returning to a time when those freedoms are regarded with suspicion?

Is it realistic to expect that the TOK course of the IB Diploma Programme (DP) can really live up to its objectives and equip IB students to meet prejudice with understanding, fallacy with validity and emotion with reason? Does it really provide them with an edge in argument, and an ability to spot falsehood and mistaken logic? Can it help them become better-informed citizens, more enlightened moral agents and more effective thinkers? Can they become like Locke and Voltaire? Can TOK students even rescue public discourse from its current descent into outrage and umbrage and bring it back to decency and compromise? Doesn't it all seem rather too ambitious?

Given that the TOK course, with its ways of knowing, areas of knowledge, and knowledge questions, confronts students with practical challenges in critical thinking and the rights and responsibilities of the 'knower', then the answer should be 'maybe'. Given also that the students receive a practical guide to logic, formal and informal reasoning and ethics, along with a mental toolbox to construct and recognize valid and true arguments, then the answer to all of the above questions should be 'yes'. Or is it assuming too much to expect that, in this new age of creeping intolerance and Twittersphere mob censure, the average IB student will be able to deploy what has been learnt in TOK lessons, let alone use it, or even be brave or confident enough to do so?

The assault on our freedoms

In many parts of the world, not least in the West, not only is the right to freedom of speech being eroded little by little, but also our traditional methods of debate are being forgotten. The Socratic idea of debate and dialogue (*elenchus*) revealed in such beautiful detail in Plato's 'Symposium,' seems a long way removed from the instant judgments of Twitter and other online forums. The formal rules of that ideal, where two or more persons enter into a discussion and question each other in order mutually to reach a new level of truth, have always been difficult to achieve since they require a genuine desire to learn rather than to preach.

Increasingly, however, across whole areas of public life, informal rules of engagement appear to have been completely set aside. In parliaments and the media, cherished institutions and universities, a relatively new phenomenon in public discourse is anger masquerading as virtue. To care more and to feel more has become more important than to think more. Humbug and hypocrisy are driving a twin assault on the freedom to disagree and the readiness to listen and reason. We have become simultaneously loud and deaf.

Intolerance and iconoclasm are recurring themes in human history. Most societies, if they survive long enough, at some time or another undergo drastic and dynamic periods of transformation, where values, certainties, cultural norms, attitudes, and allegiances are submitted to rigorous analysis, idols are torn down, and purges, violent or otherwise, are authorised. As one world view yields inexorably to another, a new priesthood establishes itself and creates its own symbols for control and oppression.

A sophisticated and stable political entity may survive and prosper anew, assimilating the new gods within its own pantheon, whilst another will eventually collapse from within. Ancient Egypt self-regenerated several times over 3 millennia BCE, but Imperial Rome died a slow death, unable to reconcile its ancient institutions with the harsh economic and demographic realities of the third and fourth centuries CE. At such times, the individual, not sure what to believe, or what he is allowed to believe, can become disorientated. And new rulers may impose new truths to which the individual may either submit or face ruin.

Change in itself is, of course, not intrinsically a bad thing and can be of great benefit. We normally speak of the Copernican revolution and the Renaissance in the fifteenth and sixteenth centuries CE and the European Enlightenment in the eighteenth century CE as ushering in an age of scientific and social progress. Together, they brought about a continent-wide intellectual liberation from the dead hand of religious orthodoxy and scientific mumbo jumbo. They overturned a 2000-year moratorium on free thinking, and replaced the rigid certainties of priests and kings with the right to discover new truths.

The struggle for freedom

In 1600, the Italian Dominican friar Giordano Bruno was burned at the stake by the church in Rome for, amongst other things, asserting that the stars were distant suns, a heresy at the time. A mere one hundred years later, no reasonably educated person in Rome or anywhere else in Europe would have disagreed with him.

The struggle for the right to be sceptical, however, has not really been won and probably never will be. Sceptics are regarded with suspicion in every age and periodically will come under fresh onslaught. The nineteenth century British political philosopher and social reformer John Stuart Mill (1806-1873) wrote of the 'tyranny of the majority', which he thought to be more dangerous to freedoms than the tyranny of government. Referring to the tendency of the powerful to silence the individual he wrote:

First, if any opinion is compelled to silence, that opinion may, for aught we can certainly know, be true. To deny this is to assume our own infallibility. Secondly, though the silenced opinion be an error, it may, and very commonly does, contain a portion of truth. (Mill, 1859)

The Russian writer, Yevgeny Zamyatin (1884–1937), wrote that "the world is kept alive only by heretics: the heretic Christ, the heretic Copernicus, the heretic Tolstoy. Our symbol of faith is heresy" (Zamyatin,1919). He wrote this just as the hopes of the 1917 Bolshevik revolution in Russia were almost overnight being replaced by the dystopia of secret police, rigid adherence to the tenets of Marxist-Leninism and terror.

Barely any society, at some point in its history, can escape the accusation of using some form of oppression in order to subdue the individual using the invented truths, however innocuous of a powerful minority. For example, for Adam Smith, 18th century author of the '*Wealth of Nations*', it was the invisible hand of capitalism, for Stalin, despotic ruler of the Soviet Union, it was the dictatorship of the proletariat. However, history has also revealed the surprising truth that, repeatedly, individuals can overthrow the power of the collective and challenge the majority view. For this reason they are nearly always persecuted. The names of Gandhi, Bruno, Martin Luther King, and Socrates, martyred in different ways, still live on when their persecutors have long been forgotten, and the truths which they asserted have become accepted wisdom.

The generic challenges to the integrity of the sovereign, rational individual are uncannily similar across ages and continents. At what point, short of physical violence and terror, does it become impossible to remain sceptical and open minded in the public domain? And does it matter anyway if our freedom to express our thoughts is curtailed as long as we can hold them in private? I will leave aside the future possibility that even our private thoughts can be controlled and manipulated.

What is free speech?

There is of course no such thing as absolute free speech. Laws exist universally to protect citizens from hate speech or incitement to violence although some free speech fundamentalists and libertarians would disagree even with that restriction. For them, any prohibition on what it is permissible to write and say diminishes our ability to debate in the open, to refute through evidence and dialectic argument. Any restriction renders us less able to destroy dangerous views by exposing them, while keeping them out of sight and concealing them risks sending them underground. Exponents of this view include Professor of Philosophy, Keith Parsons, of the University of Human Sciences and Humanities, USA who wrote:

There can be no free speech if it is required that the speech not offend anyone. There can be no free speech if only certain viewpoints or ideologies are permitted. There can be no free speech if certain topics are sacrosanct and not allowed to be touched (Parsons, 2017).

A more moderate approach is to agree that laws forbidding incitement to violence and hatred should be obeyed, but that everything else should be open to challenge, not by vilification and abuse but by reason. According to this view, giving offence through humour and ridicule should be allowed since offence is too subjective a concept to be policed. Open debate is to be welcomed but rules of engagement should be agreed beforehand.

But, increasingly, in the age of identity politics, we are witnessing a much more narrow interpretation of what is permitted to be expressed. From this perspective, any view that is contrary to some previously defined notion of what is right, or which gives offence or is likely to give offence may also be forbidden and its advocates ostracised. To guarantee conformity and acceptance, new language rules must be learnt and care taken not to upset or violate individual or group identities or sensibilities. Opinions that are deemed to go against these norms will be attacked not only as wrong but also as bad or evil. By implication, the people who express them are also bad or evil. *Ad hominem* and *ad populum* arguments rule since it becomes sufficient to attack the person to kill the argument or to appeal to a vociferous but not necessarily representative minority.

Some universities in both the UK and the USA are currently witnessing attacks on the basic academic freedom to assert new interpretations based on research and evidence. In some social science departments especially, a postmodernist orthodoxy has taken hold which foists upon its students a Manichean view of the world where good and evil can be newly attributed to historical events that may run counter to the known facts. Oxford Regius Professor of Moral and Pastoral Theology, Dr Nigel Biggar, was branded a 'bigot' by students and attacked by colleagues for an article in November 2018 in which he described the history of the British Empire as "morally mixed". Following the article, over 50 Oxford professors, lecturers and researchers signed an open letter expressing their "firm rejection" of his views (*The Telegraph*, 2018).

There is of course nothing new in this. It is a myth that universities have previously been liberal and open whereas now they are not. You would not have to go far back in time in either the UK or the USA to find academics vilified for blasphemy, heresy or championing of homosexual freedoms. These days there are new heresies and ideas you would be foolish to champion if you value your tenure, or, like Professor Biggar, your reputation. *Plus ça change.*

But it is ironic that this is happening at all in the very places where the law requires that particular attention be given to the promotion of freedom of speech. In the UK for example, Section 43 of the Education (No 2) Act 1986 imposes an obligation on university governing bodies to take reasonably practicable steps to ensure that freedom of speech within the law is secured, both on university and student union premises.

However, according to the *Spiked-Online* review of university freedoms, only 6% of British universities are completely free whilst 23% have safe space policies and 37% have no platforming policies. Moreover, 48% now publish censorious religion policies and 46% publish censorious transgender policies (Spiked-Online, 2018).

According to the British writer and philosopher, Roger Scruton, we may be on a slippery slope. He said:

> The Academy has been invaded by a new way of – a new form of study. It used to be the case that at universities – you were teaching a recognized subject with a recognized curriculum and you were carrying out research or scholarship in the humanities, which was open-minded guided by the pursuit of truth and not dismayed particularly if it came to surprising or unorthodox conclusions. Now, one of the first things that happens when a Totalitarian government takes over is that the universities are cleaned up. That is to say, people who are doing that kind of thing get thrown out. This is what happened when the Nazis took over the German universities and when the Soviets took over – and the Communists took over the Russian universities (Scruton, 2017).

A picture is emerging of dogmatism and orthodoxy both in revisions of the past and in ownership of the future. As every TOK student knows, it is a fallacy to over interpret past events in the light of current trends, and also to insert out present morality into our judgments of the past. It is one thing to be a holocaust denier. But can someone challenge the science of climate change without being labelled as a climate change denier? Is it beyond acceptable to posit a different explanation for human evolution without being an evolution denier?

In social policy, to accept gay marriage and the new laws regarding the rights of transgender people as legally correct is one thing, but can one not also challenge the underlying assumptions without being labelled 'phobic'. Can we criticise certain religions or even be allowed to be wrong about them? Few would doubt that the rapid change in social attitudes to race, religion, diversity, and gender are well intended and are having major benefits to those who might have suffered persecution in the past. But one form of persecution should not be replaced with another. Diversity cannot include everything and everybody except those who disagree.

Many universities have willingly subscribed to the contagion of writing policies on issues which have little connection with their core business of seeking knowledge. Most recently, policies on transgender rights have become popular since this issue came to the forefront of national debate. These may be justified on the grounds that they exist for the protection of students, but a policy is a statement both of values and intent. By affirming a view about something, it is also implied that the view is right and should not be contradicted. If an academic working within his subject were to question this, or reasonably to present a different perspective, then they might be subjected to professional censure, receive threats to their reputation or even risk losing their job.

The effect of all this is the hidden cost of self-censure. How much valuable research is now being withheld through fear is something that cannot be measured. However, if alternative views are being excluded from the public sphere, then the impression that there is only one permissible view becomes more marked.

How can the TOK student be a sceptic?

It is naive to assume that all IB students are immune to *groupthink* or even that the IBO as an institution is also immune. It is a brave student in a TOK lesson who will challenge a view passionately held by the majority. And TOK presentations regularly reveal old prejudices which cannot be easily exposed as false or irrelevant. If the American Declaration of Independence can state that some truths are self-evident, then why should not everyone have the right to claim their own self-evident truths which cannot be challenged by any empirical data?

But the TOK component is designed to address in practical terms the problems of knowledge which all of us encounter as free moral sovereign agents and thinkers. If, as in the IB programmes, the twin aims of education are right moral thought and action, combined with fact-based learning, then TOK is the glue which links the learner with the curriculum. It enables a process of guided reflection on subject-based knowledge with questions supported by formal rules of language and logic and insights from the discipline of epistemology.

TOK is not a history of ideas nor of philosophy. Nevertheless, it entices the student with a heady mix from the rich legacy of big ideas from the mathematical mysticism of Pythagoras and Plato, through the notions of beauty which art, music and literature represent, to Popper's demarcation between science and pseudoscience, to name just a few. Does perception trump reason for reliability or is it the other way round? Does language create our reality by being manipulated and abused, or does it have its limitations? Can we reach new truths through formal logic; can we rely on induction to make new discoveries; and are we free, and if we are what is freedom? Is it the freedom of the British philosopher, Thomas Hobbes (1588–1679) to be free of imprisonment, or the freedom of the existentialist to choose our own path out of many on offer?

The average TOK student arrives on his or her course with the typical range of prejudices, common sense notions and opinions. They will have been to a large extent indoctrinated in some form or other, but also of an age to be excited at the prospect of intellectual discovery although unsure how to separate fact from fiction, and disinterested opinion from propaganda. By the end of the course, they will have learnt to mistrust knowledge claims, to be wary of personal opinion even when it is supported by reliable evidence, and to be able to spot fallacy and falsehood in whatever forms they may take. They should have recognised their own intellectual shortcomings, subjected them to scrutiny, and taken steps to correct them as they arise. But above all, they will value reasoned debate.

By contrast, our current forums of public discourse, those shared spaces in which we meet virtually or otherwise to share and discuss news and views, often appear to have banished both reason and scepticism in favour of raw emotion, one-sided polemics, *ad hominem* fallacies, and angry agitprop. As we have seen, in our universities, parliament, Twitterspshere, and media outlets, dogmatism and ideology are back in favour. Truth seems to be the preserve of those who shout loudest, and those on the wrong side are vilified for holding wrong opinions.

Of course we have been here before. A cursory look at the past will reveal that periods of optimism, prosperity, vision and development are relatively rare. And that in fact, according to the Israeli writer Yuval Harari, by contrast, the present time should be a golden age as Mankind triumphs over nature as disease, famine and war are conquered for the first time (Harari, 2015). But, by contrast we are faced with a new challenge which centres on the sovereignty of the individual as technology gives increasing powers of control and surveillance to the state. Simultaneously, we are witnessing a policing of thought and speech, and special protections offered to ideologies and social policies held to be sacrosanct. It is a double blow to sceptics.

As a response to this, should TOK students see themselves, like the German philosopher Immanuel Kant (1784–1804), as individuals with sovereign rights and duties and as 'ends in the kingdom of ends' (Kant, 1785). Are they rational agents free to explore unorthodox views even when they go against the collective will? Or should they regard the collective as sovereign and their will subsumed within? Should they value isolation like Nietzsche, set out on new roads to freedom like Sartre, or knuckle down like most of us and seek a quiet life? How does TOK prepare them to even contemplate these issues let alone live out their examined lives, as Socrates so famously recommended? Should they demand to speak freely even if it offends others and breaches conventions? Or are there limits, which they must accept but, in doing so, also accept the consequences?

Do not beware of Greeks bearing gifts

Is it time to take solace in Plato and Socrates? Plato's '*Republic*', written around 380 BCE, has exerted a profound influence on the history of ideas and culture in Western thought. Most of us are superficially familiar with its central concept, that the most theoretically perfect political system would come close to being an unchanging entity (preferably a city state), ruled by philosophically guided guardians, educated solely for leadership, and supported by two lower castes of warriors and workers.

Of course, such a State could not exist in harmony for long before degenerating eventually into political mayhem, as even Plato himself realised. In fact, Plato's justification of the ideal and just State was equally an attempt to search for a definition of the just person, since for him, justice was the seat of wisdom, and wisdom was the path to virtue and happiness. Using a radical equivalence, he affirmed that the guardians of the state corresponded to reason in the individual, with the two lower castes equivalent to emotions and appetites. For Plato, and for most of the Greek post-Socratic philosophers, the search for serenity and balance was the supreme ethical quest for the individual. *Eudemonia*, or virtuous happiness, could only come when reason and virtue dominated the temperament and kept base instincts under control.

Reason, virtue, justice and wisdom are not of course virtues solely possessed by the ancient Greek philosophers. But Plato and his contemporaries and successors were the first to attempt to define what they meant and to note their importance both to the individual and to the State. As described by Plato, the philosopher Socrates formulated his famous dialectic to interrogate assumptions buried in premises, to search for examples which could be inferred, to look for contradictions in those examples that could lead through refined premises ever closer to the truth. In this way, the protagonists in a debate could arrive at an agreed definition of the ethical person, or the right way of behaving. Writing about the education of the future philosopher in the section titled 'Dialectic' in Book 8 of the '*Republic*', the conversation runs as follows:

"And can they ever acquire the knowledge we regard as essential if they can't argue logically?"

"No, they can't."

"But isn't this just the note which Dialectic must strike? It is an intellectual process, but is paralleled in the visible world, as we said, by the progress of sight from shadows, to real creatures, and then to the stars, and finally to the sun itself. So when one tries to reach ultimate realities by the exercise of pure reason.......one is at the end of an intellectual progress..."

"And isn't that progress what we call 'dialectic'?"

"That's perfectly true"

(Plato, the Republic)

In Plato's *Euthyphro*, Socrates skilfully leads his pious interlocutor, Euthyphro, through a series of questions to a conclusion which contradicts his original assumption that we should do what God commands, if we wish to be good. Under the relentless questioning of Socrates, it appears instead that either God commands what is good because it happens to be good or He commands what is good because He says it is good. If the former, then God cannot be omnipotent and if the latter, then that which is bad could also be good if only God says so. Either way, it seems God has little control over morality.

It is extraordinary how we take for granted the sophistication of these methods and arguments. Classical Greece in the fifth and fourth centuries BCE was surrounded by great powers such as Egypt, Persia and Carthage. But it was only the Greeks who discussed and practised such a degree of scepticism towards their gods, their leaders and governments, even though they were pious and respectful of tradition. Today, as soon as we start to debate, we are automatically using features of formal and informal logic first explained and refined by Plato, Socrates and Aristotle. When we argue about notions of purpose, meaning, truth and knowledge, we owe the very concepts to those same philosophers, concepts that later philosophers have developed but rarely surpassed.

What is truth?

The Theory of Knowledge component is intended as a practical guide to students in coming to terms with their own learning. Since it is context- and subject-based, it differs markedly from most thinking or critical skills school programmes, which are often taught as knowledge free. The pursuit of knowledge as the primary aim of education often comes under threat from skills-based programmes and child-centered methodologies. According to Dennis Hayes, Professor of Education at the University of Derby and Director of Academics for Academic Freedom, "Higher Education has adopted therapeutic forms of teacher training because many academics have lost faith in the pursuit of knowledge" (Ecclestone and Hayes, 2009).

Critical thinking skills are better developed in context since it is context which will more likely lead to more effective problem-solving and a better understanding of controversial issues such as a rise in questions of medical and social ethics. TOK students are continually required to look inwards, try to understand their own histories and assumptions, and to use this self-knowledge to explore the histories and perspectives of others. A discussion of the Pakistan blasphemy charge would be a welcome topic for debate in a TOK lesson regardless of the backgrounds and beliefs of the participating students.

The pursuit of knowledge and the Theory of Knowledge (the branch of philosophy known as epistemology) imply equally a pursuit of truth and knowledge which is a Socratic ideal. But they are not quite the same thing.

For something to be known it must be at least true, and, according to the Platonic tripartite theory of knowledge, it must also be justified and believed. According to Locke, things exist and facts are facts regardless of our beliefs, but truth is the currency which links us to them. For Plato, truth has a mystical quality, which is linked to his notion of ideals. Knowledge can only be of ideals, and anything less is mere opinion. For Nietzsche, truth does not even exist. There are only interpretations. This was not new. The Greek Sophists, itinerant teachers who flourished also in the fifth century BCE, were the first relativists and proclaimed Man to be the measure of all things. Most recently, the Postmodernist School of philosophy has set out to debunk the truths both of religion and science and taken us back to where the Sophists left us and from which Plato rescued us.

Primarily, Western philosophy is concerned with the link between reality and appearance. Plato's' famous metaphor of the cave would have most of us living in a dreamlike world staring at shadows. The French philosopher Descartes (1596–1650) picked up the theme emphatically: "The fortress of my certainty about my own existence becomes the prison of my uncertainty about the existence of a world beyond me" (Chappell, 2005). Even when we assume the existence of an outside world (which we are bound to do by common sense agreement), we cannot be sure how well we know it or by what means. For Kant, attempting to marry the empiricist view of knowledge through sense perception with the rationalist view of knowledge through reason and mental effort, we sift the world as apprehended by the senses into various mental categories and thereby make sense of it. It is as though in order to apprehend reality we put on a pair of thinking spectacles.

Truth, therefore, is not something that can be easily gained or possessed. There are self-evident truths, contingent and necessary truths, truths by correspondence and coherence, even pragmatic truths. For some there is *the truth* and for others there is *no truth*. Truth can be plausible opinion, adherence to the facts, and justified by evidence and authority. Or it can be a tool for oppression or weapon of power. For Orwell it was possession of the past to own the future, and for many religions it comes from divine revelation. How then are we to understand the truth if we all see it so differently?

The sceptical approach to truth might give us a way out. Extreme scepticism, or a refusal to believe in the objective reality or truth in anything, is a philosophically valid position but impossible to adhere to if we wish to live a normal life. As soon as we behave with moral intention, use induction to make a decision, rely on cause and effect to reach conclusions, and free will to take responsibility or hold others responsible, we are committing to an acceptance that things happen and work in a certain predictable way. We all routinely accept the uniformity of nature, because not to do so would be a form of madness.

Conclusion

Accepting a truth about something too readily may be a way of closing off all further questions. Those who proclaim the truth too loudly in the present day may have been ready to burn Giordano Bruno, and the English Catholic martyrs in the past. For that reason alone, we should prepare our students to insist on debate and evidence for beliefs and prepare them to be able to ignore the abuse which may follow. The lines between fact, plausible opinion, prejudice and propaganda are frequently blurred and too little understood. To be aware of what is at stake is also to be empowered.

In a good TOK lesson, the world comes into the classroom for dissection. Later the TOK students can, if they wish, apply their knowledge directly to the world. Beyond the obvious practical challenges facing Mankind in this century there is a more invidious one – can the individual survive as sovereign and free? Will we choose Huxley's *Brave New World* or Orwell's *1984*, or can we choose something better? Armed with a reasonable and balanced scepticism, the fortunate TOK students are better equipped to understand what is at stake. It would be better for all of us if some variant of TOK were to become a compulsory component for all educational programmes along with the reading of Plato's '*Republic*'. But I doubt that will ever happen.

References

Chappell T (2005) *The Inescapable Self*. London: Weidenfeld & Nicolson.

Ecclestone K & Hayes D (2009) *The Dangerous Rise of Therapeutic Education*. Abingdon: Routledge.

Harari Y (2015) *Homo Deus*. UK: Penguin Random House UK.

Kant I (1785) *Groundwork of the Metaphysic of Morals*.

Mill J S (1859) *On Liberty*. Kitchener: Batoche Books.

Parsons K (2017) *Freespeech*. Retrieved from www.Patheos.com/blogs/secularoutpost/2017/10/30/free-speech-fundamentalist/

Plato (1955) (Translated by H D P Lee) *The Republic*. Aylesbury: Penguin Classics.

Scruton R (2017) *Fake studies in academia*. Retrieved from lybio.net/roger-scruton-how-fake-subjects-like-women-studies-invaded-academia/people/

Spiked-Online (2018) *Free speech in University Rankings*. Retrieved from www.spiked-online.com/free-speech-university-rankings#w9mogxsozww

Theory of Knowledge.Net (2018) *What are the aims of TOK?* Retrieved from www.theoryofknowledge.net/about/the-tok-course/what-is-the-aim-of-tok/

The Telegraph (2018) *Oxford academics criticise professor who suggested people should have 'pride' about aspects of British Empire*. Available via: www.telegraph.co.uk/education/2017/12/20/oxford-academics-criticise-professor-suggested-people-should/

Zamyatin E (1919) *Tomorrow*, as translated in *A Soviet Heretic: Essays* (1970)

Chapter 2

Orientating Students to the World: Negotiating the Technicalities of TOK

Justin Laleh

Introduction

"Okay class, good morning, can we grab our seats so that we can get going please. Today we are looking at the TOK presentation. Can anyone remind us of where we start?"

"*With an RLS sir.*"

"Correct, which means?"

"*Real-life Situation.*"

"Thank you. Someone else, then what do we do?"

"*You extract a KQ sir – a Knowledge Question.*"

"Which is?"

"[Reading from notes] *An open question framed in general terms which is about knowledge in a second-order aspect.*"

"Indeed, then?"

"[again reading] *You 'progress' the presentation utilising ToK concepts to aid in your analysis.*"

"Great, thank you. Someone else, what are these concepts?"

"*Are they the WOKs and AOKs sir?*"

"Yes, but we can also use the knowledge framework, or we can look to personal and shared knowledge in order to ..."

Such an anecdote will likely sound familiar to many TOK teachers around the world, though based on my own experience it serves to draw our attention to an important issue within TOK teaching. Attempting to communicate the intent behind these technical features to a group of IB Diploma Programme (DP) students is one of the central challenges faced by teaching staff and those who are coordinating their efforts. The task is by no means insurmountable and the structural features of knowledge which the "TOK Concepts" are directed toward are accessible by a good number of students (and teachers) by the end of a course of study. However, there is an extant and pervasive issue regarding the perspicacity with which these concepts encapsulate the epistemological issues they seek to tackle. The laudable aim of these concepts and structures is to allow the DP student to interrogate the methodological issues raised in their knowledge selection throughout their DP studies. Equally laudable is the attempt to circumnavigate and, to some extent, bypass the oftentimes opaque and overly complex features of the philosophies dedicated to the task. Anyone familiar with even basic Epistemology, Philosophy of Science, Aesthetics or Logic will be aware that this type of formal philosophical endeavour is a specialist enterprise requiring its own focus (precisely why Philosophy is offered at Standard Level and Higher Level). In this chapter I will draw upon both my experience as a TOK teacher/coordinator/examiner and my experiences in academic philosophy to interrogate the successes and failures of the TOK course as well as future possibilities for its structure. I do not seek to argue for some centralised position for Philosophy within the DP, but rather to express a certain concern about the role that the metalinguistic features of the TOK course play in the process of promoting metacognition in students. In the face of this concern, and what I consider to be the most pressing problems of the DP core, I aim to show that there are some more perspicacious and, indeed, more intuitive ways to achieve our common goal of developing the capacity for 'second-order' reflection in students.

Framing the issue

Content vs Intent

Perhaps the central challenge of teaching TOK, or organising its provision, lies in negotiating the idiosyncratic technical language which has been developed for the course. The TOK course sits within the prevailing paradigm for teaching and learning: it adopts a metalinguistic approach which focuses on developing a shared but abstract language which aims at orientating students within a world of knowledge in which they find themselves. The danger here is that the language of learning becomes conspicuous in a way that obfuscates its intended function. As an IB Category Three Workshop leader once remarked, WOKs (Ways of Knowing) become 'naked and monolithic' in the hands of some students. Whilst I will argue that there are no WOKs, for there is no such thing as 'emotion' separate and distinct from 'sense perception', their invention is neither a problem for, nor a failing on the part of, the TOK course. The issue remains the extent to which the TOK concepts themselves are conspicuous or self-effacing, a question which is equally true for the assessment outcomes.

The tension when teaching concept-based and skills-based subjects is balancing out the strategic need to prepare students for assessment, and the ethical requirement of delivering a collaborative, thoughtful course. If one has a determinate 'content' to teach, and is applying a system of assessment where each and every feature of the specification could be examined, then the challenges are clearly different. One can adopt the most effective and deeply unethical approach to teaching these types of course by simply 'drilling' the students through encouraging learning via repetition. Whilst there is value in adopting this pedagogical technique in certain areas of study (introducing students to new features of languages for instance) the element of choice and therefore individuality is removed from this technique making it clearly anathema to the aims and intentions of TOK. There is no requirement to 'teach' all aspects of the TOK course, and the assessment is not limited and prescriptive in a way which requires students to have fully investigated each AOK (Area of Knowing) or WOK individually, or comprehensively. In this way the conceptual and skills-based course, which is assessed according to a global marking system, opens up a gap between 'content' (WOKs, AOKs, Knowledge Frameworks; or Induction vs Deduction, Kuhnian Philosophy of Science and so on) and the intended outcome (including orientation to the world of knowledge, and understanding the limitations of certain approaches to knowing a world). As teachers we must navigate our way through this gap however we see fit.

Treating TOK as a specification to be delivered is a notably flawed approach and one which the IB clearly resists, but schools are on the whole pragmatic and will often take the path of least resistance, focusing too heavily on the "content" and preparing students too strategically for the assessments. In my experience this problem is twofold. First there is an over-emphasis on the technicalities of the TOK concepts, and second there is an under-emphasis on certain key features of the types of knowledge students are using across their DP studies. If we look to the third TOK essay question for the May 2019 session, 'Do good explanations have to be true?', students are being asked to interrogate the nature of explanation: what constitutes an explanation, what makes an explanation good, what relationship does this valuation have to the idea of truth, what precisely is truth in this context, and so on. I imagine that all TOK teachers would agree that this is the ideal approach for students, and that this type of study is precisely what we signed up for. However, how will we go about breaking this essay question down? How will we go about preparing our students for this? What will the examiner be expecting? Inevitably we will be asked the following questions by our students: How many AOKs shall I use? How many KQs should I include? Should I signpost my KQs in the introduction? Which WOKs are the best to use for this question? Students ignore the key aspects – the proper target of a TOK question and the proper target for our course – and try to tackle it using the tools that we have given them. But by and large these are likely to be the wrong tools. For the most part they mediate and mitigate the challenge, rather than arm the students to tackle the challenge.

Issues in complexity

That this is more than just a comment on my own approach (as a teacher in a British school that offers A Levels as well as the IB Diploma: a context which I recognise as being different from that of many TOK teachers) is evidenced by the IB examiners' reports from the November 2018 session. Here the examiner suggests that there has been a decline in the standard of TOK essays from one year to the next and that essays were lacking in substance. (There are of course a number of reasons why this might be the case, including the ongoing expansion of the DP worldwide and the inevitable adjustment times required for familiarisation with the course.)

A key issue which stood out for me was the examiners' claim that too little was being done to defend knowledge from various challenges; for example, they suggest that a number of students view "reason as merely rationalisation". I am in complete accord with the idea that this is a deep problem, but what else could we expect from a course which isolates 'reason' as a way of knowing, and then establishes some standard ways of interrogating it? At the undergraduate level it takes a while for Philosophy students to grasp the idea that sceptics like Hume are not actually as sceptical as they might appear. Replacing the types of mathematical certainties established by foundationalists in the modern period with the probabilisms founded on the actual processes of natural science is not a rejection of the idea that we can know anything. However, this is a complex thought which requires some subtle work. It is unsurprising that DP students who are introduced to the idea of the problem of induction, or to the limitations of grounding knowledge in observation (WOK – Sense Perception) are likely to draw the extreme, ill-judged conclusion that knowledge, if provisional, is not knowledge at all. It is, of course, my role to dissuade students from these simplistic lines of reasoning, but to what extent are the deliverers of this course – let alone the students themselves – equipped to deal with these complexities? I therefore, in good TOK essay fashion, propose a KQ of my own: to what extent do the TOK concepts hinder the aims of the course? Rather than navigating our way through the gap between content and intent by committing to the idiosyncratic specificities of the course itself, I will argue that the delivery of TOK requires a more collaborative and adaptive approach from teachers and schools. Equally, however, it perhaps requires more perspicacity from the course itself.

The relative opacity of the TOK concepts (and this is only relative as they are indeed part of an excellent and in my view highly valuable course) appears to be a function of their complexity and their abstraction. To provide an analogy, improvements in imaging technologies have allowed for our understanding of the internal operations of organisms to be observed *in vivo* without recourse to the more invasive option of vivisection. Vivisectionists use their scalpel to investigate organic processes, but these processes have necessarily ceased at the moment of incision. In terms of TOK, we fail when we vivisect the student's processes of reflecting on their own orientation within a world of knowledge. Our aim should be to comprehend and work with this orientation, rather than to interrupt it. Students are surrounded by bodies of knowledge, processes of learning, methodologies, rigours and so on. Our emphasis on 'TOK concepts' simply introduces yet another one. This is precisely the wrong relationship: TOK can often become another subject to learn, one academic field in a series of others. I mean series here technically; there is a danger of TOK becoming incorporated into the system of student learning in a linear fashion rather than encouraging a more open approach to thinking.

To borrow from the world of Philosophy, Gilles Deleuze and Félix Guattari provide a useful distinction between two forms of complexity throughout their *Capitalism and Schizophrenia* volumes: molar and molecular (see Massumi, 1992). This distinction serves my own aim of refining the structure of the TOK course. In simple terms, the molar model of complexity allows for its component features to be integrated into well-defined boundaries, wherein the particles themselves are incorporated into a clearly identifiable whole. This type of structure is stable and rigid but less capable of changing to adapt its system to new elements. The molecular model is less stable: its component particles are not correlated in a 'rigidified' manner, but it is more capable of responding to and reforming in response to external stimuli. The latter model results in the whole structure being continually redefinable, whereas for the former, new stimuli are simply subsumed into a pre-established, pre-codified structural whole: open to the 'shock of the new' and able to deal with external stimuli without translating all unusual impulses into contexts that are already understood. A question arises here regarding the ability of molar structures to incorporate differences without turning them into identities.

Put simply, if students encounter TOK as one more set of concepts amongst others, one more cluster of technical terminologies amongst others, then they will simply incorporate the course into their pre-existent ways of thinking. They will not actually attain the level of metacognition intended by the course. If these pre-existent ways of thinking have been conditioned by the types of educational practice prevalent in, say (in my experience), the British system of education (regurgitative, repetitive, fact recollection), then TOK will be seen as one more subject to tackle in a strategic, assessment-driven way; one more series of items to learn and repeat in an ordered fashion in order to satisfy examination criteria. The IB does a good job of continually revising the TOK Guide (stressing the minimisation of set essay structures, for example) and the modes of assessment (such as the introduction of the global marking system) to guard against this. But again, the recent examiners' report indicates that, globally, TOK teachers are not getting this right. The examiner suggests that we are either too minimal in our support, or too rigid with it. The task, then, is clear: how can we best deliver and organise the TOK course in such a way that strikes the right balance in terms of student engagement? As participants in the IB, and as teachers, we must continue to reform the course, but also continue to reflect on our own practice to ensure that we are standing fast in the face of this deep challenge. Students must be encouraged to reflect on the nature of their learning, and on the nature of the pursuit of knowledge as a whole. But I propose that this essentially requires a certain shock to the system of their learning. This is certainly already provided by the course in its current form (I am sure any teacher will attest to the looks on their students' faces after the first few hours of TOK study), but is it provided in the right way? TOK has a complexity and a rigour, but it must have the right complexity and rigour in order to provide the precise type of intellectual 'shock' that I am proposing. This raises a question about the types of abstraction which are taking place in TOK.

Issues in abstraction: Getting 'meta'

At a generalised level it could be argued that the 'TOK concepts' form a type of 'metalanguage'. It is useful to think of the course in this way as it may be the case that the process of abstraction undertaken to derive the TOK concepts has been working in the wrong direction. Regardless of the actual circumstances under which they were derived, their current logical status would indicate that their utilisation results in an abstracted language which has become detached from the natural language that it seeks to order. For example, KQ, RLS, AOK *et al* are intended to allow the student to talk about various epistemological issues without requiring a fully-fledged engagement with epistemology itself. The idea here is that epistemology is far too abstract and complex – too philosophical. The opposing concept here would be that of applicability or embeddedness: the TOK concepts are somehow more proximal to actual ways in which the students would be engaging in the process of handling knowledge or orientating themselves in the world of knowledge. If one accepts this rough characterisation of the intentions of the structure of the TOK concepts as ringing true, then a question arises about the extent to which the ostensibly overly-abstract and therefore unnecessary elements of Philosophy are being repeated in the current iteration of the TOK course. The danger is that the natural language (the terms and idioms actually used in the study of Natural Science, or History, or – at a step removed – the terms utilised in Epistemology) and the metalanguage do not interact, that studying TOK does not help with the study of Natural Science, or that studying Natural Science does not help with studying TOK. If the process of abstraction has gone awry, this would be the case, and the resultant metalanguage is a philosophical abstraction of the worst kind: it describes nothing and forms a redundant set of concepts which are merely self-referential. I do not think that this is the case with TOK concepts, as they are clearly useful in some regard, but at best I would say that they are ambiguous.

At this point I should further clarify what I mean by abstraction. Ideally an abstracted layer would move away from the concrete nature of particulars and become more generalised without losing sight of that which is being abstracted away from. For example, 'Science' is a general term, 'Natural Sciences' the more concrete practice, and 'Biology' the yet more concrete practice. This simple taxonomy is of course imperfect, and has many more possible layers of abstraction and many more possible levels of concretisation. It provides a structure within which we could compare the practice of Biology to that of Physics, Social Science to Natural Science, and potentially The Arts (amongst other things) to Science. This is clearly what is happening in AOK, but there are a whole host of problematic inclusions within what constitutes the AOK because they are being adapted to fit a model of the DP rather than sitting back within the structures more readily available in the world of academia, or knowledge itself. As a potentially 'nested' metalanguage, the idea would be that each layer of abstraction conceptualises the more concrete layer below. In TOK it seems as though the abstractions are not really connected to that from which they are abstracting, meaning that they are no longer conceptualising any form of concrete practice. Rather, the concepts themselves are more self-referential and seemingly emerge from the process of having to come up with a simple and usable structure to teach something highly complex. The outcome, at its worst, is an over-simplification with two effects: the first is that the utilisation of the TOK concepts results in something facile, and the second is that they become complexly interwoven in a meaningless play of abstraction.

This is arguably true of the metalinguistic approaches to metacognitive pedagogical practices. The idea that students' reflection on their own learning (be it at the declarative, procedural or conditional level) requires a separate language is highly problematic for the reasons established above with regard to complexities. As a teacher, one is presented with many instances where these practices are taken to the extreme: students are fluent in the language of reflection but incapable of actually undertaking the complex tasks about which they are reflecting. In its lowest moments of excess, to take my opening anecdote as an example, TOK can be guilty of this too. Teachers focusing their lessons on the techniques of KQ extraction, KQ phrasing, or the nature of WOKs, starts to take on the form of a bad word game at one end of the spectrum, or a facile run-through of various optical illusions at the other. The key to correcting these excesses lies in re-calibrating the abstraction itself. I do not think that epistemology or any other form of Philosophy is a cure-all in this instance, as these endeavours can be equally problematic for teachers and students alike: the model of TOK being taught by DP teachers and not specialists is a good one, and exemplifies the types of embeddedness that we should seek after. Once again I will look to some basic resources from my own philosophical enquiries to demonstrate what this may look like.

Ways forward

Abstracting in a more productive way

There are features of Heideggerian Philosophy which inform the ways in which I think TOK could progress in its future iterations, namely some basic aspects of Heidegger's elucidations of methodology. Heidegger typically turns toward the etymologies of various terms in order to clarify their fundamental meaning. When attempting to identify a philosophical methodology he therefore analyses the original notion of 'method' itself. According to this reading, the Greek term *methodos* contains '*meta*', which means 'after' or 'behind', connoting a particular way in which we are turned toward something – the way in which we 'go after' or 'pursue' a matter. If we extract this thought and look toward the various sciences, it is clear that what determines their methods is that which they are 'turned toward'. Biology, for example, is turned towards 'that which lives', indicated in the Greek term for 'life', namely '*bios*'. The question to ask, then, is what precisely is TOK turned towards?

In a metacognitive fashion TOK seems to pursue the *procedures* of knowing themselves. This is a highly abstract and very niche approach to orienting students in the world of knowledge. It adopts a particular mode of a particular type of philosophical approach which is itself highly complex and abstract. Heidegger would refer to it as a "Metaphysics of Knowledge", namely radical abstraction from the living, breathing, everyday world of knowing (Heidegger, 1962). Rather than replace this approach with a different philosophy, I think that TOK would do well to become more determinately non-philosophical. This may sound counter-intuitive, but taking a little time to figure out what a philosophical perspective may look like could help to ensure that TOK does not end up being too abstract. Heidegger clarifies this point when he describes what it is that Philosophy would do in contrast to what more generalised approaches to 'Science' might do. For Heidegger, standard concepts (*Begriff*), ie not fundamental (*Grundbegriff*) but universal, general, particular, function according to a representative schema whereby we present 'individual items' before us according to their common aspects, always representing and determining a particular thing in relation to its identity with, or difference from, other things with which it shares properties. *Fundamental* concepts of metaphysics are 'comprehensive': they relate to the singularity and uniqueness of that which they comprehend, rather than functioning as tools for categorisation and identification. Concepts that attempt to 'grasp the whole' do not operate within the same conceptual schema as standard concepts of logic, as they do not function in a representational manner (Heidegger, 2001). If Heidegger is right, this creates a problem for us as TOK teachers, taking us back to the issue previously outlined: if what we do is radically challenging and new, our students (and indeed fellow teachers) will simply not be able to make sense of it, or will alternatively collapse it into more familiar concepts; in the case of teachers this may mean drilling, for example.

I would therefore suggest that we narrow our aspiration and do not, as has been the case thus far, try to create a structure which is 'turned toward' the whole of knowledge. Our current teaching framework is in danger of producing a 'worst of both worlds' approach, which simplifies the nuances of philosophical arguments – whether within epistemology or elsewhere – and at the same time exploits highly abstract, technical philosophical terminology to which students struggle to relate. TOK in this instance runs too far ahead of itself at the same time as it lags far behind more informed philosophical practices (either as epistemology, more advanced forms of "the metaphysics of knowledge", or philosophical endeavours such as Heidegger's). TOK should therefore be abstract in the more generalised way, where it looks to identify common aspects of actual concrete practice, rather than artificially dividing it all up and then identifying common aspects (or differences) amongst these abstractions. Again, this inability to functionally compare and contrast across AOK was highlighted in the recent examiners' report, but it is no wonder. If TOK should pursue the common aspects of concrete practice, what would this pursuit look like? It looks precisely like the essay questions. Explanation, modelling, consensus, evidence and so on are all more or less shared features of academic and productive rigours, so they should probably be the star of the show. The lack of attainment and progress on the essay is potentially indicative of the gap which exists between content and intent. The students are being asked to do the right things in the essay, but they are likely being encouraged to go about it in the wrong way. They are being asked to compare and contrast the ways in which they may have encountered 'good explanations' in order to see what they look like in different academic fields, or in their everyday lives. The general framework of TOK concepts is of course capable of yielding these types of reflections but, as I have suggested, not in the most perspicacious manner.

Teaching and programming in a more productive way

Further, there are meta-questions, and indeed meta-practices, which already exist and can be drawn upon in a far more focused and relevant way. For example, Historiography is a feature of IB studies in History; much of the TOK course alludes to certain features of the Philosophy of Science; and Meta-Ethics is a component of the Philosophy course. The disciplines which already operate at the limits of the various subjects and fields are thus already in place, and could be more readily drawn upon in TOK itself. In some regard this has already taken place in the shift toward the Knowledge Frameworks. The issue is that the Knowledge Framework still operates within the structure of the poorly, or at least problematically, abstracted structures of AOK and WOK. If the abstractions and generalisations of TOK were more firmly embedded in the everyday practice of DP teachers, the types of problems which schools experience in terms of staffing TOK could also be solved. The carousel model for teaching is of course a common practice and runs the risk of the overall aims of the course being obfuscated, but where there is a clearer connection to each subject (rather than obscurely organised groups of subjects; again History is a DP Group 3 subject but has its own AOK), there may well be more buy-in and more general understanding on the part of teachers. An Economics teacher will have a good grasp of the limitations of modelling, as will a Physics teacher. Philosophers, language teachers and historians will have a technical understanding of the limitations of interpretation, for instance. The current course tries to harness this but (if IB TOK conferences are anything to go by) it does so by primarily appealing to philosophers, mathematicians and historians, most likely because of the prevalence of meta-disciplines within those fields. A greater balance can be struck in terms of incorporating the teaching body as a whole into the practice of TOK. The more abstract the course, the more alienating it is, the more that it genuinely reflects upon and challenges embedded practice the more inclusive it will be.

This is mirrored in the student experience too. By far the most productive conversations I have had with students have arisen from discussions of their own Extended Essays and IB internal assessments. Where they have done the work of producing and interrogating knowledge themselves they are far more capable of making sense of what we are aspiring to achieve as teachers of TOK. One of my students produced an Extended Essay with a focus on the effect that a particular event had on a famous clothing brand. Where others had suggested the event was responsible for the brand's decline, she argued that this decline was attributable to the company's handling of the event. She smartly reinterpreted the evidence from a different perspective. The only issue was the following: when I asked her under what conditions I could demonstrate that her view was false, she admitted that there were none; she was convinced of her position. This type of transcendental approach (where all possible positions are already subsumed) is of great interest, and can be raised and analysed through the current TOK concepts, but again they seem to vivisect here, rather than capture them *in vivo*. Once again, finding ways to embed TOK back within the heart of what DP students do in their day-to-day activities may well serve to close the gap between content and intent in this instance. Focusing on the commonalities and the differences in the IB internal assessments (focuses, methods, modes of assessment) in a more determinate way could prove fruitful and allow the abstracting to take place in a more productive manner.

Conclusion: Staying on track

Tackling student and teacher alienation is a key way in which the TOK course can evolve and adapt. What I consider to be the central impediment to this should by now be clear: the AOKs and WOKs (perhaps even the KQ). The TOK concepts, bar the Knowledge Framework, are outmoded. To borrow from Nietzsche, they are like coins whose faces have been worn down to the point that they are now only metal, shorn of their intended power (2015). They are too abstract and simplistic, and do more to obfuscate the aims of the IB than to aid them. If one were to take a more assessment-focused approach to the TOK course and prepare for the essay alone, barring the specific wording of those essays which require two AOKs, one need not utilise this structure at all. This is clearly the intention of the course, and is well-aided by the recent addition of the Knowledge Framework. The issue here is once again a strange inclusion of the notions of Personal and Shared knowledge, which are dangerously facile – too many papers fell short of the mark in their engagement with these concepts. The current guide was a welcome reiteration of the course aims and introduced much that was genuinely productive, most of which revolved around the essay. But have these enhancements (global marking) wrought the types of change intended, or have they been hampered by the AOKs and WOKs being retained? I leave the answer to this question to the IB and await the results of the current consultation on the new guide in this regard.

To conclude, the Heideggerian view of the sciences suggests that there are concrete ways of thinking and investigating which resolve themselves into philosophical thinking, at which point they require the concepts of philosophy. At one level it is the task of the philosopher to help ground these fields, and at another it is the task of philosophy to think in pure abstractions, but this is clearly not relevant to TOK. Just as Aristotelian philosophy demarcates *Praxis* as the highest aim for thinking, but reserves a separate distinction yet for those devoted to *Theoria* (divine contemplation), so too does the history of philosophy recognise that certain levels of abstraction, no matter how important and powerful, are a kind of 'inverted world'. The world is turned upon its head such that everything which was near is now far, and *vice-versa*. Whilst this is the model of philosophy to which I am committed (and for which my philosophy students are not at all thankful!), it is not the model of TOK to which I am committed. This inverted world is perhaps too much of a 'shock' to the system for the student. Invoking my earlier analysis of complexities, we cannot leave the students so disoriented as to have no way forward (*aporia* is something reserved for the Philosophy classroom). We need to find a clearer balance between the disorienting results of the TOK course and the all-too-powerful reductive focus on outcomes prevalent in some of the more questionable pedagogical practices, and more importantly the dampening effects of echo chambers and political polarisation prevalent in the modern world. TOK continues to be an absolute jewel in the DP's crown, and despite its shortcomings it is in my experience the most forward-thinking course of its kind, focused on the most important aspect of any pre-university study: the students themselves. It sits at the core of what we do as teachers, and therefore its central position must be reasserted anew. It cannot wander off into abstraction and specialisation, just as it cannot be fully subsumed into the general course of things (one more hoop ...). As TOK continues to evolve I anticipate positive change, and hope that a general sense of conservatism with regard to old structures does not get in the way of ensuring that TOK remains the vibrant and engaging course that it is.

References

Heidegger M (2001) *The Fundamental Concepts of Metaphysics* (trans. McNeill W and Walker N). Bloomington: Indiana University Press.

Heidegger M (1962) *Being and Time* (trans. Macquarrie J and Robinson E). Blackwell: Oxford.

Massumi B (1992) *A User's Guide to Capitalism and Schizophrenia*. Cambridge, MA: MIT Press.

Nietzsche F (2015) *On Truth and Lies in a Nonmoral Sense*. CreateSpace Independent Publishing Platform.

Chapter 3

Creativity, Activity, Service (CAS): a consideration of Experience, Learning and Education

Shona McIntosh

An International Baccalaureate (IB) education has included an experience-based element, in some form or another, since its inception (Peterson, 2003). In its current form, this element is called Creativity, Activity, Service (CAS) and, like its preceding forms, stems from a belief that a balanced education prepares the whole person (Hill, 2010) for the demands of adult life which augment the knowledge gleaned from books (Hahn, 1934). To avoid a reductive education (Miller, 2000), a holistic education may include out-of-classroom experiences, with some evidence suggesting that it can support the learning of life-long skills, such as initiative-taking (Beames and Ross, 2010), as well as improving subject learning (Braund and Reiss, 2006). However, few curricula have an embedded experiential element and so the inclusion of CAS at the core of the IB Diploma Programme (DP) is unusual. Whilst fundamental to the DP's identity, CAS is, at the same time, acknowledged as something of a leap of faith (Walker, 2011). Perhaps what Walker is driving at here, which has been confirmed in a review of research conducted in this field (Gosen & Washbush, 2004), is the sense of the unknown about the precise nature of the relationship between experience and learning.

This unknown will be addressed here by drawing on the results of research that was conducted to investigate the impact of CAS on students. Indications of the perceived effects of activities undertaken to fulfil the requirements of CAS were collected from DP students, teachers involved in implementing CAS, and DP alumni. The data were analysed to understand how the experiences related to learning. Findings from the DP student data set also prompt a consideration of the extent to which CAS contributes to the DP aim of promoting international mindedness and related parts of the IB organisational mission to foster a sense of responsibility towards local, national, and global communities. This consideration will be preceded in this chapter by examining two established educational theories of experience-based learning, and the chapter ends by discussing the limits and potential of experiential learning at the core of the Diploma Programme as it is currently conceptualised.

Conceptions of experience-based learning

Learning and experience were central to arguments made by educational philosopher John Dewey about the need for schools to make the 'traditional' curriculum more relevant to the world outside the schoolroom (Dewey, 1938). For Dewey, 'experience' was connected to a project of social participation in which education could shape active and involved citizens, and was central to a progressive educational system. For Dewey, there was "an intimate and necessary relation between the process of actual experience and education" (1938, p20). Rather than the traditional forms of mass education imposed on children by others in a hierarchical system intent on acquisition of a static body of (largely uncontestable) knowledge, progressive education advocated paying attention to the experience of the learner, emphasising that it is the responsibility of the educator to make that experience worthwhile, in the eyes of the learner. One way of so doing was by giving learners freedom of choice of activity and learning through experience that was clearly relevant to the changing world outside the classroom. Successful experiences were termed *educative*: characterised by inculcating in the learner an appetite for further learning and further educative experiences. Problems that grew out of the condition of a new experience were crucial for stimulating thinking, so educative experiences were characterised by an element of "difficulty to be overcome by the exercise of intelligence" (Dewey, 1938, p79). As such, learner engagement is required for the problem to be solved, and engagement is more likely when the experience is relevant to the world the learner knows.

Real world relevance was also important in a prominent theory of learning from experience developed by David Kolb, despite not initially being concerned with the education of young people. Kolb (1984; 2014) claimed to draw on Dewey and other constructivist educational theorists such as Piaget and Levin in his experiential learning theory (ELT). ELT was based on the view that "knowledge is created through the transformation of experience" (Kolb, 2014, p49). Experience, then, is central to the ELT conceptualisation of knowledge creation for individuals: learning happens *through* experience, involving a range of senses, and values nature and the outdoors as alternative learning spaces. It is personally meaningful in a way that is not possible for traditional pre-planned curricula in systems of mass education. Kolb, in challenging the learning possibilities from a planned curriculum, is advocating conditions for the freedom of choice of activity favoured by Dewey (1938) as well as offering an alternative to 'traditional' education. For Kolb, the alternative is holistic in purpose, aiming to develop all aspects of a person rather than only the intellectual. Although Kolb's later work responded to the criticisms of ELT (Garner, 2000), some flaws are still evident, notably in his somewhat arcane conceptualisation of learning through the 'transformation' of experience. While constructivists conceptualise experience and learning as a socially mediated process (Vygotsky, 1978), I suggest Kolb conceives the individual and the environment in which their experience occurs as separate, leaving the process of transformation unexplained.

Although Dewey and Kolb agree that what one experiences can transform the way in which one understands the world, they diverge in their conceptualisation of the process of transformation. The basis of the divergence lies in how they understand learning and experience to relate to each other. Dewey's view is that progressive educators need to acknowledge that the environment – he uses the term "environing conditions" (1938, p40) – may be conducive to educative experiences, and that it is educators' responsibility to organise the conditions to maximise growth in a positive direction. The relationship between the environing conditions and the individual's experience of a situation is described by Dewey as an "interaction" (*ibid*, p42). The qualities of interactions influence the way the situation is experienced. Therefore, the learner's school experiences will lead to attitudes and behaviour developing which are helpful for or detrimental towards learning. Dewey proposes that educative experiences occur when the 'situation and interaction' (*ibid*, p43) meet the needs of the individual in a way that encourages engagement in future learning experiences and is fundamental for forming actively engaged citizens. For Kolb, experience involves two elements: feeling something, such as the experience of joy, and having participated in events. Feelings and participation occur in 'transactions' and "once they become related ... are essentially changed" (*ibid*, p47). How they become related and how they change is never clearly elucidated. It involves learning, which Kolb sees as "an active, self-directed process" (*ibid*, p48), implying an innate disposition towards active engagement, but does not account for ways in which this disposition can be cultivated or what happens to those who do not possess it.

Although Kolb recognises that interaction involves "two inseparable factors" (2014, p46), he criticises the term as "mechanical" (*ibid*, p47). Instead, Kolb offers the term 'transaction', arguing that social knowledge (external to the individual) occurs in transaction with the "personal knowledge" (*ibid*, p48) that is an accumulation of personal subjective life experiences. The choice of 'transaction' in preference to '*inter*action' emphasises that there is a gap in Kolb's ELT between person and environment that has to be *crossed*, whilst Dewey, recognising that "all human experience is ultimately social" (Dewey, 1938, p38), sees learning as arising *between* humans in the experiences they have together.

Experiential learning for Kolb is embedded in the practice of observing the moment and reflecting on what new implications it brings to one's own knowledge and perspectives. For Dewey, learning from experience is a potent educational philosophy which, through educative experiences, aims to encourage engaged and active citizens. Kolb's rather person-centred theorisation of experiential learning for individual growth is therefore working towards very different outcomes from Dewey's more expansive and inter-related conceptualisation. It is perhaps puzzling, then, that the current IB guidance on CAS (IB, 2015) cites Kolb when conceptualising experiential learning in CAS, referring to his diagram depicting the iterative and active nature of experiential learning. Puzzling because CAS sits at the core of the flagship programme of an educational organisation which includes in its mission statement the aim to:

> develop inquiring, knowledgeable and caring young people *who help to create a better and more peaceful world through intercultural understanding and respect.* (IB, 2016, my emphasis)

The Learner Profile, the organisation's "mission in action" (IB, 2015, p7), is supposed to help students "become responsible members of local, national, and global communities" (ibid, pii). Regarding the IB's aim to foster community responsibility, experiential learning (through CAS) as conceived by Dewey has a great deal to offer; indeed, it might be considered even better than Kolb's ELT, in which individual, personal growth is the goal. These ideas will be discussed later in this chapter, but first I outline two specific aims of CAS that will direct a closer examination of the evidence of learning from CAS experiences, as perceived by students.

The aims of CAS in the IB Diploma Programme

CAS is emblematic of the DP commitment to a form of education that seeks to develop students holistically, as well-rounded individuals, capable of more than just learning about the academic side of education. The current iteration of CAS envisages that the core, including also the Theory of Knowledge and Extended Essay, contributes to developing Learner Profile attributes, interacts with the academic disciplines of the DP and, somehow, helps to form students' self-awareness and their sense of identity, while fostering their international mindedness. The seven learning outcomes of CAS, related to the attributes of the Learner Profile, have to be evidenced from the CAS activities of each student. Of the six aims specific to CAS, two in particular are considered here: that students enjoy and find significance in a range of CAS experiences, and that they understand that they are members of local and global communities with responsibilities towards each other and the environment (IB, 2015a, p10). Some research sheds light into learning through CAS experiences.

Hayden and McIntosh (2018) point out that, prior to their 2017 *Impact of CAS* study (Hayden *et al*, 2017), there was little in the way of published research about CAS. Even fewer studies were concerned with students' learning or how CAS contributes to the aims of the IB. Two such studies are, however, relevant. In research carried out in a Greek school, Hatziconstantis and Kolympari (2016) found that the effectiveness of the Service strand in conveying the aims of the IB depended on whether students identified with a selfless, idealistic-humanitarian view, or a self-serving, utilitarian-instrumentalist view in which volunteering contributed to an 'ideology of meritocratic competition' (2016, p13). However, a retrospective study involving alumni of an international school in Brazil found that Service helped transform students' views of themselves, increasing their sense of empowerment to promote social change through social, political and civic involvement (Lindemann, 2012). Despite the different contexts and focus of these studies, their findings can be related to the way in which Kolb or Dewey link experience and learning. To what extent the CAS programme, underpinned by Kolb's conceptualisation of experiential learning, contributes to the DP aim of developing international perspectives is an interesting question.

Small-scale studies can be useful indicators, but to examine more fully the extent to which the IB's adoption of Kolb's ELT is apt for the learning outcomes of CAS, the findings from a large-scale IB-funded research project into the impact of CAS will now be considered. In particular, attention is paid to the aims of CAS to provide enjoyable and significant experiences, and to students becoming responsible members of local and global communities. A survey, carried out via an online questionnaire, yielded responses from 7,973 DP students, 903 DP alumni, and 533 staff with responsibilities for administering CAS in their school. These stakeholders came from 89 countries in two of the IB world regions: Africa, Europe and the Middle East (AEM) and Asia Pacific (AP). Questionnaires sought respondents' levels of agreement with a series of statements about CAS as an experience and in relation to CAS outcomes as specified in IB literature and, from students, recorded the CAS activities in which they were engaging. Student data is used here to shed light on the learning that CAS experiences support. Responses were interpreted in relation to the impact of CAS activities on a range of curricular outcomes and their contribution to international mindedness – a key aim of the DP, as well as that part of the IB mission statement pertaining to developing a sense of responsibility for local, global and international communities.

Learning from enjoyable and significant CAS experiences

CAS was perceived as worthwhile by a large majority of students in this study, with differences between the strands: Creativity the lowest (83%) and Service the highest (87%). 74% agreed or strongly agreed that CAS being worthwhile was a motivating factor in their participation. Its compulsory nature may have prompted the students' strongest response when asked what motivated them to engage in CAS: 84% agreed that it was "because it is a requirement of the Diploma". However, enjoyment of CAS was the second strongest motivator, with 79% agreeing or strongly agreeing. These responses indicate that enjoyable CAS activities motivate students to engage – but what kind of experiences gave rise to these results?

Data from this study showed many traditional school-based activities: school plays, school sports teams, and volunteering within the school were considered to fulfil the CAS requirements. Such CAS activities can be associated with feelings of belonging and enjoyment, identified by Kolb (2014) as central to the kind of experience from which one can learn. Recognising the importance of feelings associated with an experience, and its meaningfulness to students as part of a transition process into adulthood, can become further strengthened when learning associated with experience is directed *towards* something that is valued by students. What follows are examples of CAS activities related to theories of learning through experience that can begin to show how they might support self-development (Kolb, 2014) and/or be educative and growth-oriented (Dewey, 1938).

Taking part in a unique creative experience, such as performing in a school theatre production or music concert, were common examples of what students were doing for the Creativity strand. Art and design projects, cookery, crafts and photography also featured, as did photography, creative writing and debating. Many of these, arguably, sit in Dewey's categories of 'free activity' – as opposed to an activity imposed by others – and allow individual 'expression' as a result. Creativity activities could also focus on a school event, such as a prom or graduation day, with students decorating the hall, organising rotas, or ordering equipment, developing transferrable individual skills such as organisation and leadership. Other students reported that writing poems or blog posts helped them to become more mature and self-knowledgeable. There is an interesting comparison to be made between the pragmatic benefits of learning how to organise one's busy schedule and the less clearly-defined benefits of artistic pursuits. Of course, which strand is under consideration makes a difference to what students are – or are not – learning from their CAS experiences.

Students' responses for Activity showed that they were engaged in many different exercises and playing a wide range of team and individual sports: soccer, badminton, swimming, basketball and volleyball featured, along with less common examples such as martial arts, gym routines, Zumba, Thai boxing and Parkour. However, many students' Activity took place in school PE lessons or on sports days. For some students, Creativity and Activity provided a chance to depart from the school setting, while for others the school remained the focus. Both Kolb (2014) and Dewey (1938) were clear that an advantage of progressive education was freedom from pre-planned outcomes, directed by schools, while Dewey pointed out that the disadvantage of this was overlooking the life experience of the student and jeopardising their engagement and, thus, the potential for learning. The Service strand, however, was different.

Service, which has been considered to have a transformative effect on students (Lindemann, 2012), included an extremely broad range of activities which seemed to engage students. These were broadly categorised as volunteering, or providing help in some way, to the school, for charities, or in the wider community, though there were also other ways in which students volunteered. Students helped with school parents' evenings, open days, and with the studies of younger students; charities had varied beneficiaries including the elderly, displaced people, the sick, the disabled, the underprivileged and the impoverished, and included those which supported animal and environmental causes. In the wider community, students were giving their time to support the staging of sporting or cultural events, were involved in work with children's or community health organisations, or were taking part in military or community service. There is clearly a relevance and immediacy to such experiences which are likely to make an impact on students. Attending to the feelings associated with the experience (Kolb, 2014), as well as its real-world relevance (Dewey, 1938) – which is important to students coming to the end of school life – can personally connect students with issues affecting communities at local, national, or international level. But what precisely are they learning?

The questionnaire invited students' responses to a series of statements about the development of the Learner Profile attributes and other characteristics identified in the IB literature as intended outcomes of participating in CAS. Questionnaire respondents could select one of four options in response to the statements: strongly agree, agree, disagree, strongly disagree. The stem 'Participating in CAS helped me become more ...' was followed by twenty-two characteristics which participation in CAS aims to develop, including the ten Learner Profile attributes: inquirers, thinkers, caring, open-minded, knowledgeable, communicative, risk-taking, principled, reflective and balanced. Some were rephrased to fit the structure of the stem, so thinkers became 'critical in my thinking' and inquirers became 'curious and questioning'. A high percentage of agreement around a response choice was considered to be a good indicator that the characteristic was perceived to have occurred as a result of participating in CAS activities.

Students' responses to all statements were overwhelmingly positive. More than 70% of students agreed, or strongly agreed, that all of the characteristics identified from the IB literature as outcomes of CAS improved through their participation in CAS. The highest percentage returns found that students felt that CAS participation had helped them become more communicative and more collaborative, both at nearly 90%. The lowest percentage returns showed students felt CAS participation had helped them become more curious and questioning, as well as more critical in their thinking, represented by 74% and 76% respectively. The third and fourth lowest categories were only slightly higher than these levels of agreement. Students perceived that CAS helped them become more aware of their responsibilities (77%) and more internationally minded (79%). With agreement levels in the range of 74% – 79%, it could be concluded that the impact of CAS was perceived by students to be closely related to the programme aims.

Despite strong agreement, the four lowest categories raise questions. The two lowest are curious and questioning, and critical thinking, arguably important in any learning activity. The third and fourth lowest levels of agreement, relating to development of responsibility and international mindedness, concern the part of the IB mission statement that aims to develop students as active members of local, national and *international* communities. These four, then, were least likely to be perceived by students to develop as a result of participating in CAS, and have implications for achieving the second CAS aim under consideration.

Can experiential learning develop personal and international perspectives?

Development of international mindedness is a central aim of the DP (Barratt Hacking *et al*, 2018) but this study, in identifying outcomes from the IB literature, revealed that they were primarily focused on benefits to individual students through acquisition of skills and characteristics. Does learning through experience, though, support the DP aim of developing international mindedness? Although international mindedness has been criticised for lacking clear distinction from other, similar, educational concepts such as global citizenship and intercultural education (Savva and Stanfield, 2018), elsewhere it has been identified with a degree of willingness to step away from a monocultural view of the world with "open attitudes towards other cultures and belief systems" (Haywood, 2015, p87) and interest in those "issues which have application beyond national borders" (Hill, 2012, p259). If these aspects are considered important and, indeed, they resonate with the IB's mission regarding intercultural understanding and respect (IB, 2016), how do individuals' highly situated and localised experiences help them to step out of the particular and local in ways that enable them to develop international perspectives? The questionnaire data included examples from students that showed that personal experiences can engage students with issues beyond their local community in ways that might contribute to the development of international mindedness.

Many schools had craft groups, where students were learning to knit, crochet or sew. One respondent stated that the Knitting Club at their school was engaged in a project in partnership with a local refugee charity. The gloves and scarves the school club was knitting were delivered to the charity, which shipped them to Syrian refugees in time for the coming winter. This example shows how Creativity has been intentionally connected with an international issue, involving students with events beyond their local context in ways not possible for students whose Creativity involved, for instance, continuing to learn a musical instrument. For the Activity strand, there were many examples where students engaged in physical activity in relation to ecological or environmental issues, such as mangrove planting, forest conservation, or beach cleanups. Service had multiple examples of local volunteering with, for instance, disabled people or animal shelters. There were also many organisations with a specifically international focus for which students volunteered, including the Red Cross, Amnesty International, the Global Issues Network, and Hospital Ships. Other examples showed how Service was an avenue through which students could experience issues of global significance, such as inequality and social injustice, and begin to make the connection between how they themselves could be related to the issues and, importantly, how they might be able to act upon them.

One final example which illustrates this last point well is taken from a detailed account given by one respondent about their CAS project. At the time the data were collected, the project required that students engage in teamwork and bring two or more strands together for a significant duration (IB, 2008). This particular project described how DP students attending a school in a South-East Asian capital city set out to collect and record the life stories of people who were living on the streets. They had met the people through their Service activity while volunteering with a local homelessness charity. The account given by the respondent describes the realisation that the homeless people and the students were in fact all citizens of the same place. The stories were recorded and made part of a website intended to communicate the street people's backgrounds, and to inform other people about how to help them. This project, like the examples above, shows that students can actively connect their CAS experiences to issues of international significance, but that this may have to be intentional. Activities which have an intentionally active international focus may not be limited by the fact that they take place within the school; the key is for students to step outside the international school 'bubble' and engage with issues that are more diverse than those they find within those walls.

This argument challenges that put forward by Belal (2017), who contends that, from evidence gathered in one Egyptian IB school, the diversity of the school population is more effective in developing international mindedness than is engaging with diverse communities outside the school. However, there is evidence that CAS experiences can be the environing conditions (Dewey, 1938) that support students' learning beyond their individual growth (Kolb, 1984; 2014) and relate closely to the stated programme and organisational objectives of active international mindedness. I conclude that adopting a Deweyian theorisation of experiential learning, with its focus on social participation, can better support the DP and IB aims than can Kolb's more individualist theorisation of experiential learning.

Concluding reflections

This chapter set out to contribute to the debate about what is learned through experience, drawing on Dewey (1938) and Kolb (1984; 2014) to examine how differences in the way they theorised experience and learning relate to differing educational aims and outcomes. The way in which experience, learning, and education are theorised influences the way in which the curriculum is interpreted and enacted, as well as influencing priorities and values. This was made clear when two learning outcomes of CAS were considered: learning through significant and enjoyable experiences, and learning to be responsible members of local, national and international communities. When these aspects were related to the aims of the DP and the IB more widely, some questions arose, particularly when considering the DP aim of developing international mindedness and the part of the IB mission statement that relates to developing students as responsible members of local, national and international communities.

Although the relationship of the DP to the IB's mission has been criticised for lacking clarity (Lineham, 2013; Belal, 2017), examples of CAS activities that intentionally focus on international issues and step out of a monocultural world view lead to active involvement in experiences that support the development of international perspectives. If a Deweyian lens is turned on these examples, any social aspect in the experiences assumes greater importance for fostering responsible community members. Perhaps future research can help to develop a more precise account of the way in which experiential learning through CAS activities articulates with the development of international mindedness.

Consideration of the intended aims of the theories of experiential learning included in this chapter raised questions about how they relate to the aims of an IB education. For instance, consider the effect of itemising individual characteristics at the centre of an educational programme with claims to being holistic. At the heart of the DP curriculum are a set of ten Learner Profile traits associated with an idealised *learner* which troubles Savva and Stanfield (2018) for its view of character that derives from the modern West but also influences interpretations of what is important, and what CAS activities are aiming to develop. Focus on becoming a learner puts classrooms, books, and academic learning in the foreground, rather than characteristics of an active and responsible member of local, national and international communities. It may also be argued that both holistic and experiential learning are somewhat limited by ten characteristics: is it possible to separate into individual characteristics the knowledge gained by the students whose knitting was sent to refugees? The Learner Profile attributes of being caring and principled might be emphasised in this activity, but could it be assumed that these were the only ones?

It has been argued that the theoretical lens through which experiential learning is considered may affect the emphasis on the outcomes of CAS. The experiential learning theory proposed by Kolb (1984; 2014) originates in the field of management, is intended for adults, and its purpose is personal development. This is a rather more individualistic educational purpose than that of Dewey (1938), for whom the purpose of education was to ensure that young people had positive learning experiences that laid the ground for their continuing active involvement in social and democratic processes. Through CAS activities which embody educative experiences (Dewey, 1938), and from which individuals learn how to connect to wider issues in the world, experiential learning complements a conceptualisation of international mindedness that typifies a growing awareness of one's self in the world. Such a process has been described as one of "'reaching out' to relate to others and 'reaching in' to understand ourselves" (Barratt Hacking *et al*, 2016, p38). While this process resonates with the Kolbian educational purpose of self-development and holistic education, a Deweyian conception of the purpose of education goes a step further. In asserting the inextricable links between people, we are not so much reaching out (perhaps) as acknowledging our inter-relatedness with the world.

References

Barratt Hacking E, Blackmore C, Bullock K, Bunnell T, Donnelly M & Martin S (2018) 'International Mindedness in practice: the evidence from International Baccalaureate Schools', *Journal of Research in International Education*, 17(1) 3-16.

Barratt Hacking E, Blackmore C, Bullock K, Bunnell T, Donnelly M & Martin S (2016) The International Mindedness Journey: School Practices for Developing and Assessing International Mindedness Across the IB Continuum, Research Report to International Baccalaureate. Available via: www.ibo.org/globalassets/publications/ib-research/continuum/international-mindedness-final-report-2017-en.pdf

Beames S & Ross H (2010) 'Journeys outside the classroom', *Journal of Adventure Education & Outdoor Learning*, 10(2) 95-109.

Belal S (2017) 'Participating in the International Baccalaureate Diploma Programme: Developing international mindedness and engagement with local communities', *Journal of Research in International Education*, 16(1) 18–35.

Braund M & Reiss M (2006) 'Towards a more authentic science curriculum: The contribution of out-of-school learning', *International Journal of Science Education*, 28(12) 1373-1388.

Dewey J (1938) *Experience and education.* Chicago: Simon and Schuster.

Garner I (2000) 'Problems and inconsistencies with Kolb's learning styles', *Educational Psychology*, 20(3) 341–349.

Gosen J & Washbush J (2004) 'A review of scholarship on assessing experiential learning effectiveness', *Simulation & Gaming*, 35(2) 270-293.

Hahn, K (1934, November) Radio broadcast: The practical child and the bookworm. (reprinted) *The Listener.*

Hatziconstantis C and Kolympari T (2016) 'Student perceptions of Academic Service Learning: Using mixed content analysis to examine the effectiveness of the International Baccalaureate Creativity, Action, Service programme', *Journal of Research in International Education*, 15(3) 181-195.

Hayden M C, Hemmens A, McIntosh S, Sandoval-Hernández A and Thompson J J (2017) The Impact of Creativity, Action, Service (CAS) on students and communities. The Hague: International Baccalaureate. Available via http://ibo.org/contentassets/d1c0accb5b804676ae9e782b78c8bc1c/cas-finalreport-2017-en.pdf

Hayden M and McIntosh S (2018) 'International education: the transformative potential of experiential learning', *Oxford Review of Education*, 44(4) 403-413.

Haywood T (2015) 'International-mindedness and its enemies', in Hayden M, Levy J & Thompson, J (eds.) *The SAGE Handbook of Research in International Education*, 2nd Edition. London: SAGE.

Hill I (2010) *The International Baccalaureate: Pioneering in education*. Woodbridge: John Catt Educational Ltd.

Hill I (2012) 'Evolution of education for international-mindedness', *Journal of Research in International Education*, 11(3) 245–261.

International Baccalaureate (2008) *Creativity, Action, Service Guide*. Cardiff: International Baccalaureate.

International Baccalaureate (2015a) *Creativity, Action, Service Guide*. Cardiff: International Baccalaureate.

International Baccalaureate (2015b) *IB Learner Profile Booklet*. Cardiff: International Baccalaureate. Available via: www.ibo.org/benefits/learner-profile

International Baccalaureate (2016) *International Baccalaureate Mission Statement*. Available via: www.ibo.org/about-the-ib/mission

Kolb D (1984) *Experiential Learning as the Source of Learning and Development*. Englewood Cliffs, N.J.: Prentice-Hall.

Kolb D (2014) *Experiential Learning: Experience as the Source of Learning and Development*, Second Edition. PH Professional Business, Safari online.

Lindemann I M F (2012) *Perceptions of former International Baccalaureate Diploma Programme (IBDP) students on the transformational impact of the Service element of Creativity, Action, Service (CAS) on their lives: a case study from Brazil*. Thesis (EdD). University of Bath.

Lineham R (2013) 'Is the International Baccalaureate Diploma Programme effective at delivering the International Baccalaureate mission statement?' *Journal of Research in International Education*, 12(3) 259-282.

Miller R (2000) 'Beyond reductionism: The emerging holistic paradigm in education', *The Humanistic Psychologist*, 28(3) 382–393.

Peterson A D C (2003) *Schools Across Frontiers: The story of the International Baccalaureate and the United World Colleges*. Peru, Illinois: Open Court Publishing Company.

Savva M and Stanfield D (2018) 'International-Mindedness: Deviations, Incongruities and Other Challenges Facing the Concept', *Journal of Research in International Education*, 17(2) 179-193.

Vygotsky L S (1978) *Mind in society: the development of higher psychological processes*. Cambridge, MA: Harvard University Press.

Walker G (2011) *The Changing Face of International Education*. Cardiff: International Baccalaureate.

Chapter 4

The Issues and Challenges of Assessing TOK

Julian H Kitching

Preamble

This chapter is the product of my observations and experiences, and my appraisal of initiatives launched by the IB over my eight years as chief assessor for Theory Of Knowledge (TOK), and, more broadly, as a TOK teacher and examiner for the past three decades. I hope it will contain some useful observations on a range of important issues for assessment in this signature IB Diploma Programme (DP) course that may not only set the present arrangements in context but also provide some salient backdrop for future developments.

Since 2001, TOK has been assessed using an externally assessed essay of 1,600 words and an internally assessed individual or group oral presentation with a duration of approximately 10 minutes per presenter. The internal assessment will take a different form from 2022, but this development is unlikely to invalidate my observations about TOK assessment as the challenges it presents transcend different assessment models as a result of the core nature of TOK itself.

I would like to divide my comments into five parts – each of them connected to a key aspect of making assessment judgements in TOK.

1. Feasibility: does the far-reaching ambition of the TOK course render it too difficult to assess student work?

2. Validity: are the periodic changes in the nomenclature of the central concept of the TOK course an indication of the difficulty in setting valid assessment tasks?

3. Authenticity: in the digital age, is it reasonable to expect responses to TOK assessment tasks to show original thinking from students?

4. Quality: is the current points weighting of TOK in the IB Diploma optimal for producing high-quality work of the kind that is appropriate for the course?

5. Reliability: what is the best mechanism for generating fair outcomes in a course that encourages such a high degree of complexity and variation in response to its assessment tasks?

How feasible is it to assess performance in TOK?

It is often correctly observed that the TOK course is unique to the IB Diploma. It is hence not possible to rely upon any prior disciplinary consensus among those with the tasks of teaching and assessing it, and there is a need for particularly well-articulated descriptions for those students who follow it. Achieving and documenting this consensus are tasks that are arguably complicated further by the sheer scale of the remit of TOK. For all of these reasons, there is value in reviewing the various ways in which the nature of the course has been described over its history in order to tease out the key aspects.

Perhaps the best entry point here is to revisit the perceived circumstances that promoted the genesis of TOK. These were identified by Alec Peterson in his memoir of the early IB years as "...the tendency of students to study subjects in watertight compartments", and "...the failure to make explicit the different forms in which academic learning and knowledge take place". He goes on to write that "...the intention of the course was to help the student to think about the questions which underlie the nature of knowledge as presented in the school disciplines and in his daily life." (Peterson, 1987, p48)

It seems clear from these observations that a prime intention behind TOK from the start was the promotion of an awareness and understanding of the architecture of knowledge in the various academic disciplines that DP students follow. This focus on the landscape and dynamics of knowledge would permit comparisons to be made across the academic curriculum. Furthermore, in an indication of the educational philosophy of the IB that is now so much more widely disseminated, it is suggested that understanding should be attempted through a process of enquiry. The final words of Peterson's description crucially broaden this field of questioning beyond the boundaries of the student's academic curriculum and legitimise the scrutiny of the contact the student experiences with all forms of knowledge.

So here we have a vision of TOK as enquiry aimed at the exploration of fundamental questions about the structure and functioning of knowledge across academic disciplines and beyond, developing an appreciation of similarities and contrasts, and of the opportunities for connections.

Meanwhile, the current IB TOK subject guide advises that TOK is "...a course about critical thinking and inquiring into the process of knowing, rather than about learning a specific body of knowledge." (IB, 2013, p8). And in a recent companion book, students are told that "...from the outset, the Theory of Knowledge was identified as an important element in promoting critical thinking which could be applied to the DP's six subject disciplines." (Bastian, Kitching and Sims, 2014).

On the surface, these extracts appear to place a stronger emphasis upon the approach that should be taken to the task of mastering TOK, which is closely identified here with critical thinking (indeed the last extract suggests that critical thinking comes first in some sense). This might amount only to a somewhat more explicit rendering of what Peterson meant by "thinking about the questions that underlie the nature of knowledge", but the focus upon critical thinking here may still have ramifications for how the course is understood by all varieties of stakeholder. Teachers are influenced by their own interpretation of what the TOK literature states, with obvious follow-through to the composition of the course in different schools and the learning experiences to which students are exposed. At an administrative level, these statements can shape the expectations of school leaders with respect to what they imagine to be the role of TOK in the wider curriculum. Student output in the form of responses to the assessment tasks may reflect some of these local factors.

So the content of specific TOK courses in schools varies in subtle ways – sometimes from a rather dry and detached examination of the nature of a range of academic subjects to a much more freewheeling and situated exercise in enquiry into the students' own life experiences. TOK may be conceptualised as a kind of shield or weapon for intellectual self-defence, or as a course advancing more assertively the development of critical thinking skills with looser connections to particular disciplines.

Presented baldly, with some exaggeration for effect, TOK might be construed as taking the following alternative forms:

i   A dispassionate study of the architecture of knowledge in different academic areas

ii   A vehicle for discussing the basis for students' knowledge in their lives as a whole

iii A set of tools that can help distinguish genuine knowledge from falsehoods, lies, spin, etc.

iv   A course for the development of critical thinking skills in each individual student

The fact that some of the current objectives of the course seem to map onto these conceptions of TOK suggests that all of them might have some legitimacy. By the end of the course, students are expected to be able to (i above) "examine how academic disciplines [...] generate and shape knowledge"; and (ii above) "...demonstrate an [...] understanding of different perspectives and be able to relate these to one's own perspective"; and (iii and iv above) "...identify and analyse the various kinds of justifications used to support knowledge claims". (IB, 2013, p15)

It is interesting to compare these statements of expectations in TOK alongside those for courses in critical thinking. For example, a recent version of the Oxford, Cambridge and RSA A-level course in Critical Thinking is designed to provide opportunities for students to: "understand the importance of examining knowledge and beliefs critically; recognise, analyse and evaluate their own and others' beliefs and knowledge claims in a variety of contexts; recognise and evaluate assumptions; evaluate reasoning of different kinds, including common and important species of reasoning; make connections and synthesise information and arguments; generate their own arguments and express them clearly." (Oxford, Cambridge and RSA Examinations Advanced GCE in Critical Thinking, 2013; H452)

It is instructive to note that most of these capacities would be regarded as necessary but not sufficient for success in TOK, thus illustrating the magnitude of the expectations of the TOK course. While value in dedicated critical thinking courses and TOK resides in the ability to apply critical thinking skills beyond the courses themselves, it would seem that TOK additionally places an instrumental value upon these critical thinking skills applied to the course content. This is surely because the subject matter of TOK involves dealing with a degree of complexity and uncertainty that demands particularly clear thinking and explains the historical link in TOK between the study of the nature of knowledge and the capacity for highly-developed rational thought.

It is often argued that recent developments in politics and world affairs – with the rise of 'post-truth' and the rapid spread of new means by which dubious claims and outright falsehoods are propagated – have rendered the need for mastery of critical thinking skills or intellectual self-defence ever more urgent. It is difficult to argue against the notion that young people should be given every opportunity to develop these skills or that formal education must form a crucial part of the array of potential measures that protect the quality of public discourse.

But whether or not such developments are singled out for accommodation in future iterations of the TOK course, the fact is that this strand of the TOK project remains only a part of the remit. The daunting scope of the course is accompanied by weighty implications for the task of assessing it, and arguably the challenges are magnified by the interpretive latitude offered to the teacher in the provision of learning experiences.

At the same time, developments in academia indicate significant changes to the intellectual landscape which might one day render the structure of a TOK course organised around an appraisal of traditional school disciplines somewhat dated or even obsolete. It is to be hoped that the structure of the DP as a whole will continue to evolve in order to reflect such changes, and at the same time provide a template for the composition of the TOK course.

In the last few years, TOK has been available as an assessed course to students who are not studying for the whole DP, or indeed any of it. This is a welcome development if it is accepted that the educational value of the course survives the severing of some (or all) links to other DP courses, or at least outweighs the loss of input that such courses naturally might provide. Attitudes are likely to hinge upon the degree to which the educational philosophy of the IB resonates across all elements of the DP.

TOK places heavy demands on teachers as a consequence of the breadth of knowledge and the course aims, and there is little doubt that the new teacher is faced with a steep learning curve. Quality of teaching and learning requires that this stage is negotiated successfully. In similar vein, examiners are expected to demonstrate at least some familiarity with knowledge from a wide range of disciplines to enable them to make reliable judgements about student work. Some examiners may not stay around long enough to grasp fully these requirements, and practical considerations may mean that some may need to be appointed before they have developed them. By contrast, dedicated critical thinking courses tend to strip out content and focus almost exclusively on the reasoning processes involved. With TOK, examiners often need to make vicarious evaluation of the students' own personal and cultural input, mediated in diverse classrooms around the world – something once memorably described as celebrating blooms we do not recognise; whereas critical thinking courses stick to publicly verifiable qualities of argument.

Is it feasible to assess performance in a course that has such a broad remit? Dealing with critical thinking alone would be an easier project. How can the threads outlined here be balanced and treated in a consistent way? What seems to be needed is a kind of virtuous circularity in which students' ability to deploy critical thinking skills is stretched by the nature of the content of the TOK course and then applied back to provide a deeper understanding of the content itself.

What is the central object of study in TOK that ensures that assessment tasks are valid?

Problems of knowledge

One of the consequences of the unique origins of TOK is the desirability of providing a vocabulary that can be understood by all, guide practice, augment achievement and steer the process of assessment. Of particular importance here is how the central object of study in TOK is framed. Early efforts to describe this object arrived at the concept of a problem of knowledge, and so, in 1999, students and teachers were presented with a new IB TOK guide urging them to ask: "How do I, or how do we, know that a given assertion is true, or a given judgement is well grounded?", and advised that "…the difficulties that arise in addressing these questions are […] known as 'problems of knowledge". (IB, 1999, p3)

These problems were alluded to indirectly through the provision of a total of 269 questions, organised by course component and sub-headings after brief introductory sentences. Only in one of the assessment criteria was there some unpacking as to what the problems might consist:

The phrase 'problems of knowledge' refers to possible uncertainties, biases in approach to knowledge or limitations of knowledge, and the methods of verification and justification appropriate to the different Areas of Knowledge. (IB,1999, p45)

The effort to problematise knowledge-making generally helped to focus TOK discourse on knowledge itself and thus perhaps distinguish it from that commonly found in other subjects. But while uncertainties, biases and limitations clearly seem to be categories of problems, methods of verification and justification, despite their challenges, could equally be viewed as attempts to find solutions. By including these aspects under the umbrella of 'problems', TOK students were arguably encouraged to see all of them in a negative light.

Nevertheless, a particularly successful exposition of the notion of problems of knowledge is shown below (Sims, R. Workshop Materials, IB TOK Workshop Oporto, October 1999) – in which problems reside in the epistemological gaps between two categories of objects.

Knowledge Gaps

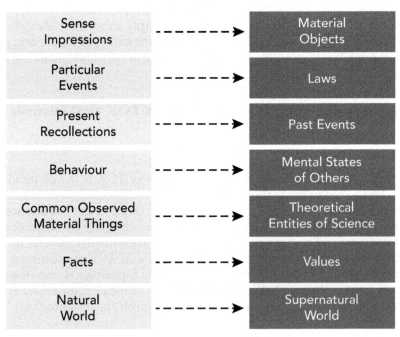

Figure 4.1: Knowledge Gaps (Sims, 1999)

Notwithstanding such successful conceptualisations, the negative implication of 'problem' tended to reinforce a widely held perspective that TOK was a subversive activity directed at undermining confidence in what was learned elsewhere in the DP and beyond. It tended to support the interpretation of TOK as a course in which the pillars of confidence in knowledge that scaffold learning are first kicked away and then replaced with a more modest set of prospects for the enterprise of knowing. Given the connotations of problems of knowledge, those involved in the IB's TOK curriculum review process felt that a sustained acknowledgement of the magnificent edifice of human knowledge was required. The 'demolish and rebuild' model is an unlikely strategy for success as it fails to empower what the student already thinks she knows. The apparent meaning of 'problems' led to the suggestion that it could be balanced with 'strengths of knowledge', but this formulation never really caught the imagination and was never followed up by the IB – possibly because of the danger of promoting a rather mechanical approach to analysis.

Knowledge issues

Concerns of this nature inspired a shift for the 2006 edition of the TOK guide in which 'problems of knowledge' were superseded by 'knowledge issues' – a term whose provenance lay in the name of one of the assessment criteria in the earlier guide. Here was an attempt to portray the business of TOK in more neutral terms. This phrase can be found 78 times in this document, including three instances alone within the course objectives, referring to "…areas of knowledge, ways of knowing and students own experience as learners"; the "understanding of different perspectives on knowledge issues"; and the ability to "draw links and make effective comparisons between different approaches to knowledge issues…". (IB, 2006, p5)

'Issues' supported the notion that the point of TOK was not merely to identify difficulties with knowledge but rather to discuss them. However, what exactly the parameters of such conversation should be were hard to pin down, and this difficulty is perhaps manifest in the guide itself:

> In the broadest understanding of the term, knowledge issues include everything that can be approached from a TOK point of view (that is, in accordance with the TOK aims and objectives as they are formulated) and that allows a development, discussion or exploration from this point of view. (IB, 2006, p10)

Knowledge questions

And so discussions during the lifetime of the 2006 TOK guide moved the debate on towards a further clarification of the key target of TOK. The idea of 'knowledge questions' became increasingly attractive as the term seemed intuitively simpler and easier to grasp – who doesn't know what a question is? But doubts were expressed about a change in terminology in such a key aspect of the course seeming to accompany every seven-year curriculum review by the IB. Nevertheless, the change was made for the 2013 TOK guide:

> Knowledge questions are questions about knowledge. Instead of focusing on specific content, they focus on how knowledge is constructed and evaluated... [They] are open in the sense that there are a number of plausible answers to them. The questions are contestable... [and] should be expressed in general terms, rather than using subject-specific terms... (IB, 2013, pp20-21)

In contrast to problems of knowledge, knowledge questions make an appearance in the course objectives, and examples are provided – in general and for each area of the course:

> Not a knowledge question: "How can we predict future population growth in Africa?" This is not a knowledge question because it is a technical question within the discipline of population studies.

> Good knowledge question: "How can a mathematical model give us knowledge even if it does not yield accurate predictions?" This is now sufficiently general and explores the purpose and nature of mathematical modelling. (IB, 2013, p22)

There is little doubt that the introduction of the concept of knowledge questions has assisted teachers in providing focus for their TOK lessons. To this extent, its introduction into the vocabulary of the course has been a success, but its alignment with assessment tasks has brought up a number of issues requiring further analysis and adjustment. The 2013 guide advises that:

> [Essay] titles are not meant to be treated only in the abstract, or on the basis of external authorities. In all cases, essays should express the conclusions reached by students through a sustained consideration of knowledge questions.... (IB, 2013, p52)

And essay examiners are tasked when faced with student work with answering the question:

> Does the student present an appropriate and cogent analysis of knowledge questions in discussing the title? (IB, 2013, p60)

While knowledge questions can be deployed in a variety of ways in the classroom, their centrality to the assessment process dictates that their use must be specified with more precision. The instrument for the TOK oral presentation demands that there be a single central knowledge question around which the entirety of the task revolves. Hence any failure to formulate it well produces a severe knock-on effect for the quality of the response as a whole. The essay instrument directs the examiner toward an evaluation of knowledge questions (plural) in the work and to the answers that are provided to them. But a series of explicit knowledge questions, each followed in turn by an answer, is not a promising formula for a stylish and convincing piece of prose. So what we see here is an asymmetry between the effectiveness of knowledge questions for teaching and learning, and for structuring responses to assessment tasks – unless those tasks are shaped in such a way to avoid these unintended consequences.

Comparing the formulations of the central objects of study

All of the formulations of the key focus of study in TOK discussed above are about recognition of some unresolved matter concerning what we know. All are aimed at fostering and maintaining dialogue at a second-order metacognitive level – an emphasis on *how* we know as the primary object of attention, one step away from an exclusive focus on the content of *what* we know. Each one of them has advantages and drawbacks, and can be summarised as follows:

- Problems of knowledge: largely about uncertainties, biases and limitations, tends to direct the student towards a negative perspective on knowledge; but emphasises the need to look critically at it

- Knowledge issues: everything approached from a TOK point of view – too amorphous; but arguably comes closest to describing the desired kind of discourse in TOK

- Knowledge questions: open, contestable, general questions about knowledge – more emphasis on the starting points of TOK discussion rather than the subsequent content: but there is a strong focus upon enquiry consistent with IB philosophy

It is clear that all of these attempts to capture the essence of TOK enquiry result in assessment tasks that are highly demanding for the student. In the IB's TOK curriculum review process, there is always a risk of over-correction in the longer term, but change is often delayed in the shorter term as a result of the time needed for the absorption and assimilation of the new. An accurate understanding of changes in the specification and requirements for TOK assessment is mediated through the careful deployment of language – an aspect of particular importance for an organisation operating at an international level and whose clientele is growing rapidly. Whereas at an earlier stage in the development of the IB, common understandings seemed to spread osmotically, there is now a more urgent need for precise terminology. The danger is that such terminology expands into the realm of what some might describe as jargon, and explanations turn opaque as obscure terms come to refer to each other.

The goal must be a sweet spot between the unjustified assumption of implicit collective understanding or an intuitive grasp of TOK matters on the one hand, and the overproduction of an extensive bespoke vocabulary, or 'jargon' of terms unique to TOK. If the legitimate scope of TOK is an important consideration, so surely is the nature of the key concept at its heart. At least a single concept at the heart of TOK helps to focus the attention of students, teachers and examiners. Not only should we consider what is to be assessed, but also how that assessment is to be prompted.

How can examiners judge the authenticity of candidates' work?

The metaphor of the intellectual journey is an attractive one in education, and no less so in the more restricted sense of TOK. A successful TOK journey relies upon the gradual assimilation of new ideas, skills and concepts, and a growing facility in marshalling them in new contexts. It requires that there be sufficient space in the process for students to include their own knowledge and intuitions, and subject them to the new input. Crucial also is that input is measured by the teacher according to the stage of the student's development, and tailored in a way that encourages him/her to fill that space.

Since the turn of the millennium, growth in students taking the IB Diploma has been such that there has developed a significant market for assistance for TOK students in the form of TOK books, blogs and websites. There is an obvious tension between the kind of input that provides good scaffolding for the student's own thinking and that which has the primary goal of making the TOK assessment tasks 'easier'. At best, the latter kind of input 'short-circuits' the developmental process; at worst it contaminates the student's thoughts with those of the 'helpers' in a way that makes it extremely hard for examiners to recover an authentically individual perspective on the task.

Online help sites thrive on the premise that many students do not receive sufficient support from their own teachers in order to fulfil their potential in the TOK assessment. This is undoubtedly the case in some schools, but it is in the interests of those in the 'help' business to exaggerate the extent to which this is true, and perhaps to overestimate their ability to know that it is so.

In these circumstances, it is tempting to favour a return to modes of assessment that render outside interference difficult or impossible. But there is a deep tension between giving students the space to explore and articulate their ideas and the attempt to evaluate student performance in a controlled environment. Under these circumstances, there is a need to keep faith in the value of the task and the integrity of most participants in it, despite the most valid and authentic task also being the most vulnerable.

One measure that the IB has taken in response to the concerns in this area has been to require each candidate to keep a record of interactions with the teacher over the period of 'gestation' of the TOK essay. This also carries the advantage of placing a strong emphasis on the process by which the candidate's work was created rather than just on the product. At the same time, the teacher is tasked with developing habits of mind in the student that resist what might seem to provide instant fixes and promote measured and deliberative thinking. This might well be a key characteristic of the nature of the DP core as a whole.

The ubiquity of material from 'help sites' does present a dilemma for examiners who often find themselves confronted with a regrettable uniformity of examples and arguments from students around the world. Too often, candidates suffer from including such material without having had the personal experiences in class that would guide them as to its suitability or what it actually means in context. Much of the advice is not good advice in the first place.

How can intellectual opportunity and concrete reward be balanced in the interests of quality of work?

Newcomers to the world of the DP and TOK often express surprise that a course that seems to speak to such an important and noble purpose attracts such a meagre reward in the context of the Diploma: about a point and a half is allocated to TOK out of a DP total point score of 45. The course is assessed on a scale of grades from A to E, and then combined with an award on the same letter scale for the Extended Essay through a matrix that generates a maximum of 3 points in total. Arguments have been advanced for finding a way to associate it with a greater haul of points in order to bring reward into line with intrinsic educational value, or the effort required for success.

There are strong grounds for believing that any move in this direction would corrode the nature of the TOK enterprise in fundamental ways. A potential score of 7 – the highest score in any DP course – for instance, would bring with it demands for accountability and assessment reliability that are almost certainly impossible to fulfil in this course. This could probably only be achieved by a deliberate narrowing of the scope of the course, and would result in candidates 'playing safe' with their responses to assessment tasks. It would also vastly increase the market for unsolicited advice.

Taken to the other extreme, it has also been argued that the best solution for TOK assessment is to liberate it from any points score at all. This would have the effect of avoiding pragmatic exigencies, and TOK could be monitored in a similar manner to another component of the DP core, Creativity, Activity and Service (CAS) through intermittent evaluation of each school's provision rather than focussing upon students' performance within it. The danger here is that the motivation to excel in tough, demanding summative tasks might well be diluted to the extent of depressing the quality of the student's engagement with the course as a whole. Additionally, it may be easier to support interest in the experiential learning of CAS rather than TOK through a means other than points availability.

The argument for the current model revolves around sticking with a happy medium that avoids an unhealthy overemphasis on assessment, while maintaining some motivation toward practical reward. It gives students a space in which to engage in some intellectual exploration without the threat of serious deleterious overall effects being associated with limited success.

However, the decision a few years ago to designate the lowest TOK grade of E as a failing condition for the whole Diploma has created a strong imperative among students to ensure enough engagement with TOK in order to avoid the weakest level of performance, but this 'stick' is arguably not balanced by any correspondingly attractive 'carrot' to encourage students to excel. Instead, candidates have to be encouraged to interpret the receipt of the highest grade (grade A) mostly as a stand-alone acknowledgement of excellence, with its value to be recognised rather than assigned as a reward. It may be that some further limited form of recognition might boost overall quality of work in TOK in a manner that would be discernible to examiners.

What assessment instrument and process is most likely to generate realiable outcomes?

It is clear that TOK presents multiple challenges for reliable assessment. For many years, TOK assessments were made with the help of a number of analytic criteria designed to identify discrete aspects of each assessment task. For example, the 2006 TOK subject guide presented four such criteria for each of the assessment tasks as: understanding knowledge issues, knower's perspective, quality of analysis of knowledge issues, and organisation of ideas. Assessment instruments of this type are predicated upon a certain degree of independence of the attributes that each criterion is designed to measure.

It is debatable as to whether desired attributes in TOK possess sufficient independence to merit placing them in separate categories. In the 2006 edition of the TOK subject guide, the challenge in viewing each criterion as a separate entity meant that, in practice, differences in judgements about TOK essays were easily magnified as stricter or more lenient awards of marks were reiterated across the criteria. Furthermore, the assessment instrument stretched over four pages due to the level of detail included in the levels of description in each criterion – generating a high cognitive load for the examiner that made retention of the details of the instrument extremely difficult.

In 2015, separate criteria were replaced by single marking scales of 0 to 10 for essays and for presentations. The descriptors at each level of these instruments referred to all attributes of the response worthy of reward together – an arrangement known as global impression marking. This move was designed explicitly to address the difficulties encountered in the multiple criterion model. Rather than a focus on the intrinsic meanings of words in the assessment instrument as applied to TOK, examiners were tasked with developing an understanding of these meanings by working through exemplars and other essays to which marks had already been attached. An understanding of standards arose from hands-on experience with examples rather than elucidation from the words in the descriptors themselves. With a single mark scale, there was no prospect of component marks 'conspiring' together to inflate or depress overall awards, and, with the instrument slimmed down to five bands of descriptors in total, the whole could be presented on a single page for the examiner to retain or easily revisit.

More recently still, there has been interest in adopting a radically different method of conducting assessment. Adaptive comparative judgement (ACJ) literally does away with marking as a concept altogether and, instead, presents the examiner with the task of comparing essays – two at a time – and making a judgement as to which is the better one. Over a sustained process of such comparisons, carried out by a large number of examiners, a rank order for all of the essays can be established. This is comparative judgement, and the process can be adjusted by applying a particular level of adaptation, which controls the process of pairing of essays according to the aggregated outcome of previous judgements.

ACJ presents exciting possibilities for 'democratising' assessment in contrast to the strict pyramid methods of quality assurance that have been employed up to now with a chief examiner whose standards are considered golden and which serve to be emulated as far as possible by other examiners down the hierarchy. However, a number of concerns remain. The system demands a lot of comparisons to be made by each examiner at a fairly consistent pace throughout the marking period. This is not how some examiners operate at the moment. The need for quick work raises worries about examiners merely skimming texts or making final judgements at an early stage in the reading, and these practices might be difficult to detect. Furthermore, the effort to reduce the cognitive load on examiners that was part of the attraction of global impression marking might be undone by the need to hold in the mind the content of two essays at the same time in order to make a comparative judgement about them. And finally, there is the danger of the 'wisdom of the crowd' dominating judgements in a way that diverges from what was intended by those who set the essay titles and those who may hold positions of authority in the assessment system.

Nevertheless, there are exciting and radical possibilities here for TOK assessment that will doubtless be explored further by the IB in the near future.

Reflections

When contracted to assist the IB in developing the latest TOK assessment instruments, Doug McCurry of the Australian Council for Educational Research memorably described assessment in TOK as "the perfect storm". The reasons for this conclusion would include the following from the perspective of the examiner:

- The difficulty for less experienced examiners of understanding the nature of second-order discourse, and hence making judgments about what is a valid candidate response
- The breadth of the suite of desired attributes in a successful response and the need to take account of all of them at the same time, leading to cognitive overload

- The fact that candidate responses are highly variable in their approach and their content, as a result of the ambitious scope of the course
- The credibility of material included in responses that is overtly personal and unverifiable, or seems to have been taken wholesale from sources designed to sidestep the normal developmental processes of construction
- The need to avoid punishing candidates for poor expression due to linguistic shortcomings when it may be that the thinking behind it is worthy of credit
- The poor quality of responses from some unmotivated candidates
- The volume of work that is expected of the examiner over a fairly short period

Elements in this list – particularly those towards the top – affect students and teachers as the other major stakeholders in the business of TOK assessment. The least we can do is to recognise that the storm can be calmed to some extent through conscious reflection and action on the aspects of TOK explored in this chapter – from an enhanced awareness of the multidimensional shape of the course, to a deep understanding of the nature and functions of knowledge questions, through interventions designed to maximise student ownership of the development of their work, and the application of an assessment instrument that is rigorous enough to shore up reliability while respecting the diversity and intellectual breadth that lie at the heart of TOK.

References

Bastian S, Kitching J, and Sims R (2014) *Pearson Baccalaureate Theory of Knowledge 2nd Edition*. Harlow: Pearson Educational Ltd.

International Baccalaureate (1999) *Theory of Knowledge guide*. Cardiff: International Baccalaureate.

International Baccalaureate (2006) *Theory of Knowledge guide*. Cardiff: International Baccalaureate.

International Baccalaureate (2013) *Theory of Knowledge guide*. The Hague: International Baccalaureate.

OCR Critical Thinking, www.ocr.org.uk/qualifications/as-a-level-gce/critical-thinking-h052-h452

Peterson A (1987) *Schools Without Frontiers*. Chicago: Open Court.

Sims R (1999) *Knowledge Gaps*, Workshop Materials, Oporto, International Baccalaureate.

Chapter 5

The Cohesive Power of the IB Diploma Core

John Cannings

Introduction

Right from the outset, the structure of the IB Diploma has had many traits which align it with a holistic education. John Hare, in his position paper written for the IB (2010), argued that all three of the IB Primary Years Programme (PYP), Middle Years Programme (MYP) and Diploma Programme (DP) are examples s of holistic education. Before that, in a speech given in 2008 the then Chair of the IB Board of Governors, Dr Monique Seefried, outlined the qualities of an IB education that contained many of the characteristics of holistic education. However, holistic education has been notoriously difficult to define (Forbes and Martin 2004; Rudge 2010). Hare identified some of its qualities and listed some learner outcomes, which are remarkably similar to the attributes of the IB Learner Profile – although his paper did not fully embrace some of the concepts and ideas of holistic education. Since Hare's paper there have been references in introductory remarks made by Adrian Kearney at the 2018 IB Global Conference to the IB delivering a holistic education, but no further developed statement on its meaning.

The core of the IB Diploma (the Extended Essay, CAS and TOK) is a framework designed by the IB that has the potential to facilitate a holistic education. However, it is really for individual schools to realise this potential fully, and doing so presents many challenges. Anecdotal evidence from workshops in which I have been involved, both online and face-to-face, suggests that in some schools strands of the core are in fact quite isolated from the rest of the Diploma programme. Figure 5.1 is my own representation of how I understand many teachers to perceive the IB Diploma and its level of cohesion.

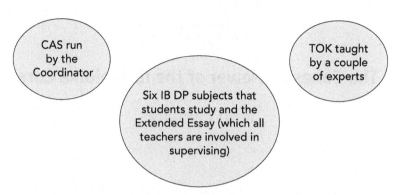

Figure 5.1: Teachers' perceptions of cohesiveness in the core

Experienced DP teachers are likely to recognise the importance of the academic subjects, which they and others teach. They are also likely to see that the Extended Essay is relevant to students' learning, as they have to supervise those with a focus on their subject area. In my experience, however, many teachers appear to know little about the Theory of Knowledge course and are not able to identify its basic structure or content, perceiving it to be the domain of identifiable experts on the staff with whom they have little interaction. Again in my experience, CAS is often considered to be the province of a CAS Coordinator and to take up an inordinate amount of school time.

This chapter will examine the qualities identified by Forbes and Martin, Rudge and others about holistic education, and consider the role that the core plays in developing these qualities. The core is at its most cohesive when a number of strategies are developed to enhance its power in not only linking its three strands (Extended Essay, Theory of Knowledge and CAS) with each other, but also in forging links between the core and the subjects.

An important aspect of the power of the core is revealed by the role played by the process of reflection, as it is a common feature of all three core strands. Reflection is different in each part of the core and yet the three strands can complement each other. In CAS, reflection is based on authentic experiences the student has had, while the Extended Essay requires the student to reflect critically on their research process, and for the Theory of Knowledge students are expected to analyse how knowledge is acquired. A challenge in developing understanding of the reflection process, however, is that in many students' minds and also in some teachers' minds, reflection is seen as a product. Stirling Perry (2018), in an IB conference presentation, quoted a Turkish student whose view echoes those of many other CAS students: "I think reflection is something that we have to do, so it's not very helpful". Students may feel that what they are doing is producing something that the teacher wants to hear, rather than what the students think, feel or learn about themselves, and feel constrained by the fact that it has to be a piece of written prose. Some teachers

I have encountered (especially new CAS Coordinators) may not yet have learned how to be very creative in facilitating different forms of reflection through, for instance, audio, group discussions, poetry, art and music.

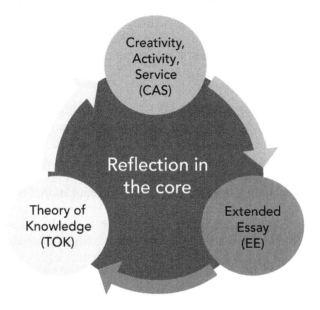

Figure 5.2: Reflection in the core (IB, 2015)

Arguably, CAS, TOK and the Extended Essay can play an important role in helping to develop a student's understanding of themselves and the subjects they are studying through the process of reflection (see Figure 5.2). Through the TOK course students start to develop a sense of metacognition, where they develop an overview of the different ways in which knowledge is acquired from different subjects. This occurs particularly when subject teachers are also able to support TOK by reflecting on how knowledge is created in their subjects – though this may not always be the case in reality if subject teachers have not yet developed that level of expertise with TOK.

TOK can also provide the framework for carrying out research for the Extended Essay. Any Extended Essay raises a number of knowledge questions, which are at the heart of TOK, although this potential is not realised in all schools. CAS is able to link with the skills and knowledge of the individual subjects through the pedagogy of service learning, where students research an authentic need and then use skills learned in the classroom to undertake service. Again, the extent to which such links are made is dependent on subject teachers being aware of the potential link as well as on the students involved.

This chapter will discuss the meaning of holistic education and whether or not the IB Diploma is (or could be) a good example of such an approach. The extent to which the DP can move more effectively in the direction of holistic education may rest on just how mindfully schools integrate the core into their practices and lived values. The second aim of the chapter is to consider the unique role of the core within the DP and examine its potential for delivering holistic education. In particular, we shall look at relationships and (particularly) reflection elements within the core which can make it cohesive and encourage the potential for stronger relationships between the core and the subjects.

Holistic education and the IB

Miller (1990, in Rudge, 2010) argues that "holistic education is not to be defined as a particular method or technique; it must be seen as a paradigm, a set of basic assumptions and principles that can be applied in a number of diverse ways." Miller (1990, in Rudge, 2010) and Forbes (2003) made the first attempts to analyse the meaning of holistic education. Forbes (2003) has argued that a holistic education should develop two major concepts: Ultimacy (in which the person experiences spiritual enlightenment, or is psychologically well developed and reaches the highest possible state: sometimes described as self-actualisation) and Sagacious Competency (which equates with wisdom). A person reaching this state experiences inner freedom, good judgement, metacognition, social ability, refining of values and self-knowledge. Rudge (2010) identified ten basic qualities of holistic education:

a. It should be focused on human development

b. It recognises the uniqueness of each individual as a learner

c. Learning is primarily experiential

d. The concept of wholeness should be at its heart

e. Educators should facilitate the learning which is considered to be a natural process

f. Students have an opportunity for choice throughout

g. It should educate for citizenship in a democracy

h. It should educate for global citizenship

i. It should educate for global sustainability

j. It should educate for spirituality

As noted earlier, Hare (2010) wrote that the IB programmes (at the time DP, MYP and PYP) were forms of holistic education, stating that "Holistic education does not exist in a single consistent form. It is best described as a group of beliefs, feelings and general ideas that share a family resemblance (Forbes, 2003, p2). It is more than the education of the whole student and addresses the very broadest development of the whole person at the cognitive and affective levels".

Hare goes on to say that the aim of such an education must be to produce an individual who wishes to lead a productive life, contribute actively to the society in which they live and be a lifelong learner. He argued that holisitic education produced a set of outcomes not dissimilar to the IB Learner Profile. It has been argued by Martin (2018) that Hare's paper "failed to address some of the theoretical conflicts between a productive life that is good for a society versus the self actualization and wisdom needed for human beings to develop toward goodness or other 'higher' goals, where they live in society, while not necessarily being 'of society'". Martin went on to explain that this distinction essentially distinguishes between Forbes' use (2003) of 'social ability' and what are often referred to as 'social skills'. Social skills are easy to teach, whereas social ability must be nurtured and facilitated in more experiential ways, with reflection being an integral part of the learning process, integrated according to students' own learning processes and not imposed artificially.

Dr Monique Seefried (2008, p4), then Chair of the IB Board of Governors, argued – without explicitly using the term – that the IB programmes had many of the qualities of holistic education:

> An IB education places emphasis on 'learning how to learn' and on developing attitudes which students will retain throughout their lives. The opportunity for learning by doing rather than learning by receiving is an integral element ... The fundamental themes of all IB programmes are:
>
> - developing citizens of the world – cultural and linguistic development as well as learning to live together
> - building and reinforcing students' sense of identity and cultural awareness
> - fostering students' recognition and development of basic human values
> - stimulating curiosity and inquiry in order to foster a spirit of discovery and a joy of learning
> - equipping students with the skills to learn and acquire knowledge, individually or collaboratively, and to apply this knowledge to a broad range of areas
> - providing international content while responding to local requirements and interests, encouraging diversity and flexibility in pedagogical approaches
> - providing appropriate forms of assessment and international benchmarking

She went on to say that "From the outset, IB programmes have aimed to develop students' minds as well as hearts not only through formal teaching but also through service to others."

Many characteristics of holistic education can be found in the points made here. Two key points that are hallmarks of holistic education are that students 'learn how to learn', and that the IB programmes aim to develop minds as well as hearts, with the learning through the heart coming from service experiences outside the classroom. Research by Forbes, Martin and Miller has identified many school systems which claim to offer a holistic education, including the Waldorf, Montessori and Quaker schools. The IB Diploma Programme exemplifies many of the characteristics of holistic education defined above. It aims for students to be internationally-minded, based in local and global contexts, to encourage students to develop metacognition and to learn from experiential education. Moreover, it aims to educate the whole person, and helps students to clarify and develop their values. These are aims that the IB itself has decreed for students and schools, raising the question 'Can IB schools move solidly in the direction of holistic education?'

Characteristics of the DP core that help to create opportunities for holistic education

Theory of Knowledge

The Theory of Knowledge course encourages students to be aware of how they acquire knowledge. It aims to achieve this through the lens of Areas of Knowledge, which broadly overlap with the academic subjects that students study in the IB Diploma: Mathematics, Natural Sciences, Human Sciences, History, The Arts, Ethics, Religious Knowledge systems, Indigenous Knowledge systems. Each of the Knowledge Areas considers the scope and application of the area, specific language and concepts used, methodology used to acquire knowledge, how knowledge in that area has developed over time, and a person's individual connection to that area. Students are expected to see similarities and differences between how knowledge is acquired in the different Knowledge Areas. They examine Knowledge Areas through the lens of different Ways of Knowing identified by the IB as Language, Emotions, Sense Perception, Reason, Memory, Intuition, Faith (used here in the sense of trust) and Imagination. These Ways of Knowing affect the acquisition of knowledge, helping students to develop what Forbes and Martin (2004) describe as metacognition (one of the characteristics of holistic education).

The IB Theory of Knowledge guide claims that knowledge is unique to each student and that it derives from two sources: personal knowledge and shared knowledge (see Figure 5.3), implying that every individual has a unique store of knowledge derived from their own experiences and shared with others. Knowledge can be sourced in a variety of ways through individual subjects. It highlights one of the principles of holistic education noted by Rudge above about the individuality of each learner.

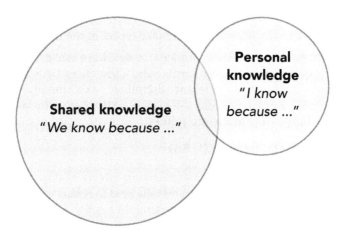

Figure 5.3: Personal and Shared Knowledge (IB, 2015, p 17)

Central to the TOK is that students can ask questions about knowledge. Knowledge questions are expected to be about how they have acquired knowledge or how knowledge has been created. These questions tend to be open-ended, which allows for interpretation about a particular issue from different perspectives. The questions themselves tend to be general in nature. One example of such a question is 'How certain is scientific knowledge?', which suggests the review of various examples of paradigm shifts that have occurred in science, and particularly the review of how changes in methodology have brought about refinements in our understanding of the environment.

TOK's cohesiveness with the academic subjects through reflection

In TOK, students have to reflect on claims about the truth in various disciplines or knowledge areas, create Knowledge Questions and analyse them using examples from real life and their academic subjects. They have to consider the role that the Ways of Knowing have played in developing this knowledge. When TOK is truly functioning well in a school, subject teachers are able to reflect on their subject through a TOK lens, seeing both the strengths and limitations of how they know what they know. Teachers can make the link to their knowledge area and refer directly to it in their classes. They can highlight the language that the subject uses and, in particular, the methodology they are using to acquire knowledge in their subject area. Moreover, they can assist students in identifying and developing potential knowledge questions in their subject areas. In addition, they are able to respond in a knowledgeable way to students when they identify a link to TOK. However, my own experience of responses received from participants in online workshops has been that their knowledge of TOK is limited, they have difficulty in helping students to make links to TOK, and they have real issues trying to phrase Knowledge Questions. Lack of knowledge of TOK also appears to be an issue where the DP is being offered in conjunction with national programmes, and teachers are involved with teaching their subject in both programmes. Teachers in this context are committed to their subject, but may struggle to engage with this broader aspect of the DP.

TOK provides an opportunity for students to develop a sense of metacognition where they can compare the similarities and differences between knowledge that they have acquired in different disciplines. Additionally, students are able to recognise similarities and differences with respect to how they have acquired that knowledge in the disciplines.

Creativity, Activity, Service (CAS)

CAS and Holistic Education

Creativity, Activity, Service (CAS) "enables students to enhance their personal and inter-personal development through experiential learning." (IB, 2017). Knowledge is created through an individual's reflection on experiences that enable learning to occur. The learning process involves much more than just the experience; it also involves research, planning, acting, observing and reflecting. In the enactment of these experiences, individuals develop relationships with others and with the communities to which they belong. The results of this learning prove to be the creation of knowledge at a very personal level. Students are expected to make their own choices of experiences in a way that ensures that they come to no harm, while the role of the CAS Coordinator is to support the students, ensure their safety and enable them to make choices appropriate to their abilities.

The seven learning outcomes of CAS that students are expected to exhibit focus on personal development. They ask students to identify their own growth from new challenges, to show commitment and resilience, demonstrate the ability to work with others, connect with global issues and recognise that they have acted in an ethical way. Achieving these outcomes enables students not only to develop socially, but also to realise their role as part of a global community and to clarify their own values.

CAS then can help to provide several of the qualities of holistic learning described by Rudge (2010):

1. It can facilitate human development.
2. It provides for individual learning.
3. Students should have choice of activity throughout.
4. Learning is primarily experiential.
5. It facilitates a sense of global citizenship
6. It aims to develop the whole person.

A key factor in learning from CAS is the process of reflection. The American educational writer, John Dewey (1910, pp 209-210), had this to say about reflection: "The working over of a vague and almost casual idea into a coherent form is impossible without a pause, without freedom from distraction ...

[Reflection] is indispensible for the development of coherent and compact conclusions."

Considerable effort was made in the 2017 CAS guide to stress the importance of reflection (it is mentioned 93 times) and to highlight the need for students to carry out reflection on an on-going basis. However, research undertaken by Perry (2018) in Turkish schools indicated that in fact reflection was taking place after experiences rather than before, during and after experiences as advocated by the 2010 and 2017 CAS guides. Moreover, Perry's research also highlighted that students' reflections were often presented in such a way as to satisfy what the CAS Coordinator wanted to hear. Brodie's (2014) research on CAS also highlighted that students found reflection difficult and that it was the part of CAS that they found most tiresome. While there has been a growing recognition that teaching of reflection is necessary, there are still schools that do not formally timetable lessons for CAS, which may lead to students lacking in basic skills.

Cohesion of CAS with DP Subjects

In the 2017 CAS Guide a tentative link between CAS and the pedagogy of Service Learning was made through the use of a five-stage experiential learning model developed by Cathy Berger Kaye for carrying out CAS experiences and demonstrating learning. Service Learning has been defined as:

> an approach to teaching and learning in which students use academic knowledge and skills to address genuine community needs.

Service has traditionally been a well-recognised element of CAS and part of an IB school's ethos. Service Learning is a part of CAS Service as shown in Figure 5.4, and not the only way in which Service can be practised.

Figure 5.4: extract from unpublished presentation at the IBAEM Conference (Wynten, Robeau and Cannings, 2015)

Many DP subject teachers struggle to make links between CAS Service and their subjects, even though it is a formal requirement that they make the link in their unit plans. In the US, where the pedagogy developed has seen a good uptake of Service Learning, perhaps the greatest successes have been where Service Learning was included as part of the IB Middle Years Programme (MYP) and clear links have been established between subjects and Service.

Extended Essay

The Extended Essay and Holistic Education

The Extended Essay has traditionally been a piece of research that students undertake and write up in 4,000 words on a research question of their choice in a subject discipline. The assessment criteria have recently been revamped to include reflection on the research process as a compulsory requirement. Here it can benefit from reflection skills learnt in the Theory of Knowledge. The World Studies Extended Essay is a recent development that allows students to study a global issue at a local level through the lens of two different subjects. The IB states that:

> A World Studies Extended Essay must focus on a topic of global significance. This encourages the student to reflect on the world today in relation to issues such as the global food crisis, climate change, terrorism, energy security, migration, global health, technology and cultural exchange. (IB, 2018a)

CAS can provide opportunities for World Studies Extended Essays in particular. Students are dealing with issues such as refugees, the elderly, working with people suffering from a variety of illnesses, and environmental sustainability – global issues with which they engage in a local context through CAS and which can provide an opportunity for an essay. An example of such a link arises from a student working with sickle cell disease sufferers in London who, using the disciplines of geography and biology, wrote an essay about the distribution of sufferers in London.

This relates to the characteristics of holistic education noted by Rudge of developing global citizenship and awareness of global sustainability. However, it must be noted that while the World Studies Extended Essay is growing in popularity, only 1,264 of 79,635 Extended Essays were submitted in May 2017 (IB, 2017). Individual essays may address global issues, but the Extended Essay has not proven to be the major vehicle for holistic education that the other strands have provided.

Reflection within the Extended Essay

Students are now required to reflect formally on the Extended Essay. They are expected to reflect on three separate occasions with their Essay supervisor and record this on a form in 500 words. Students are able to use feedback from their supervisors in generating their reflections. The first reflection should enable students to describe the topic they have chosen and discuss some of the materials used in the initial research. It may also include such things as mind maps of the topic. The second reflection should include the research question and a clear vision of the method of research to be carried out. It should be critical of that approach and also set a clear timeline for the research. The third reflection should occur after the Extended Essay has been submitted. The student should have a clear idea of whether or not they have answered their research question, and provide a clear analysis of the Essay's strengths and weaknesses.

The cohesive power of the Theory of Knowledge with the Extended Essay

A great opportunity arises to apply the reflective and analytical skills of the Theory of Knowledge to reflection on the Extended Essay. When a student chooses an Extended Essay topic they often do so based on their own personal interest and knowledge, using the personal knowledge they have acquired and starting to tap into shared knowledge. The Area of Knowledge framework can be used to support the student in reflecting on their Essay research question and preparing for the second Extended Essay reflection. Every Extended Essay will be based within one of the Knowledge Areas. The research question itself should fit within the scope or application of the subject area, though sometimes it is not clear to students whether that is the case. The Essay should be written using terms and concepts that are applicable to the subject chosen, and this is recognised in the new marking criteria. The new subject guides recognise key concepts for each subject. Geography, for example, has four key concepts: Power, Place, Processes and Possibility, with subsidiary concepts of scale and spatial interactions (IB, 2018b).

In the second reflection, it is important that the student is very clear about the methodology of collecting data for the Essay as this is an important aspect of the research process. In addition, the student has the opportunity to consider how the data will be analysed. They are able to receive feedback on whether the process they are following is likely to support them in carrying out their research properly. The historical development of the subject area may need to be discussed in the Essay; within the subject there may have been a number of significant paradigm shifts that need to be considered as the Essay develops. Lastly, every Extended Essay makes a number of claims about knowledge that underpin the research question, and asks some fundamental questions about how knowledge may be acquired. The last reflection the students have to make requires them to evaluate their Essay. It asks students to be self-critical of their methodology and to suggest improvements for research within the topic.

TOK therefore has the potential to facilitate the research process in the Extended Essay by use of the TOK knowledge framework. The Ways of Knowing may play an important role in carrying out the research. This cohesive link between the two strands of the core has the potential to heighten the bonds of unity within the Diploma. However, anecdotal evidence suggests it is not often used by Extended Essay supervisors, and that many supervisors appear to be struggling with appropriate advice for students in carrying out reflections for the EE. My own observations from supervising a number of geography Extended Essays suggests that many students could have benefitted from having a greater understanding of the link when making their reflections.

The cohesion between CAS and TOK through reflection

When TOK and CAS are linked together in a joint experience and reflection, they can help students to clarify their values and develop an ethical identity. Maria Ines Piaggio (2012) has described an individual's ethical identity as the ability "to own his/her life"; in other words, the ability to judge what is right or wrong and to decide on the key influences that they wish to follow in life. It goes further than that, however, including the ability to take decisions that are ethically valid and to do so in a free and autonomous way that ultimately determines what makes a person happy. Piaggio argues that both CAS and TOK form a part of ethical education, alongside DP policies relating to academic honesty and experimentation. She identifies four major aims for ethical education:

1. The developing of a coherent ethical identity: free, autonomous, accountable for and able to take ethically valid decisions.

2. A respectful and peaceful co-existence between people, groups and cultures and countries celebrating diversity as well as wealth of humanity.

3. Intercultural understanding, safeguarding the identity of people and communities involved.

4. The clarification of and development of values.

It is argued that ethical education requires the development of both cognitive and affective qualities and is carried out through experiential education.

What implications does this approach to ethical decision-making have? In response to this question, Piaggio (2012) argued that the following benefits arise:

a. Acceptance of some general values (the values presented by the IB mission statement and Learner Profile)

b. Awareness of different ethical systems (through TOK)

c. Reflection on the reality of decisions made

d. The ability to make the transfer between the knowledge of values and how one behaves

e. The ability to build relationships based on respect and self-respect for others

Theory of Knowledge helps students to do this by examining morality. Dombrowski et al (2007, p226) state that "In TOK, we will consider morality to be our sense of right and wrong, and ethics to be the Area of Knowledge that examines that sense of morality and the moral we develop from it." A number of ethical systems are examined in TOK:

1. The source of morality is human nature (Kohlberg's ideas on moral development, Maslow's hierarchy of needs and Rousseau and natural man)

2. The source of morality is religion. Both theist and non-theist religions teach codes of morality based on a supreme being or forces beyond the material world

3. The source of morality is observation and/or reasoning (Kant's categorical imperative and John Stuart Mill's principle of utility)

4. The source of morality is emotional empathy (Carol Gilligan's ethics of care)

5. The source of morality is social and political: the laws of a particular society or international agreements that override them (UN Declaration of Human Rights)

Reflection on CAS experiences provides one important opportunity to examine the ethical system or systems that an individual uses in making a decision. A discussion in a TOK lesson provides the opportunity to decide whether or not the students have met the seventh learning outcome of CAS:

LO 7 Recognize and consider the ethics of choices and actions: ... Students show awareness of the consequences of choices and actions in planning and carrying out CAS experiences. (IB, 2017)

In my experience, many CAS Coordinators find this to be the most difficult of the learning outcomes for students to understand. However, linking CAS to TOK in a lesson can help students to understand the full implications of their actions and to be able to reflect meaningfully on them. A challenge for many schools is being able to make these two parts of the core truly cohesive and facilitate the development of an ethical identity.

There are other ways in which CAS and TOK can be mutually beneficial. It would be possible to use a real-life situation from CAS as the basis for a TOK presentation. The presentation might have as its genesis an ethical dilemma that has arisen from CAS. For instance, a school has traditionally supported a school for girls in Tanzania, and students have visited it and worked there. Now, however, the school finds that some of the money sent and buildings constructed are being used for other projects. A dilemma for the students and the school is whether to continue to support the Tanzanian project. A Knowledge Question that could be developed and that could be the basis for a TOK presentation is 'How much does reason guide our ethical decision making?'. This could be linked to other situations that the student may have come across academically, such as the amount of aid money that a country donates at a time of high local unemployment.

CAS can also help to provide real-life situations to support an answer to the TOK essay. The TOK essay is different from the presentation in that the students are given a choice of six titles from which to choose. Not all essay titles will provide students with the opportunity to reflect on a CAS experience, but what follows are two topics that were suggested to students in the past:

> Are reason and emotion equally justified in making moral decisions? (November 2007/May 2008).

This could have been partially analysed by examining an ethical decision made in a CAS experience and considering decisions made in history, such as Germany's decision to go to war in 1914.

Another question that was posed highlights the possible nexus between CAS and TOK:

> Moral wisdom seems to be as little connected to knowledge of ethical theory as playing good tennis is to knowledge of physics (according to Emrys Westacott). To what extent should our actions be guided by our theories in ethics and elsewhere? (November 2008/May 2009).

CAS and TOK when linked together provide many opportunities for the development of holistic education. The knowledge created in CAS provides the opportunity for critical reflection by students. It can help them to define their own values and to achieve a better understanding of themselves and the way they act, moving towards the human development of the whole person. This comes through the process of reflection, which is an essential part of both strands of the core.

Conclusion

No single education system offers all of the qualities that Rudge uses to define holistic education, nor can this be decreed by a particular system. The IB Diploma core framework certainly seems to provide many of the characteristics of holistic education noted in this chapter. It encourages a sense of global citizenship (through its emphasis on international mindedness), it aims to develop the whole person and provides, not only through CAS but also through some of its subjects, the opportunity for experiential education. Moreover, the core of the IB Diploma helps to clarify and develop a set of values from which to work.

In this chapter, it has been argued that the core of the Diploma has the ability to develop in students a series of holistic education experiences. If the core can be delivered in such a way that it strengthens the links between the strands of the core, and between the core and the subjects, then it will make the Diploma more cohesive. A key to this cohesiveness is the ability to use the process of reflection to link the core strands. It has been argued that this has great potential but it is not always realised.

The potential of TOK to be reflected on by students within their subjects is a challenge, if subject teachers struggle to understand it and see its relevance. This is particularly so in schools where the DP is not the only pre-university course being taught (such as the many public high schools in the US, and schools in other countries that also have to offer a national curriculum). Similarly, the symbiotic relationship between CAS and TOK is not fully realised when the two operate separately, and there is little chance for joint reflection or for CAS experiences to provide real-life knowledge to be drawn on in TOK assessments.

The formal requirement for reflection in the Extended Essay caused many students and teachers some consternation in its first year of operation. Using the TOK Knowledge Areas framework could help students to be more critical and focused in their reflection on the Essay, rather than simply producing descriptions of their research process.

CAS experiences may lead to development of a subject-specific or World Studies Extended Essay. While this approach to the EE is slowly but surely being encouraged in DP schools, there is fear amongst some EE Coordinators that students will find difficulty in coping with the transdisciplinary approach required.

It should not be forgotten that while the IB can present the philosophy and framework for holistic education to be developed within schools, it is for the individual schools to see the potential that exists and develop that potential. In my experience such a development is at present still rather piecemeal. It may be that the adoption of the following approaches and strategies could improve the situation:

1. That school leaders understand more fully the value of the core in facilitating holistic education, and reflect that understanding by making greater provision of time and resources to teaching it.

2. That the core teachers operate as a team, and plan activities for the students that give real cohesion to the core and establish the links of reflection between the strands.

3. That subject teachers are involved in attending student presentations on TOK and CAS so that they have a better understanding of them.

4. That students are taught about the different types of reflection that are needed within the core, and their value.

The growth of such approaches and strategies in DP schools may well, in due course, lead to the core being seen truly as a cohesive force in promoting holistic education.

Acknowledgement: Many thanks to Dr Robin Martin for feedback and suggestions in developing this chapter.

References

Brodie T (2014) *The perception and practice of Creativity, Action, Service in the IBDP for students, teachers and schools*. The Hague: International Baccalaureate, Available via www.ibo.org/contentassets/4ccc99665bc04f3686957ee197c13855/finalexecutivesummaryandappendices.pdf

Dewey J (1910) *How we think*. Available via https://ia801406.us.archive.org/17/items/howwethink000838mbp/howwethink000838mbp.pdf

Dombrowski E, Rotenberg L and Bick M (2007) *Theory of Knowledge: Course Companion*, Oxford: Oxford University Press.

Forbes S (2003) *Holistic Education: An Analysis of Its Ideas and Nature*, Brandon, VT: Solomon Press.

Forbes S and Martin R (2004) *What holistic education claims about itself: An analysis of Holistic Schools literature*. Paper presented to American Educational Research Association Conference, San Diego

Hare J (2010) *Holistic education: An interpretation for teachers in the IB programmes, IB Research Paper*. Geneva: International Baccalaureate.

IB (2015) *Guide for Theory of Knowledge*. Geneva: International Baccalaureate.

IB (2017) *Guide for Creativity, Action, Service*. Geneva: International Baccalaureate.

IB (2018a) *World Studies Extended Essay*. Accessed via www.ibo.org/programmes/diploma-programme/curriculum/extended-essay/world-studies/

IB (2018b) *Guide for Geography*. Geneva: International Baccalaureate

Kearney A (2018) *Unpublished remarks in opening plenary session*. Vienna: IB Africa, Europe, Middle East conference.

Martin, R (2018) *Personal communication*.

Perry S (2018) *Implementing Effective Reflective Strategies*. Unpublished paper presented at IB Africa, Europe, Middle East conference, Vienna.

Piaggio M I (2012) *A Theoretical and Practical Approach to developing links between TOK and CAS*. Unpublished notes for an IB workshop in New York, IB Americas, February 2012.

Rudge L (2010) *Holistic education: An Analysis of its pedagogical application*. Lambert Academic Publishing.

Seefried M (2008) *Unpublished introductory address to International Baccalaureate Peterson Lecture*.

Wynten C, Robeau D and Cannings J (2015) *Unpublished presentation at the IB Africa, Europe, Middle East conference*.

Chapter 6

The DP Core: helping to create a Better and More Peaceful World

George Walker

Introduction

The Theory of Knowledge, the Extended Essay and Creativity, Activity, Service – these three elements of the IB Diploma Programme (DP) have become known collectively as the programme's 'core'. This accurately describes their compulsory nature but the term 'core' suggests more than that; it implies that they form the foundation on which the DP is constructed. This is evidently not the case because in practice the core, the heart of the DP, is composed of the student's six chosen academic subjects, at one time displayed visually in the shape of a hexagon (Figure 6.1).

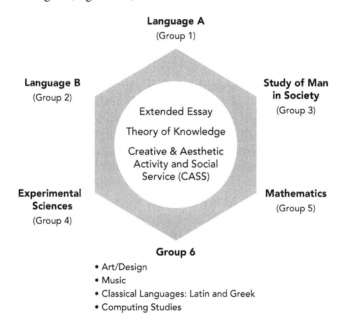

Figure 6.1 The hexagon model of the IB Diploma curriculum (after Thompson, 1983)

In this chapter I examine the relationship between the hexagon and the core. I believe the IB student can use the core to 'unlock the knowledge' contained in the hexagon in order to study it in a global context. The academic subjects are enriched by the core, enabling the student to contribute an informed opinion and propose considered action on issues that threaten global stability. As the IB Learner Profile expresses it:

> We develop and use conceptual understanding, exploring knowledge across a range of disciplines. We engage with issues and ideas that have local and global significance (IB, 2017).

I explore the origins of the three so-called core elements and describe attempts to bring coherence to the tripartite structure. I examine the important role played by these elements in achieving the IB's ambitious mission of "helping to create a better and more peaceful world" (IB, 2017) at a time when the IB's values are under unprecedented threat.

The enrichment of the hexagon subjects by Theory of Knowledge (TOK), the Extended Essay (EE) and Creativity, Action, Service (CAS) is what makes the DP a unique learning experience. However, I identify a risk that the hexagon and the core might go their separate ways, wasting the opportunity to reflect on, and then to react to, some of the most important issues of the day. The global threats of growing nationalism, populism and fake news create an environment of mistrust and fear. DP students must be encouraged to use their unique combination of knowledge, values and skills to write, speak and act in support of the classical virtues of truth, beauty and goodness.

A misnomer

Thompson's iconic diagram depicting the DP in the shape of a hexagon (Figure 6.1) has been one of the programme's enduring images (Hill, 2010, p126). Like any good model it is simple, accurate and helpful, summing up at a glance the curricular breadth and balance that are the programme's distinctive features. I shall use the hexagon as a visual shorthand for the six academic subjects that students must study, three at Standard Level and three at Higher Level, in order to satisfy the DP's assessment requirements.

Nonetheless there is more to the DP than the hexagon. Three compulsory elements – TOK, the EE and CAS, are to be found inside Thompson's diagram and are described as the 'core'. This description implies that these elements form the bedrock of the DP on which the hexagon of subjects is constructed, the very heart of the programme. But this is not the case whether we measure the relative importance of hexagon and core in terms of teaching time or points awarded in the final assessment (just three out of forty-five). In practice none of the three elements exerts an influence on the programme in a way that would justify the use of the term 'core'.

The IB organisation's ambivalence over the purpose and position of the core is illustrated by the core's steady retreat from the centre of the official DP curricular diagrams. In 2006 the original Thompson model was replaced by one with concentric circles that accommodated the newly-launched IB Learner Profile at its centre (Roberts, 2018). Ten years later another concentric circle, representing 'Approaches to Teaching and Approaches to Learning', pushed the DP core still further from the heart of the programme. (See Figure 6.2)

Figure 6.2: The current Diploma Programme model

Nonetheless the core remains a compulsory part of the DP experience, "central to the philosophy of the programme" (IB, 2015). It is what distinguishes the IBDP from other comparable pre-university programmes. According to one knowledgeable IB observer, the core:

> grew from the IB Founders' notion of what an educated person ought to be, and became the parts of the programme that students praise most often (Mathews and Hill, 2005, p48).

Cores and keys

The three elements of the IB core have different origins; none was planned with the others in mind. The most radical has been TOK, a course designed to encourage students to reflect on the nature of knowledge and on the assumptions that lie behind their use of knowledge. Alec Peterson (2003, p47), who had a profound early influence on the curriculum of the DP, argued that there was little point designing a broad and balanced hexagon of subjects if there was no opportunity to study important issues from the different perspectives provided by those subjects. A typical TOK assessment question, for example, would be

> Using history and at least one other area of knowledge, examine the claim that it is possible to attain knowledge despite problems of bias and selection (IB, 2014).

This example confirms the relationship of TOK to the hexagon, namely it is the hexagon (in this example history and one other chosen area of knowledge) that forms the bedrock core of the DP. TOK enables us to unlock the different parts of the hexagon in order to understand the contribution each distinct area of knowledge makes to our overall understanding of a concept, an issue or an argument.

Another important factor influenced TOK. The course represented an important compromise between two very different educational traditions, French and British; a way of balancing the French commitment to philosophy for its own, intrinsic sake with the more pragmatic approach that the Anglo-Saxons found useful in the classroom.

> They discussed this problem and arrived at the idea of including an element of reflection in the IB programme that would not be called 'Philosophy' and which would not be examined (Hill, 2010, p52)

One is reminded that a curriculum, especially a curriculum that must satisfy the demands of the world's most prestigious universities, is likely to be shaped by political as well as educational factors.

The second element of the DP core, our second key, is the experience known currently as Creativity, Activity, Service, abbreviated to CAS. I write 'currently' because CAS has been (in IB terms) a relatively unstable element of the DP, having changed its title twice. After a muddled start it first appeared as Creative, Aesthetic or Social Service, abbreviated to CASS; in 1989 it became Creativity, Action, Service. Students are now required to engage with at least one CAS project during their DP studies. A CAS project "is a collaborative series of sequential CAS experiences lasting at least one month" (IB, 2015) which, in turn, is made up of one or more of the three CAS strands.

Once again, politics played an important part in the early design of CAS. The hexagon contained (and indeed still contains) an enduring weakness: it left the Arts subjects without a fully protected place on the hexagon. CAS, and particularly its creativity and activity experiences, was seized upon as a compromise solution to this problem. A major research project, commissioned by the IB (Hayden et al, 2017) concluded that CAS helps students to be better at taking on new challenges, learning to persevere and developing better interpersonal skills. Our CAS key unlocks the possibility of widening the scope of the hexagon by identifying opportunities for experiential learning, and it is this aspect that has attracted the most attention.

The third element of the DP core is the Extended Essay, a 4,000-word report of a piece of research carried out either within the remit of one of the hexagon subjects or as a study of an issue of global importance involving two DP subjects. The EE had its origins in the Trevelyan Scholarships, founded by the distinguished educationalist Kurt Hahn, to counter-balance what he saw as an excessive emphasis on external examinations, particularly for candidates seeking entrance to Oxford and Cambridge (Sutcliffe, 2013 p104). It is often assumed (Alchin, 2011 p30) that Hahn, given his promotion of outdoor activities, helped to shape the CAS element of the DP core but that is not so. Hahn's direct input to the design of the IBDP was small but his indirect influence, through the pioneering work of Atlantic College in South Wales, which he helped to found in 1962, was huge. Atlantic College played a crucial role in translating the unfamiliar learning techniques of the DP core into concrete curricular and extra-curricular experiences.

In summary, a study of the historic origins of the so-called DP core confirms the view that the tripartite experience of TOK, CAS and the EE does not lie at the heart of the DP. Rather, it consists of a set of keys that the student can use to unlock the hexagon in order to enrich the six subjects and to link them to the issues that dominate our globalised world.

Cutting keys

The different origins of the three DP core elements present a challenge to the international educator who is seeking common qualities that might be used as keys to develop the six-subject hexagon. Roberts for example (2018, p36) states that the role the core subjects "play as a literal core to the programme can be debated". Satisfied that the importance of the core has not been compromised by its demotion in the later diagrams, he searches for the factors that make the core elements interactive "in that they support each other in terms of embedding the skills needed by 21st century learners" (2018, p36). He identifies three. The first is the role of reflection, which Roberts argues provides a common thread in each of the three elements.

> The role of reflection has been central and fully articulated within the CAS programme since its inception...it can also be argued that the writing of a 4,000-word research project ...is also a reflective task...In terms of TOK, given that the development and application of thinking skills is one of the key requirements of the course, the idea of reflection is built into this" (2018, p38).

Roberts' second interactive factor is ethics and he argues that, in addition to acknowledging the ethical dimension to TOK, CAS and many Extended Essays, it is important that students have the tools to resolve ethical tensions that exist in many of the hexagon subjects. The process of unlocking the hexagon will almost inevitably lead to questions of an ethical nature. His third factor is experiential learning, which is central to CAS but also important in the search amongst the hexagon subjects for learning resources that are tangible and relevant and take the student, at least in spirit and often in the flesh, outside the classroom. The Model United Nations is one such example, a sophisticated simulation which encourages skills of negotiation, compromise and the building of alliances. Roberts concludes:

> The interactive core as reflective, experiential, ethical learning becomes a place where students understand that they can undertake their own learning without being told what to think and how to think (2018, p42).

Alchin (2011) criticises the isolated nature of each of the three core elements as a weakness of the DP and he seeks coherent themes that might provide a unifying basis: "some bedrock for the core" (p38). He proposes three such themes: thinking skills, global outlook and self-awareness and identity. Cognitive skills, suggests Alchin, are developed in the EE and TOK while the emotional, affective component of thinking is developed in CAS. However, he argues that this simple model ignores the global context in which this thinking takes place, a context that I have described elsewhere (Walker, 2018) as a combination of diversity, complexity, sustainability and inequality. Alchin is sensitive to the political implications surrounding these categories and wonders if: "any move towards an overtly political agenda may not do the IB any favours with some individual students, teachers, parents and even states around the world" (2011, p34) at the same time acknowledging the overtly political agenda that is already implied by the IB's mission statement and the much-used IB phrase 'a better and more peaceful world'.

Alchin's third theme is self-awareness and identity, the three elements of the DP core offering opportunities: "for students to become more aware of their identities, to self-consciously develop these identities, and hence to become the people they want to be" (p35).

Roberts and Alchin are seeking a unified model for the DP core; skills and concepts that knit the three elements together despite their different origins. They identify the following six qualities that the core elements – TOK, EE and CAS – can offer:

- reflection
- ethics
- experiential learning
- thinking skills

- a global outlook
- self-awareness and identity

but they fail to show how they connect with the subject hexagon which, I have argued, is the true core of the DP. Indeed, the absence of any reference to the academic subjects in both Roberts' (2018) and Alchin's (2011) papers might lead one to the unhelpful conclusion that the more united the core, the more detached it becomes from the hexagon. There is an ever-present risk that the DP will split into two disconnected parts: the hexagon which maintains the programme's academic credentials, and the core which underpins the visionary nature of the IB's mission. It is only by linking these two that the true potential of the DP can be released.

A crucial decision was taken in the early days of the DP's development to allow students to study parts of the programme rather than the whole Diploma (Hill, p70). This was of particular benefit to schools in the United States where, to this day, many students study free-standing hexagon subjects and, if they achieve a passing grade, receive an official IB certificate. The decision was controversial at the time and it is appropriate to ask whether the policy can be justified today when the power and influence of the DP depends upon the interaction of the core elements with the hexagon: all the core elements and the complete hexagon. Let us not underestimate the challenge of delivering the academic expectations of higher education – worldwide – while at the same time developing young people who are inspired to help create a better and more peaceful world. We must question the wisdom of the IB in offering an easy option that destroys much of the Diploma's unique combination of hexagon and core.

Let us take a closer look at the IB's mission in order to explore the relationship of the core to the hexagon.

The mission of the IB

From its earliest days, the IB DP has set ambitious targets that reach far beyond its recognition as a quality preparation for entrance to university. Peterson, for example, who became the IB's first Director General, described the educational aim of the DP as follows:

> to develop to their fullest potential the powers of each individual to understand, to modify, and to enjoy his or her environment, both inner and outer, in its physical, social, moral, aesthetic and spiritual aspects (Peterson, p 33).

Five years later, Hagoort, the President of the IB's governing Council of Foundation, proposed the following mission statement (IB, 1992a):

> Our mission is the shaping, through education, of individuals in every area of the world who are better able than others to function effectively,

constructively and peacefully amidst a diversity of nationalities, cultures, languages and religions – individuals who will be good citizens not only of their communities and their nations but also of the world.

The IB's first 'official' mission statement was published in 1992 under the title 'Education for life':

Beyond intellectual rigour and high academic standards, strong emphasis is placed on the ideals of international standing and responsible citizenship, to the end that IB students may become critical and compassionate thinkers, lifelong learners and informed participants in local and world affairs, conscious of the shared humanity that binds all people together while respecting the variety of cultures and attitudes that makes for the richness of life (IB, 1992b).

The current mission statement has, remarkably, remained in place for more than sixteen years:

The International Baccalaureate aims to develop inquiring, knowledgeable and caring young people who help to create a better and more peaceful world through intercultural understanding and respect. To this end the organization works with schools, governments and international organizations to develop challenging programmes of international education and rigorous assessment. These programmes encourage students across the world to become active, compassionate and lifelong learners who understand that other people, with their differences, can also be right (IB, 2017).

Finally, the introduction to the IB Learner Profile states that

IB programmes aim to develop internationally-minded people who, recognizing our common humanity and shared guardianship of the planet, help to create a better, more peaceful world... (IB, 2017).

These mission statements all contain the seeds of action, using words and phrases such as:

- to modify and to enjoy
- shaping through education
- participants in local and world affairs
- active, compassionate and lifelong learners.

The three elements of the core – TOK, CAS and EE – can unlock and enrich the hexagon's six subjects that provide the balanced diet of academic study, creating the means to deliver the IB's mission. This is the fundamental difference between the DP and more conventional pre-university courses: the DP has the tools to unlock the hexagon subjects in order to achieve the IB's mission to create a better and more peaceful world.

Creating a better and more peaceful world

The true core of the DP is the hexagon with its important balance of academic subjects which guarantees a comprehensive accumulation of different realms of knowledge, capable of addressing the world's 21st century problems. We can imagine this knowledge stored partly in the human mind, partly in written form but increasingly in digital media accessible from the internet and retrievable in different formats to satisfy different demands – to pass an examination, to earn a living, to develop a hobby, to pursue an argument. The so-called core provides tools to study those parts of the hexagon's knowledge which contribute to the achievement of the IB's mission of "helping to create a better and more peaceful world" (IB, 2019).

It is easy – depressingly easy – to identify issues needing urgent improvement in the contemporary world. For example, there is increasing disquiet at the rejection of the values of the Enlightenment that have underpinned learning institutions like the IB for centuries. So there is a reluctance to accept 'scientific evidence' or to trust 'experts'; a tendency to prefer 'tradition' to 'reason'; to rely on 'opinion' rather than on 'fact'; to accept 'fake news' rather than the 'true account'. Now, each one of those words put between inverted commas, post modernism tells us, is contestable, even 'scientific evidence', as the bitter arguments on climate change confirm. But we have three keys – TOK, CAS and the EE – that enable us to unlock and interrogate the subject hexagon and thereby join in the debate. For example, what do I learn from TOK about the statistical evidence for climate change? What does chemistry tell us about the greenhouse properties of carbon dioxide? Could I write an Extended Essay arguing the case that rising global temperatures are caused by solar rather than human activity? Can I join a local environmental group that is determined to reduce atmospheric pollution caused by vehicle exhaust?

> To be open to the world we need to understand it. IB programmes therefore provide students with opportunities for sustained inquiry into a range of local and global issues and ideas (IB, 2017 p1).

Another area of concern is the threat to 'democracy' posed by the rapid growth of digital media which have the capacity, concealed under the cloak of anonymity, to sabotage elections, encourage mobs onto the streets and libel individuals who have no means of redress. But note once again those inverted commas, a warning that not all cultures accept the Enlightenment's description of democracy nor subscribe to the fine detail of the Charter of the United Nations. By studying 'democracy' we recognise the crucial importance of political systems to human happiness and achievement. We start with the hexagon and what must surely be a concept discussed in the context of World Literature, of History and of Global Politics. What can we clarify using the new TOK optional theme 'Knowledge and politics' (IB, 2018)? Does CAS enable us to engage with experiential learning, perhaps as a committee member of a local society? Can we study, then write into 4,000 words, for an EE, the notion that one size and shape of 'democracy' does not fit all?

Future faith

In this chapter I have examined the relationship between the two constituent parts of the DP, the hexagon of six subjects and the core of three elements. I have concluded that the true core of the Diploma – the bedrock on which the programme is constructed – is provided by the hexagon. The core elements (I have suggested that we think of them as 'keys') are able to unlock the hexagon in order to create a learning environment that encourages reflection, ethical values, experiential learning, thinking skills, a global outlook and self-awareness, thereby laying the first stepping stones towards the IB's ambitious mission to create a better and more peaceful world.

All this had its origins two generations ago so we must ask if the DP core requires structural change. Have we failed to keep up with new elements of learning that should be reflected in the DP? One obvious area that has changed out of all recognition in the past fifty years is communication. The internet, social media and smart phones are transforming the way we access information, the way we share it and the way we make use of it. Unfortunately it is often the negative aspects of the digital revolution – trolling, grooming and plagiarism, for example – that occupy the headlines. Is there a case for requiring all DP students to complete a significant piece of work that confirms their computer literacy (including their ethical behaviour) and tests their skills of digital communication? There must be thousands of DP students whose skills of digital communication are marginal; at best they just get by, concealing their weakness but that is no longer acceptable and unless they improve their skills they risk being left behind.

Creating a better and more peaceful world may seem to be the introduction to a Utopian fantasy, far removed from the daily news bulletins of fractured societies. But "words not only have meanings, they have power, the power to change states of affairs and the power to bring about action" (Allan, 2013, p149). The IB Diploma Programme has the keys to the powerful use of words (TOK); to the power of well-researched arguments (EE); and to the power that converts an issue from the printed word into a form, however modest, of community action (CAS).

References

Alchin N (2011) 'The identity of the IB Diploma Programme core', in Hayden M and Thompson, J (eds) *Taking the IB Diploma Programme Forward*. Woodbridge: John Catt Educational.

Allan M (2013) 'Understanding International Education through Discourse Theory', in Pearce R (ed) *International Education and Schools*: London, Bloomsbury.

Hayden M et al (2017) *The Impact of Creativity, Activity, Service (CAS) on Students and Communities*; Bethesda MD, International Baccalaureate.

Hill, I (2010) *The International Baccalaureate: pioneering in education.* Woodbridge: John Catt Educational.

IB (2002a) Paper from the 1992 North American Regional Conference, Breckenridge, Colorado, USA.

IB (2002b) *Education for Life.* Cardiff: International Baccalaureate.

IB (2014) *TOK Subject Brief,* The Hague: International Baccalaureate.

IB (2015) *CAS Subject Brief,* The Hague: International Baccalaureate.

IB (2017) *What is an IB education?* The Hague: International Baccalaureate.

IB (2018) Draft new *Theory of Knowledge guide* for 2020: The Hague: International Baccalaureate.

IB (2019) *Mission,* Accessed via www.ibo.org/about-the-ib/mission/

Mathews J and Hill I (2005) *Supertest.* Chicago: Open Court.

Peterson A (2003) *Schools Across Frontiers.* Chicago: Open Court.

Roberts, W (2018) 'The role of Theory of Knowledge, Creativity, Activity, Service and Extended Essay within the IB Diploma Programme', in *International Schools Journal* XXXVI, 2, 36-42.

Sutcliffe, D (2013) *Kurt Hahn and the United World Colleges with Other Founding Figures.* UK.

Walker, G (2018) 'Living in a global world', in Fabian J, Hill I and Walker G (eds), *The International Baccalaureate.* Woodbridge: John Catt Educational.

Chapter 7

Disrupting the DP Core

James MacDonald

Introduction

The IB Diploma programme (DP) has shown itself, over its 50-year history, to be a remarkably forward-looking curriculum model. Adoption rates of the DP have been consistently impressive. The fact that it has stood the test of time and its basic structure remains fundamentally unchanged since its inception (Walker, 2011, p5) is a testament to the foresight of the original designers. When discussing how we can take the core of the DP forward, we need to first recognise that it has taken 50 years to establish the DP and earn global recognition.

As someone who is frequently asked by parents and others what is the difference between the DP and other high school pathways, there are two things that stand out: the requirement that students take a balanced range of subjects (rather than just selecting a collection of courses as with Advanced Placement (USA) and A-Levels (UK) and the core made up of Extended Essay (EE), Theory of Knowledge (TOK) and CAS (Creativity, Activity, Service). These features, and the confidence in the validity and reliability of the DP external assessment system, have led to the DP often being called the 'Gold Standard' of high school qualifications.

What if, like the well-worn Confucian warning that 'your strengths are your weakness', the very success of the DP, and the Core components within it, is giving birth to a weakness? More specifically, could the success of the DP, and the fact that it has taken so long to establish and so much has been invested in earning the recognition of the qualification in universities around the world, mean that there is a naturally strong resistance to change? After all, no person wants to be the one accused of spoiling a successful programme and experience suggests that in large organisations success can foster a type of inertia and even resistance to change.

Furthermore, if we accept the premise that one reason why the DP has been so successful is that it was forward-looking to begin with, then it follows that its continued success will be dependent upon it being a forward-looking programme and qualification for the next 50 years. We must acknowledge that in today's changing world, something designed in the 1960s and unchanged in structure since its inception may not be fit for purpose for the next 50 years. For example, 50 years on the DP still has six subject groups and the core, and even something such as CAS is largely unchanged, although originally it contained an extra 'S' – 'Social Service' versus just 'Service' – (Tarc, 2009, p11). At the very least, we must pry open the door that allows such questions to be seriously examined.

We are fortunate that there is considerable experience within our IB community that we can draw upon to shape the conversation about taking the DP core forward. However, we must acknowledge that generating ideas and implementing ideas are very different things, requiring differing skills and competencies. In fact, my experience in leading schools and groups of schools is that generating ideas can be relatively easy. Sometimes I refer to this as the "Ken Robinson effect", whereby some of the strongest advocates for change in education have a tendency to forcefully prescribe the change for others, but show little interest in partaking in the complex and hard work required to make change happen in an environment like a school. Implementing change in schools can be deceptively difficult; prescribing it on a stage with a microphone is much simpler.

In practical terms, when change efforts fail this is often not because of the quality of ideas behind the change, but instead because the management of change was not good enough. Therefore, any conversation about taking the DP forward needs to focus not just upon generating fresh ideas of what could be, but on the heavy lifting of managing the change and sharing ideas for how to turn good ideas into practical reality.

Based upon this premise, this chapter outlines a theory for disruptive change. In the words of educational change guru Michael Fullan, "give me a good theory over a strategic plan any day of the week" because, he argues, a good theory can be a powerful and practical guide to "understanding complex situations" while pointing to actions that are likely to be effective within a particular context (Fullan, 2008, p1). If there is an appetite for seriously considering disruptive change, and not just incremental improvement to the current model of the core, then the change process must be structured properly, managed carefully, and it will be necessary to articulate why the change is needed, who will be involved, what will be accomplished and how the change process will work. This is what this chapter is intended to be all about.

How the pace of change is affecting organisations

It is something of a management axiom to claim that what makes one successful today may not be what is needed for success tomorrow. Consider some statistics that emerge from tracking the 500 biggest companies in America. Only 12% of companies on this list in 1955 remained on the list in 2015 (Perry, 2016) and, extrapolating statistics, half the companies on the list now will be replaced in the next ten years. Statistics like this remind us of the turbulent nature of the business world, where today's giants have no guarantee of retaining their position. Even Jeff Bezos, the CEO of Amazon, predicts that his company will eventually be disrupted (Hamilton, 2018). There is a Darwinian element to it all, sometimes called 'creative destruction' where a dynamic competitive market environment ensures the future belongs only to those that can adapt and evolve.

But education is not business, and certain educational institutions have proven themselves to be remarkably resilient to disruption. Take, for example, universities like Harvard, Yale, Oxford and Cambridge: in contrast to business leaders from 100 years ago, the global standing of these institutions remains largely unchanged from a century before. Reputational success in education, at least at the highest levels, seems to offer something of a long-term sustainable competitive edge.

While education may not change so quickly as in other sectors, however, competition is increasing, especially in international education, as multi-billion dollar businesses (eg. Cognita, Nord Anglia, GEMS) are moving into the education space with great speed. Business can be very responsive to opportunities as for-profit organisations have an inherent incentive to grow in pursuit of profit and wealth creation. Not-for-profit organisations do not have the same types of incentive to expand and this helps to explain why so much of the growth of the international school sector is driven by for-profit organisations.

Organisations like the IB will remain a critical part of the international education ecosystem, but do not be surprised when other curriculum and assessment bodies seek to undermine the IB approach, increase their market share and erode the IB's position. This is not just conjecture: aiming to disrupt the *status quo* to their advantage, the College Board, in the USA, in 2014 began to offer the Capstone Diploma (College Board, 2018) which features elements quite similar to the DP. If nothing else, this is a competitive move by the College Board to erode some of the appeal of the IB Diploma in the US market and at leading overseas American schools. Meanwhile, Cambridge International Examinations (CIE) already operates in 160 countries, offering an increasing variety of internationalised curriculum options as it continues to expand its global reach (Cambridge, 2018). It is noteworthy that both the College Board and CIE are not-for-profit organisations, but their strategic activities demonstrate that not-for-profit does not mean not competitive.

For better or worse, economic forces and business interests are shaping our schools and, ultimately, our curriculum. It is essential then that, as educators, we resist the creation of an echo chamber of voices and ideas that originate from within our IB circles. We must stay open to allowing theories and ideas from other domains to help us refine our approaches. With this in mind, the discussion now turns to a selection of research and theory from the realms of economics and business.

A predictable path of development

The genesis of the IB is a well told story; one of the coming together of different individuals to create an organization that "has brought order to international education" (Walker, 2011, p3). It has been a remarkable success. Yet despite its unique qualities, the IB has followed a pathway natural for many organisations: beginning as a relatively loose network of entrepreneurially-minded individuals sharing a common vision, who saw their original creation eventually morph into a hierarchical organisation with established systems, structures and policies. Consider the following about organisational life cycles and ask if this also describes the IB's development:

> They begin with a network-like structure, sort of like a solar system with a sun, planets, moons, and even satellites. Founders are at the centre. Others are at various nodes working on different initiatives. Action is opportunity seeking risk taking, all guided by a vision people buy into ... over time, a successful organisation evolves through a series of stages into an enterprise that is structured as a hierarchy and is driven by well-known managerial processes: planning, budgeting, job defining, staffing, measuring, problem solving. (Kotter, 2014, p5)

Start as a network (system of interconnected people) and grow into a hierarchy (a structured approach to organising people by rank and relative authority); it is the classic organisational evolution. It is useful, for our purposes, to highlight some of the differences between networks and hierarchies below (Table 7.1).

	Network	Hierarchy
Structures	Relatively flat structure, often authority is less formally allocated through contribution to the team	Clear reporting lines between superiors and subordinates according to job descriptions
Approach to change	Focus on a type of innovation; adaptation valued; seeking emergent opportunities	Incremental improvement of systems; control and predictability valued
Interactions guided by...	Personal interactions	Management procedures, policy, performance metrics
Metaphor	Constellation of planets	Pyramid

Table 7.1: Differences between networks and hierarchies

But why is it that organisations, as they scale and become better established, seem to follow a natural path of evolution that takes on the attributes of a hierarchy once again?

As Kotter (2012) explains, hierarchies bring "expertise, time-tested procedures, and clear reporting relationships and accountability so that we can do what we know how to do with efficiency, predictability, and effectiveness. Hierarchies are directed by familiar managerial processes for planning, budgeting, defining jobs, hiring and firing, and measuring results." The development of such systems is not a bad thing, even if our society tends to celebrate a 'start-up' culture over the more staid view of the bureaucratic organisational hierarchy. Consider, for example, that most of things in your immediate environment were produced and delivered through hierarchal organisations (and probably almost all of them for-profit as well). As IB educators we benefit greatly from the now highly refined structures of the IB organisation. Do we prefer the IB's assessment system to run as a flexible startup venture, or through a well-established system that has been improving incrementally over many years of development?

On a more local level perhaps, if one was to identify the areas within a school where the strongest hierarchical controls restrict freedom, this might shed new insights into why schools have historically been so immune to disruption. For example, what if the school schedule, which has been optimised to ensure efficiency of teaching resources, could be organised differently? What if the teachers, students and learning locations could be organised through network principles, instead of through the command and control systems of the hierarchy?

But therein lies a paradox as the strength of hierarchy is also a weakness: "even when minimally bureaucratic, hierarchies are inherently risk-averse and resistant to change" (Kotter, 2012). So hierarchies do evolve over time, but by their very nature they will resist revolutionary change as they are built to last. Networks, by contrast, are much looser by nature and when we see disruptive change occurring, the genesis of the change can probably be traced back to people being organised in some type of network (Ferguson, 2018, p32). So how can a successful organisation which has evolved into a hierarchy create conditions for a disruptive change if a hierarchy, by its very nature, will resist such disruption?

The innovator's dilemma

There is a term in the business world meant to describe this paradox: the 'innovator's dilemma'. How can leaders invest in potentially disruptive new areas without usurping the presently successful and established organisation? Christensen provides an astute insight into organisational dynamics, stating that "the logical, competent decisions of management that are critical to the success of their companies are also the reason why they lost their positions of leadership" (2000, xvi). While Christensen is referring to broader strategic issues, I can see how a collection of small, individually correct decisions can actually undermine an overall objective. Here is one example. As a school head, each year I would work with a team of leaders to recruit and select the best teachers we could. We often used a collaborative process including department heads. But I noticed over time that we were losing some of our overall diversity on staff because, for example, younger teachers without much experience were consistently losing out to more veteran applicants. In every case we made a 'right' decision, but because these were independent decisions we ended up with, in my opinion, an aggregate of the decisions which was actually sub-optimal for the organisation as a whole. What I learned from this is that we needed to find a way to include collaborative approaches to recruitment, while taking into account a bigger picture as well. In a similar way, could incremental improvements without a proper strategic re-evaluation threaten the IB's leadership?

If you are a leader of a successful organisation, there will be a natural inclination not to 'break anything' by chasing innovations that end up leading nowhere, but, as discussed above, it is rare for leading businesses to remain in the top spot as rivals are constantly seeking ways to erode their competitive advantage. Standing still, it seems, is never an option. On a smaller scale, readers may have encountered a personal version of this dilemma if they have contemplated changing careers: do you continue with your current career, or take a leap into an innovative direction, forsaking the safety that comes with the present situation?

'Dual-system' theory contends that this dilemma is a false dichotomy, in the sense that it is not an either/or proposition. Instead, propose some business thinkers, leaders can create the right structures to allow an innovation network to exist alongside the main organisation. How to do this, at least according to the theory, is the topic of the next part of the chapter.

Applying the duel-system to the IB: the basic theory

So, imagine that you are leading a successful organization and know that you must remain agile and responsive to changes in your environment if you are to remain relevant in terms of your mission. This point is underscored through the statistics around the churn rate of Fortune 500 companies shared above. To paraphrase Fullan, we need a good theory to guide us – which leads us to Kotter.

According to Kotter, the solution is not to dismiss what is already known and established, but to introduce "in an organic way, a second system – one which would be familiar to most successful entrepreneurs. The second system adds needed agility and speed while the old one, which keeps running, provides reliability and efficiency" (2014, vii). This is a 'dual-system' approach.

On the surface, it is quite straight-forward: create a network alongside the hierarchy, and the network should be "populated with a diagonal slice of employees from all across the organisation up and down its ranks" (2014, p20) while adhering to a number of other important principles:

1. Solicit volunteers who like the idea of working with others on a project bigger than themselves from throughout the organisation, and not just the usual few appointees.

2. Appeal to people's emotions and idealism as well as their practical thinking in the call to action.

3. Ensure relevant connections and communications flows between the hierarchy and network throughout the project, so that when it becomes time to integrate the outcomes of the network into the hierarchy, the change does not seem overly "awkward, wrong, or threatening" (Kotter, 2014, pp23-25)

Can we use existing IB networks to create a dual-system approach?

Those familiar with the IB organisation will know that much of its strength is derived from the broader IB community. There are regional networks, the IB Educators Network (IBEN) and events such as the IB annual regional conferences which are often seen as 'networking' events. In addition, curriculum review cycles are strongly supported by practising educators, whilst much of the capacity for school authorisation visits and workshops is provided through IB educators, whose primary commitment is to another organisation, normally a school, contracted on a part-time basis by the IB.

We need to acknowledge that Kotter's theory was developed for more traditional Fortune 500-type companies, with strong existing hierarchies. The IB does not quite fit this mould, as it has well-established structures outside of the hierarchy referred to as 'networks'. However, according to the dual-system, these IB networks do not have the attributes needed to fulfil the role of a parallel system. Key networks, like IBEN, are ultimately overseen by members of the hierarchy and activities are managed through clear processes and policy. These networks were certainly not created as a free flowing network with a mandate for innovative disruption.

What the theory around disruption advocates is an unbridled network operating alongside the main organisation, with freedom to pursue innovation without the restrictions that come with a hierarchy. So, in this regard, the existing IB networks do not fulfil the disruptive role prescribed in the business literature around a dual-system approach. The current IB network is thoughtfully designed to support and reinforce the structures within the IB, not to disrupt them.

A process for change

Therefore, what is needed is a different type of IB network, tasked with coming up with disruptive innovation. For our purposes – consideration of change in the DP core – this will be referred to as the 'Core Disruption Team'. There are four main activities for the IB leadership: articulating to important stakeholders 'why' the core should be reviewed; creating the team and deciding 'who' will be on it; creating the structure of the team ('how'), and then evaluating its work and monitoring its progress and function ('what').

The Why

As made famous by Simon Sinek, great leaders 'start with why' and strive to communicate the 'cause for action' ahead of a 'course of action' (2011, pp6-7). Different authors in the field of change management, including some of Kotter's earlier work cite the need for communicating the need for a change as the first vital step delivering sustainable change to an organisation. In a mission driven organisation like the IB, where much is already accomplished through goodwill, the importance of this step in inspiring people to act should not be underestimated.

The Who

Deciding who will be on the team is critical. It is essential that those involved are volunteers, with a genuine interest in the project and a high degree of intrinsic motivation (similar to how the IB selects participants for its curriculum review teams). When considering who is on the team, the leadership needs to think beyond the immediate output of the team and ahead to wide implementation. These people will be champions for change and, if the innovation is to be deemed worthy of wider adoption, these individuals will be critical to supporting the change in their home setting. So, for example, perhaps some individuals on the team should be IB employees within the DP curriculum team, others from leading and innovative IB schools, and others from IB governance. The Core Disruption Team should be selected very strategically, and must report directly into the highest levels (likely the Director General and, possibly the governors) with updates given to the Heads Council (an advisory body to the Director General, elected by heads of IB World Schools). As a reminder, Kotter clarifies that this is not meant to be a "cross-unit 'task force' or a new 'initiative' built into this year's plans" but rather a "whole new system that is much bigger, more powerful and involves far more people" (Kotter, 2011).

The How

There is also the question of how the Core Disruption Team might come together to do their work. Obviously with a global organisation such as the IB, it is almost certain that members will be spread around the globe, so coming together will be a challenge. Technology can no doubt help, and there are two established models that have been used successfully to stimulate and guide change in schools that could provide some guidance.

Horizon Project: The Horizon Project predicts some of the most influential trends in educational technology with different time horizons. But how do you predict the future, especially around technology? The approach is both simple and powerful: identify some of the leading thinkers in educational technology, and then using technology readily available (like Google), ask the experts what they think will be the biggest trends in the coming years and synthesise their responses through a voting/ranking procedure to gauge the level of support for the various suggestions. While this is no guarantee of the future, by gathering some of the best-informed minds in EdTech, asking them the same question and then summarising their answers, the rest of us end up with a distillation of some of the best thinking available. I see no reason why a similar type of approach, soliciting ideas from some thought leaders associated with the DP, could not be used.

PELP Approach: Another approach, which is used at the Harvard Graduate School of Education, is the PELP approach. Using a framework and skilled facilitator to guide discussions, schools or districts will send a leadership team for a week to Harvard to work through a 'problem of practice'. Over the course of a week, the team uses a framework and analyses and fully defines the problem they are trying to address, develops a 'theory of change' and analyses various contextual issues that need to be considered. While the specifics of the process may not apply to the work of a Core Disruption Team, the basic concept of working together over an extended period of time with a skilled facilitator and framework for dialogue (and perhaps even informed by a Horizon Project-like research project) some great thinking and perhaps even a new model could emerge.

The What

The team's task is to design a disruptive model that could reasonably be trialled alongside the current DP core. The remit from the leadership should be relatively open, allowing the team to come up with a creative proposal. Any new model would need to be approved by the IB leadership ahead of any pilot being launched, but throughout the process the team must be protected (or even fire-walled) from interference from the main organisation. This approach will allow time properly to test innovations so that they may effectively be evaluated.

Conclusion

When discussing how we can move the DP core forward, we need to pay at least as much attention to the process of change as to the ideas for the change, which is the 'what'. As IB educators we should be discussing not only what types of changes we might want to see but also what processes we think are best suited to seeing that the changes are properly implemented in a manner that will have the maximum benefit for students. Often in education, if you get the process right the outcomes will take care of themselves.

The IB organisation is a prime example of a hierarchal organisation that has shown great capacity for incremental improvement, but little appetite for disruptive change to existing programmes. It is possible that the IB could slowly drift into the complacency trap where its strengths could undermine future success, and this is why setting up systems to explore new opportunities is so important. Perhaps, as it celebrates its 50th anniversary, the time has come to ask where, when and how disruptive change could come to the IB. And maybe, just maybe, it could start in the centre, at the core of the Diploma Programme

References

Cambridge Assessment International education (2018) Cambridge Pathway. Available at: www. cambridgeinternational.org/programmes-and-qualifications/ (accessed 25 January 2019).

Christensen C (2000) *The Innovator's Dilemma: When New Technologies Cause Great Firms to Fail.* Boston, MA: Harvard Business School Press.

College Board (2018) AP Capstone Diploma Program. Available at: https://apcentral. collegeboard.org/courses/ap-capstone (accessed 25 January 2019).

Fullan M (2008) *The Six Secrets of Change.* USA: John Wiley & Sons.

Ferguson P (2018) *The Square and the Tower: Networks and Power, from the Freemasons to Facebook.* New York: Penguin Press.

Hamilton I (2018) 'Amazon will go bankrupt': Jeff Bezos keeps talking about Amazon's inevitable death'. Available at: www.businessinsider.com/jeff-bezos-keeps-talking-about-amazons-inevitable-death-2018-12 (accessed 25 January 2019).

Kotter J (2011) 'Hierarchy and Network: Two Structures, One Organization'. Available at: https://hbr.org/2011/05/two-structures-one-organization (accessed 25 January 2019).

Kotter J (2012) 'Accelerate!' https://hbr.org/2012/11/accelerate (accessed 25 January 2019).

Perry J (2016) 'Fortune 500 Firms 1955 vs 2016'. Available at: www.aei.org/publication/fortune-500-firms-1955-v-2016-only-12-remain-thanks-to-the-creative-destruction-that-fuels-economic-prosperity/ (accessed 25 January 2019).

Kotter J (2014). *Accelerate: Building strategic agility for a faster-moving world.* Harvard Business Press Books. Boston, Massachusetts. USA.

Sinek S (2011) *Start with Why.* New York: Penguin Group.

Tarc P (2009) *Global Dreams, Enduring Tensions.* New York: Peter Lang Publishing.

Walker G (2011) *The Changing Face of International Education: Challenges for the IB.* London: IB Publishing.

Part B

The Core in Practice

Chapter 8

TOK: promoting Attitudes and Dispositions that foster Lifelong Learning

John Sprague

I'm at the beginning of the school year and about seven lessons into the first year of our IB Diploma Programme (DP). Despite our best efforts I still had one of my own students this week ask, in something of an unguarded moment, "So what is TOK supposed to be all about?"

Theory of Knowledge (TOK) is one of the subjects that the students entering the DP hear most about from their predecessors, but it remains the subject of which they have the loosest grasp. Some teachers may have cracked it, but in my experience many TOK teachers are still faced with this question. I, for one, have been faced with it from students at the beginning, middle and end of all the iterations of the TOK course I've developed over 18 years of teaching TOK and 15 years of assessing it. My first year DP parents' evening is next week and I'm dusting down my explanation to this question, as I've done every year. Still we persevere. TOK is the glue that binds the DP, but it is a real challenge for even the best and most experienced teachers to get right. In this chapter I hope to articulate some of the reasons why this subject presents a unique challenge in the hopes that we can better understand the challenge and perhaps feel less alone as we try to meet it.

One reason why TOK is a challenge to teach is that it is, by design, at the cutting edge of what students at this age are able to do; it stands at the front edge of their cognitive development. The TOK course represents a genuine shift in thinking; it asks students to jump to a parallel track which runs alongside their normal thinking and in the first instance represents a genuine 'code' shift – a shift into a new domain where the old rules of classroom learning don't apply in the same way.

Ultimately, we hope that the students shift towards and maintain a 'second order' view at all times, asking themselves "How reliable is this knowledge?" "Are these methods appropriate to the nature of the knowledge I'm producing?" or "Is my own perspective adding value or weakening the knowledge I'm producing?" The first-order learning within subjects and the second-order reflection on that learning and knowledge construction are not mutually exclusive, but that dual coded approach is certainly out at the fingertips of even the most gifted 17 or 18-year-old student. Which is why good teaching is essential as we are guiding the students through this Zone of Proximal

Development (ZPD) (Vygotsky, 1981) where the students, initially, are struggling? unable to find their way.

Students arrive at TOK mastery at different times and in different order, an important point for school leaders and parents to understand. Some students excel in their six DP subjects aiming high and succeeding in each of their first order activities, but they may find the shift to TOK too much of a challenge. This shift involves moving away from learning subject-based content and skills to thinking about second order questions such as how knowledge is constructed, and for some students, initially, it may be a a bridge too far. Alternatively, some students find the narrow, more closed questions of traditional academic disciplines something of a constraint, but the risk-taking, free thinking involved in TOK far more natural.

School leaders and parents nevertheless will argue that because students do well in DP subject groups 1-6, this fact alone should indicate that they will therefore do well in TOK and any break down in this correlation is the fault of assessment or the teaching. Granted, success in the DP subjects often correlates with success in TOK, because the students are good at a variety of skills. When the correlation breaks down, however, it is less likely that it is the assessment model that is at fault and more likely, given the developmental age of the students, that they have simply yet to develop the particular skills necessary for success in TOK.

The challenges facing TOK teachers

It's not terribly controversial to suggests that TOK is a genuine challenge for students; our experience in the classroom, assessment results and feedback from students and parents bear this out. Neither is it controversial to suggest that teaching TOK is a significant challenge, but it is worth considering the nature of those challenges from the perspective of the teachers so as to clarify them, if not to solve them, so that we can better muster our resources and resilience.

My claim here is that what is at the developmental edge of our students' abilities is also at the developmental edge of our own. I've mentored, coached and supported new TOK teachers throughout my own teaching of it and all of us have been challenged by the different approach in the same way as are our students. Our saving grace, I feel, is that while students have two years to demonstrate success, provided we remain on the TOK staff, we have a career to work on it. Every year my thinking on certain elements of the course develops and shifts. This sometimes represents a genuine 'paradigm shift' where my new approaches are incommensurable with what they were before (my current approach towards the Ways of Knowing (WOKs), for instance, is one such shift), but other developments are more of a 'settling' into a belief, pushing ideas around until they fall into place like a puzzle. If I were to offer a single piece of advice in relation to this, it would be to listen to your students and learn from them. My approach to the Arts, for instance, finally began to settle during the lingering conversations with a particular Higher Level Visual Arts student. These conversations often continued after a last period of the day TOK lesson, both of us standing with our books in our hands, at the classroom door, while she struggled to articulate her thoughts about shifting from thinking of art as a creator to thinking of it as a TOK student. I listened and let her deeper experience and knowledge of creating art feed my own thinking about Art as an AOK (Area of Knowledge). I owe much to conversations such as these.

That we think carefully of the challenges of teaching TOK is also important because the challenges we face ultimately impact the students' own experience of TOK. At one extreme, if a teacher doesn't understand a foundational concept like "the knowledge question", then the trickle-down effect means that student almost cannot succeed. As a moderator of TOK internal assessment, the comments that teachers offer when they justify their marks speaks volumes and often this brings into sharp relief some deep misunderstandings of the subject. Or, a teacher may not fully understand the content of one of the AOKs and though still managing effective second order discussions of that AOK, may not be able to model good use of examples, thereby giving students a model of shallow thinking. Whilst in the first case teachers must work hard to get their understanding calibrated with the subject guide, the latter is somewhat unavoidable, given our relatively narrow specialties and backgrounds. This is simply a call to model life-long learning.

Being honest about the level of our own understanding, and having strategies to manage the worry about our depth knowledge and skill, is important in order to become a better TOK teacher.

No degree for TOK

No one comes out of university with a degree in TOK. This presents at least a couple of challenges. Firstly, school leaders, when assigning the course to teachers, will be missing a ready-made step in the vetting process. Quite literally, all the teachers on staff have the requisite qualifications for teaching TOK (there are none!) and therefore from this perspective any teacher might be the right choice. So what criteria remain to help with the choice?

I've heard many times something along the lines of "Mr Tanner seems like a good choice, he's got the right sort of personality and approach". But just what does this mean? Generally, it is a suggestion of several things, from "gets along with teenagers", to "likes to ask really 'deep' questions" to "is really smart". Having these qualities, of course, are a mark of distinction to a teacher (we should all be so lucky to be thought of in these terms), but equally obvious, especially in the IB, these are the qualities of all good teachers. In the context of TOK, however, these qualities do, in fact, make for a better experience for reasons I'll outline below. Suffice to say here, these qualities do fit the course in that the approach conducive to a TOK classroom requires a certain level of modelling and an even higher level of trust. Teachers who can both show comfort in the seemingly esoteric and rudderless world of TOK and who can leverage good relationships in guiding students through that landscape, are bound to reach a larger proportion of the students and thus lead them to a genuine change of attitude toward knowledge. As teachers we should accept this change of disposition as the aim (as opposed to a narrow obsession with top marks on the assessment), and the shift away from performance in an assessment towards mastery of an approach requires teachers with a certain skill set. So if you're teaching TOK because "you seem like the right person to teach it", consider this a win.

Just as often, however, and it's possible that the above might be a rationalisation for this next reason, teachers are often 'given' TOK simply because there is room in that person's timetable. In terms of all the teachers new to TOK that I've supported over the years, this seems to be the most common reason why teachers find themselves in front of TOK students. One of my first questions to my attendees at an IB TOK workshop is "How many of you were given TOK because you had to make up hours in your time table?" and every time there is a sizeable proportion. From the perspective of school leaders, this is an obvious solution to a practical problem. From a teaching and learning perspective, however, this is clearly a mistake. This is not to say that the teachers who finds themselves in the TOK classroom for this reason cannot be excellent teachers of TOK. Rather, the point is that this strategy more often than not leads to a kind of revolving door mentality; teachers are on the TOK staff for a couple of years, but then are pulled back into their own subject, once the hours for that subject have returned. However, successful teaching in TOK takes time, and we improve with experience. Using TOK as a lay-by in which to park those teachers who need some topping up on their hours, creates a TOK environment where deep expertise cannot be built. There could however be a boon to this revolving door model, namely that after a few years there may be a staff room populated with a number of teachers who 'used to teach TOK'. This, of course, is both good and bad. Good in that some knowledge is trickling down through the staff room, bad in that that knowledge is often half-baked and superficial, and hence inconsequential. Overall, I think it is preferable to have a smaller, better-skilled TOK community in the teaching staff who can then support non-TOK teachers in developing their knowledge of the subject and in creating opportunities to bring TOK into their classrooms.

Where does the fact that there is no degree leave the individual teacher faced with learning how to be a TOK teacher? Firstly, as any experienced TOK teacher will be the first to tell you, we learn alongside of the students. The *only* reason I feel minimally competent in TOK is because of the experience gained through 18 years' worth of students with whom I've struggled through the course. Every year a new facet makes itself known; some years I will backtrack on some particular element, or I might completely reverse my approach, all in the course of working through the ideas with the students and learning with them. This is why certain teachers may be better qualified to undertake the teaching of TOK in terms of their character: they are relatively comfortable in that 'rudderless' environment and are happy to change tack, try something new and raise their hands in supplication when faced with exasperated students wishing to know "the answer".

Two sources of guidance present themselves to the new TOK teacher. First, in so far as they are teachers, the TOK Subject Guide, the annual TOK Subject Reports and the TOK Teacher Support Material are the 'official' IB guidance. These mark out the boundaries of the TOK landscape and act as the focus dial for the concepts. So many of the problems in terms of assessment, in my mind, could be minimised were the teachers simply to work through the official material presented in these IB documents. I subscribe and contribute to several Facebook groups and the same old questions and debates are bandied around there as if they were still contentious. Many are not. They are written down in black and white in the official documentation for the TOK course. We bemoan the fact that students, when asked to do some research, will run straight to Google rather than look at the carefully vetted material we present in the classroom, yet so often teachers looking for answers will likewise run to the internet for questions which are clearly anticipated and answered in official IB material. And again on Twitter, minute and local issues are often blown all out of proportion from the soap-boxes of our social media feeds. These unofficial networks certainly offer invaluable advice and collegial support, but they must be tempered with, and constrained by, what is actually in the formal IB documentation.

In so far as teachers are also learners, I always recommend commercially produced TOK textbooks as excellent source material for teachers, especially as summer reading in the run up to the course. And I prescribe more than one source, since triangulating our understanding of a topic is sage advice. The books on offer are generally quite good, exhibit a lot of detail in terms of the main structures of the course and provide a fit-for-purpose approach from which TOK teachers can later expand and develop. But the textbook is not the course.

Lastly, even though there's no 'degree' in TOK, I always remind teachers that in nearly every case, they know the TOK of their own subject pretty well. Historians and scientists have a natural advantage, I feel, in that their training has emphasised a sensitivity towards and reflection on method, and this awareness in their own circumstances can easily be extended into other AOKs. But the point remains that in all university degrees there will be some awareness of the methods, historical development, key concepts and general scope of the discipline embedded in the training. So, although there is no formal degree in TOK, degree programmes in general will have sensitised teachers to the knowledge issues of TOK. Our job as teachers is to apply the TOK course concepts back to what we already know about our subject, then forwards into other subjects. Fortunately, that projection forward doesn't require a ground level, first-order, understanding of the subject itself, just an awareness of the corollaries between it and our own subjects and expertise. This fact provides an excellent opportunity to develop a strong TOK team. In one of my schools we developed a carousel where a historian taught the History AOK unit, a scientist taught the Natural Science unit, a mathematician the Mathematics unit etc, and the students cycled through each teacher in three-week segments. This placed a huge burden on the timetable as the classes had to be block-scheduled, but after a few years we had a dozen teachers comfortable with TOK in their own subject, and ready and experienced enough to take on the AOKs in other subjects.

Genuine cognitive challenge

Understanding that there is no formal training for TOK, but committing yourself to persevering nonetheless, there remain several challenges that should not be ignored or underestimated.

Open-ended

The TOK course is notoriously open-ended. This again means that the best TOK teachers are those who are comfortable with the ambiguity inherent in the course and in the discussions, but skilled enough to avoid an "anything goes" open-ended debate. This goes for students as well; students who are, perhaps, less wedded to facts but who can spin about in abstractions, may have an inherent advantage over students who wish to drill down and find the truths. Again, however, I think all teachers who are genuinely devoted to their subject will understand that at the cutting edge of their subjects there is a great deal of ambiguity and many unanswered questions. The chemist who simply expects students to memorise the periodic table, or the economist who simply wants students to describe the various supply and demand curves, or the mathematician who only wants students to solve equations, might have lost sight of the unanswered, open-ended questions at the edges of their disciplinary maps.

From these kinds of teachers, you may hear the old nugget, "at the end of the day our students need to pass their exams." Certainly, this is true in one sense: at the end of the process students do actually engage in assessment. But this should never be the sole guide of the model we choose to guide our day to day best practice. Perhaps this is something of a caricature of "the worst teachers we see," but the point is that we don't have to think long or hard to find teachers who incline in that direction. I would say that any of us, during our particularly uninspired moments, sometimes lean in that direction. The remedy to the open-ended nature of the course is not to close it down or make it narrower, it is to accept it genuinely as a strength. Not all teachers are comfortable in that space.

No content *per se*

There is no 'course content' as such in TOK; none, at least, in the way that we recognise content in other subjects. This can completely flummox students who come to class pens-a-ready to write down what they need to know. Teachers can be equally set adrift. We spend a fair bit of our time at the board or screen, pointing to ideas and facts that we want the students to know, by which we sometimes mean memorise and write down again later. In terms of the content of the course, the IB TOK Subject Guide certainly has a plethora of words and ideas in it, most of them consciously presented as tools to frame the exploration; they are meant to guide our attention towards other ideas, which is the real point of it all. Knowing that there are AOKs, WOKs, and a "Knowledge Framework", of course, is not the learning objective. Memorising and then later arguing "that there are eight Ways of Knowing" is a pretty clear signal to an examiner that the essay is not going in fruitful directions.

Some TOK teachers manage to turn the nuances of the course into something which can be too-easily 'packaged' in these concept-shaped containers. More importantly we want our students to think about are the Knowledge Questions (or "Knowledge Issues" and "Problems of Knowledge" from previous iterations of the course). The framing concepts in the general IB documentation help to guide the exploration, but are not the object of that exploration.

The students and their learning are really the true content of the TOK course. I mentioned the skills and expertise of the Visual Arts student above, but there are also Higher Level mathematicians, and historians, philosophers and literary critics in your class. In fact, every DP student is a mathematician, a literary critic, a scientist and a linguist. Make use that student expertise, especially in the cases where you have less expertise than they do.

Shift to 'second order' thinking

If there is no content, what is going on in TOK classrooms? We are modelling a certain approach to knowledge, one that is characterised by the distinction between first and second order thinking. There is no doubt that for students this is one of the biggest challenges, but teachers also will struggle with this distinction and this is made evident through the students' own assessments. Since the IB started moderating the TOK presentation through the PPD, where we now have the students' own knowledge questions and, importantly, the teachers' evaluations of those knowledge questions, it has become evident that many teachers struggle alongside their students in trying to identify and maintain a genuine second order approach. This is not easy, even for the experts in the room.

That being said, there are some sharp edges around the concept of what a "second order" claim or question is; the concept is not so broad that it will withstand an 'anything goes' approach. TOK is clearly about something specific – how communities of knowers construct their knowledge of the world and what role individual knowers play in that construction. This is at the heart of what we mean by second-order thinking, and while the TOK subject guide offers a tripartite definition (about knowledge, open and general), unpacking these elements takes a fair bit of time and thought from the teacher. The demands of TOK on the teacher should not be underestimated, especially by school leaders. There is no easy solution to this, but time, experience, trial and error and support from more experienced colleagues are obvious directions.

Transdisciplinary requirement

In addition to the complexity of the first and second order thinking distinction, the other primary challenge facing TOK teachers is the transdisciplinary and interdisciplinary approaches that lie at the heart of the course. TOK is inherently comparative; we analyse how knowledge is constructed in one AOK in order that we might compare that with other AOKs. Unless you're a true renaissance man or woman, transferring these ideas and reflections across disciplines can be a challenge. I would suggest that TOK teachers comprise the highest percentage of what we could call 'true renaissance' teachers. I am continually impressed with the breadth of knowledge represented in TOK workshops.

In this sense, then, TOK is transdisciplinary – it represents a holistic approach that moves beyond any one of the approaches within an AOK. This is the goal, but the course usually starts at a multidisciplinary level, whereby we are expected to have something of a working knowledge of the methods and application within AOKs across the board, but in which we've not been trained. This means stepping well outside of our comfort zones and engaging directly with the unknown. However, the level of genuine knowledge of the methods and outcomes of these disciplines needed by the TOK teacher can still be relatively shallow (relative to experts in the disciplines); the students will often be far more sophisticated in their understanding of the content in these other disciplines. This is TOK's saving grace, we need not be practitioners in these new AOKs, only voyeurs – we only need to be able to spot the relevant TOK elements in these AOKs in order to discuss them. This is the interdisciplinarity of TOK – we use a series of concepts (Knowledge Framework and WOKs) which then are used to see the similarities between them. For instance, I can rely on my own first-year university calculus knowledge, from nearly 25 years ago, to give me enough of an understanding of mathematics to know (generally speaking) how its basic axiomatic approach and deductive logic make it importantly different from how the traditionally conceived "historical method" works in History. Granted a Mathematics and TOK teacher will certainly be able to guide the students into more sophisticated discussion of Mathematics, but then my own students will benefit from my own training when exploring Ethics or Religious Knowledge Systems. Similarly, never having studied Economics, I can read up on the role of models and challenges in studying how humans respond to incentives, in order to discuss the differences between this and relatively straight forward (though undeniably complex) behaviour of molecules in Chemistry. This again, however, takes up a great deal of time and energy.

Still, few of us are as well-equipped or experienced when we start teaching TOK, so trying to make sense of how it works in other subjects presents a genuine challenge. The subject guide offers a life-line in that not every AOK needs to be explored, suggesting that six of the eight would be 'appropriate'. Which six, and the depth of each, is left to the teacher to decide and should start from his or her own expertise.

Given the multi-, inter- and transdisciplinary expectations heaped on the TOK teacher, it is no wonder that we spend an inordinate amount of time utterly confused and vulnerable when wading into the morass of unknown AOKs. This takes a cognitive toll (we're going to be thinking harder than we have in years) and it takes an emotional toll (we spend our days in the constant fear of looking ill-informed). This is hard work, much harder work than I have to put into my own discipline. In a DP subject, the hardest work is usually the graft of marking and planning, but in TOK, the understanding itself adds to the graft.

The added cognitive challenges presented by both the TOK approach (the second order thinking) and the cross-disciplinary nature of the course is not easy to measure, but school leaders must recognize that adding a TOK class to a teacher's workload is a shift in the kind of amount of work. The open-ended nature of the TOK course is often overestimated but, at the same time, the work and cognitive load that it takes to do the job well can be underestimated.

School structure of work

I have outlined the challenges presented when teachers are asked to join TOK teams simply because they have room in their timetables, but there are additional structural challenges facing TOK teachers.

In many school contexts TOK is allocated far fewer hours in the DP timetable than other subjects. This is probably appropriate, and indeed the IB suggests only 100 hours against the 150 hours for Standard Level subjects. However, the relatively fewer hours means that it often gets overlooked and is given even fewer than the 100. Many coordinators of TOK have to push to have those hours made up in a variety of ways, not all of them effective in terms of teaching – but effective in terms of meeting requirements.

From an individual's perspective, teachers must manage their own time to make sure that they give TOK the time required to bear the cognitive load and produce effective lessons. This may take a disproportionate amount of time and can lead to either resentment ("It takes up too much of my time!") or complacency ("it's all about debate anyway...").

Students are the first to draw conclusions when TOK is given fewer lessons or see the struggle that their teachers are facing. The students are already faced with the same kinds of cognitive challenges that their teachers face, but then they also have an added burden of being assessed. If they see a teacher straining under pressure, or they rarely see the inside of the TOK classroom, or they exist in a school structure which doesn't take TOK seriously, they are quick to tune-out. A critical mass of disinvested students lowers the effectiveness of a class, thereby lowering the effectiveness of the overall Diploma Programme at the school.

Assessment

The challenges faced by the IB's assessment structure for TOK seem to draw together and heighten all the challenges described above. That TOK is only part of three points of the overall score (maximum 45 points) means a couple of things. Firstly, it underscores the point about the challenge presented being at the edge of the students' cognitive development, so it is not expected that every student will succeed, and when they do not, it doesn't over-penalise the student: the 'A' grade in TOK is a genuine discriminator. Secondly however, that it represents so few points does not mean that it is taken less seriously. Many teachers to whom I have spoken suggest that it should be worth more points, 'because then students and school leaders will take it more seriously.' IBO, I think this is a mistake both pedagogically and strategically. Trying to gain the interest of the students through the piling on of assessment is always suspect and focusing on performance in TOK assessment might be desperately unfair given the challenges of the course.

The nature of the TOK assessment presents challenges as well. Whilst many teachers praise the open-ended nature of the course, an equal number (and often the same teachers) will complain that the assessment is not rigorous enough. This raises some complex issues. One one hand the course promotes a skills-based approach to content, but on the other hand the assessment must be of the type that assesses those skills in a valid manner, but in a way that allows for any number of plausible approaches and responses. The TOK essay, at least, helps to constrain the field by offering only six titles but, on the other hand, the TOK presentation can be about anything so long as it demonstrates TOK skills. Trying to strategise about 'what will get good marks' in TOK is something of a superfluous task and the old methods we teachers employ when shifting to 'exam strategy' often don't work in TOK; results often don't mirror expectations. Having examined TOK for many years, I don't think this is only the fault of the examiners nor of the assessment model. There is not the space here to go into the strengths and weaknesses of the TOK assessment model (there are many of both), but let it be recognised that reliably and validly assessing the kind of practice we hope to instil through the TOK course, while maintaining the applicability, creativity and rigour of good TOK skills presents unique challenges. I think the fact that there are relatively few points hinging on TOK helps assuage some of this worry.

If teachers feel that they don't understand TOK assessment, one solution is to work as an examiner. Every year the IB must recruit more and more examiners and engaging in the examining process is excellent professional development. My view is that teachers gain a level of charity, humility and understanding towards both the process and the subject when faced with 200 TOK essays, which cannot be gained in any other way.

The TOK assessment model however serves as a reminder of the real focus of what we do. A short externally assessed essay and a short internally assessed presentation cannot possibly serve as a proper summative assessment of all that we know the course to be. This then underscores the value of what we do day-to-day in our lessons. Next Wednesday's lesson on the role of selection in History is not directly aimed at performing well in the final essay, but it is important, it is what the course is about, and it will make the students better thinkers.

TOK is worthwhile

The long and the short of it is that teaching TOK is hard, and maybe it's not for everyone. What I hope to have presented here are a number of reasons why the struggles are genuine and not uncommon. TOK has been, however, the source of some of the most rewarding teaching I have done and some of the most effectual. We've all had the experience of students returning to us years after leaving school or after a couple of years at university to say, "I finally understand what TOK is about!" As teachers who hope to promote attitudes and dispositions that foster life-long learning, this is high praise indeed.

References

Vygotsky, L (1981) *Thought and Language*. The M.I.T. Press, Cambridge, Mass.

Chapter 9

Independent Learning in TOK: a Case Study

Edward Allanson

Introduction

Our school has been an IB World School since 2013 and we have around 70 students taking the IB Diploma Programme (DP). The Theory of Knowledge (TOK) course is taught by four teachers each of whom also teaches another DP course. Previously to the innovation described here, we ran our TOK course on a carousel system, with each teacher specialising in two Areas of Knowledge (AOK) with the students moving between groups. We are part of a Jesuit network of schools, colleges, and universities throughout the world. There are somewhere in the region of 2000 Jesuit educational institutions teaching 2.5 million students. In October 2017 Jesuit delegates from around the world gathered in Rio de Janeiro to discuss the future aims of education within the network (Jesuit Institute, 2018). From this congress came an action statement. One of the action points was entitled 'Tradition and Innovation', and it encouraged us to reflect on our pedagogical models. The emerging project, the focus of this chapter, forms part of a response to that request.

There has been a recent rise in teachers interacting with educational research. Although there have always been pockets of interest, research has remained largely the domain of universities. Social media, as well as the development of such bodies as the Chartered College of Teaching together with a rise in practitioner research publications, have allowed teachers to engage at some level with research which has reignited a desire to professionalise the role of the teacher. Now that there seems to be easier access to research, and to practical guides to apply it in the classroom, schools are becoming more research-informed and willing to try out these ideas. Books from practising teachers (Hendrick and Macpherson, 2018 and Sherrington, 2017) allow other teachers to apply research in an uncomplicated and brave new way. This chapter is one such attempt. The project is not fully developed but it is an attempt to engage in a new and experimental way with research-informed ideas as well as encouraging risk-taking within the staff body.

The school has four TOK classes in each year of the DP, and it was decided to trial a new lesson structure with one of these classes. All four classes have access to the TOK content online, with one class moving to what I have termed the 'independent structure'. The remaining three classes have retained a more instructional approach to lessons, more akin to a 'normal' lesson in any other subject. We are generally very happy with the quality of our lessons and so the project was intended to find out whether we could enhance students' independent learning, their time-management, and their participation in the TOK classes. The three 'normal' groups were not control groups however, and it may be that there are other factors affecting the conclusions drawn from the review. This is a case study looking at a project which attempts to use the flexibility and pedagogical approaches encouraged in the TOK course (provided by TOK) to improve the school's own teaching. We have gained interesting and helpful insights which we hope will be of use to others. We share these with you on that basis.

Background to the case study

As in all walks of life, there is discussion surrounding much of what teachers should do (or shouldn't do) in the classroom. Terms such as child-centred, teacher-centred, progressive, and traditional are used both to explain one's own teaching style and, at worst, to undermine the practice of another. The purpose of education continues to be under much scrutiny: is it to develop a love of life-long learning, a 'good' in its own right, for employment, for developing the skills needed for the future, or even for employment which can't yet be imagined? These discussions all play a part in forming how teachers see themselves and their role.

Teaching TOK provides an opportunity for a teacher to rethink how they teach in a way not necessarily open to teaching any other IB subject. This is in part related to the nature of the course. Teaching in my Philosophy class is different from teaching in my TOK class, and different again from teaching in my Religious Studies class. There is a freedom inherent within the TOK course which places the content in a different context. The first page of the TOK Subject Guide lays this out: "Teachers are not obliged to follow the suggested examples and ideas presented here; this guide offers a framework rather than prescribed content" (IB, 2013, p1). This does not mean that there is no content, but rather that there is flexibility around what is chosen. The nature of the TOK assessment also means that there is a good deal of flexibility; there is no required content, but content is required. A course which fulfils the key aims to examine "how we know what we claim to know..." and does this by encouraging students to analyse knowledge claims and explore knowledge questions (IB, 2013, p8) will be likely to be successful. Of course, with freedom comes a degree of fear, as a lack of a solid structure and a new way of teaching mean that there is a certain amount of unknown.

Mention the role of technology in learning and educators will quite happily share their love or loathing for tablet computers and mobile telephones. What is often forgotten is that pedagogy must always come before technology. Faddish use of technology without a clearly defined role to play in learning will sooner or later fail, leaving a trail of exhausted staff less inclined to participate fully next time. It was important for us to design a course which started with clear outcomes and a clear pedagogical style. Only at this point would we then ask what could help us achieve this. There is little doubt that technology can play a positive role in learning: the very fact that this book is printed demonstrates this. The rise of MOOCs, distance learning university courses and the Khan Academy, for example, show that there are ways in which technology can provide independent learning opportunities.

We were aware of the dangers of removing expert teacher guidance from the classroom. Independent learning can mistakenly be viewed as the withdrawal of the teacher from the learning process: the educational equivalent of throwing the student in at the deep end and watching to see if they can swim. We believed that the role of expert guidance was an essential element of the course, especially in the early stages of learning a new concept: "when teaching new content and skills to novices, teachers are more effective when they provide explicit guidance accompanied by practice and feedback, not when they require students to discover many aspects of what they must learn" (Clark *et al*, 2012, p6).

Although we did not wish to remove the teacher from the classroom, we did want to engage with some of the benefits of moving the focus away from the teacher and back towards the students. We wanted to make sure that the start of the process of learning was covered in such a way that the pupils were able learn the content most effectively. We then wanted to move beyond this to engage them in critical discussion of the knowledge claims and questions. We also structured the course to allow groups to have ownership of their learning to a greater degree than had happened before with teacher-led classroom environments. Technology allowed us to do this. Placing content online meant that students could work at a monitored and yet independent rate. This ownership of learning became an important theme in the review of the course.

Assessment of knowledge and the development of skills are important. This is one of the reasons for including the teacher discussion element of the class, which follows below, as well as the testing of content and the TOK-style essays. As much as it is important that students develop the skills needed, we also had to make sure that they were able to apply these in a way which would result in good assessment grades.

What we do

The students in the 'independent structure' class were split into three teams and were expected to collaborate to help the group learn together. They were given guidelines at the beginning of the TOK course to advise them on how to work well as a team, and consequently they have since developed their own rules for learning. These include: 'No one is left behind', 'No showing off', 'Build each other up, not knock each other down'. The students went through the usual team-building issues of ignoring all their own advice, but they slowly developed into highly effective teams and mini-learning communities. Each student has access to an online programme of study which provides them with the learning content needed for TOK. This generally include videos, newspaper articles and links to academic articles. The students are given questions to help focus their study but certainly not to stifle alternate areas of interest. The questions are open and allow the students to respond to the stimuli that they have been given.

Many schools have their students keep a TOK journal and they report differing levels of success with this. We have found in the past that some students start off well but that the enthusiasm drifts as the course progresses. Our own TOK journal has been changed so that it is also a record of the discussions and answers to the prompt questions given during the lesson. This has had a positive effect in that, as the students are recording in the same Word document each lesson, they are more inclined to record other thoughts. Using the same Word document has the added benefit of easy access to their previous answers, as well as seeing their own progress throughout the course.

The students come in to their TOK classroom and have immediate access to the material. They are all at different points and so start work (off themselves) without expecting the teacher to be the 'leader'. This took a little while to settle but they are now able to come into the room and start without too much delay. The students are developing the skills that they need in their independent study of TOK, such as revision and homework, as well as beyond their life at school. During each lesson it is expected that groups will divide their time between three main activities: learning from the stimuli online, learning from each other in discussion, and developing their learning through discussion with their teacher.

The students spend some time engaging with the TOK content with which they have been provided. For example, this may be through learning about the observer effect, Paschal's Wager, or deductive reasoning. It is important that students understand that learning is not simply about having an opinion, but that their learning will be strengthened by using foundational knowledge as a treasure trove from which to draw. This knowledge is tested with short, no-risk online testing which gives the students their score. At first a few students simply kept taking the test until they gained a 'high enough' score without learning the material. As soon as they realised that the tests were for them rather than for the teacher's mark book there was a change, and they became more interested in the learning than in the score; they wanted to retake the test after going back over the material. This change in attitude did not take an insignificant amount of time, but the result was worth it and we devised other ways to assess learning too so that no one fell too far behind.

An important part of each lesson is also to make sure there is time set aside for the students to discuss the TOK issues raised by the content. There is a freedom in the discussion and some of the connections made between the TOK Areas of Knowledge (AOK) have been truly impressive. The teacher is not expected to interact with the students at this stage (although they are available to support them if needed) and this means that further questions are developed by the students: they learn what they do not know. During the discussions it is expected that notes are taken in their TOK journals so that there is a record of the work, and also to help with the third element of the lesson, a discussion with the teacher.

The final element of the lesson involves the students leading a discussion with the class teacher. They begin by summarising the content before moving to sharing the discussion in which the group has already engaged. This usually brings up all kinds of issues: further questions about the implications of some of the material they have chosen, disagreements within the group about certainty of knowledge, the role of experts, or the fact that some students struggle to deal with ambiguity. These are high-level discussions which require the students to assimilate what they have learned and to develop an understanding of the wider pool of knowledge and its interconnectivity

At the end of a study of an Area of Knowledge the students produce an essay which involves them developing those skills needed for the TOK Essay part of the IB's assessment, which is also intended as a formal way of structuring their own thoughts on what they have covered to that point. It allows the teacher to be confident of the student's ability to write in a way which is appropriate for TOK as well as providing a record of the learning journey the pupils are taking. Essays are formally assessed according to the TOK grade descriptors, and feedback given as usual.

The TOK journal is also periodically submitted to see what has been discussed in the groups but which may not have been aired in the teacher discussion element of the class. Students also record which aspects of TOK they have identified during the week in their other classes, in newspapers or in their everyday life. We ask the students to change the text colour for this so that it is easily identifiable to us and to them. As mentioned above, this is bet ter used than in previous years, partly due (we believe) to the students feeling greater ownership of their TOK learning, but also because teachers ask whether anything has come up during the week during their group discussion with the students.

Outcomes and adjustments

As part of the review of the whole TOK course we asked all students to complete questionnaires as well as taking data from the assignments they had completed, and their TOK journal. It is important that the course develops organically and so we will make adjustments as we go along. The review was much more informal than rigorous academic research, but we intended to gather as much good quality information as was possible. To begin, we asked the students via an anonymous questionnaire about their enjoyment of TOK lessons, with the same questions asked to those who were part of the 'independent structure' described above as well as to those who were not. There were some helpful responses which allowed us to make adjustments to the course.

The students in the 'independent structure' course maintained that they felt in control of their learning and that the teacher discussion part of the lesson meant that they all have to speak and so were more engaged: "there is less room to hide". They appreciated the fact that they could control the pace of their learning of the content: "I like that I can go back and watch the video again". These simple dimensions of the course seem to be working. However, the students from the other classes said that they felt more secure during lessons than the independent class: "I like that the teacher explains things until we understand them', 'My teacher answers questions really well". This will be interesting to monitor going forward. Robert Bjork's work on the idea of 'desirable difficulties' may also be able to help us here and it may indeed be that feeling less 'safe' leads to a higher degree of challenge and success (a point developed below). There was a slightly higher level of enjoyment expressed by students in the questionnaire in the 'independent structure', with mention by two students that they have only begun to enjoy the lessons after struggling for a few weeks. This is in some way to be expected as this is an entirely new way of the students working. We expected that there would be a settling in period but maybe there is more that we can do to help ease that difficulty.

Next we looked to see if there was evidence of differences between the groups in terms of the degree to which the course encourages the students to see (and record) TOK observations outside of the classroom. This was measured in two ways: entries into TOK journals, and evidence from essays. It seems that there was a higher degree of 'non-class content' within the 'independent class' structure, which was pleasing. Most significant was noticing that the class which followed the 'independent structure' course had all work completed and on time. All students, regardless of course structure, have the same deadlines for the TOK essay-style questions. It was only the class in which this new course structure was followed where all students had the work complete (as well as being completed to a very good standard) at each checkpoint in the course. This may suggest that for these students there is a higher level of ownership over their learning. It may also be that they have more time to complete the work as they have moved through the course at a faster rate. We will monitor this going forward to see if the course is indeed having the impact it seems to be having in this respect. Nevertheless, this was the most significant difference between the groups. Over time one would expect that students holding the belief that they have a high degree of ownership over their learning should have a positive effect upon the outcomes.

However, looking at the four classes there was little difference in the average quality of the essays produced as compared to the students' overall baseline data. There was, however, evidence of much wider engagement with material outside of the course content. It may well be that the structure of the course has little impact upon the quality of written work or that we need to adjust the course to include more of a focus on how to write an essay which, in turn, may be better facilitated in classes which have a higher level of teacher input.

Overall we believe that there are encouraging signs in the review even at this early stage. The higher levels of enjoyment and ownership were key aims for the project. We hope that this will allow for even more progress to be seen in the TOK assessment outcomes this year.

Following the review, we have looked for ways to make sure that we continue to improve the learning of the pupils. There are three main areas we hope to develop; two following the review and one which comes from our reading of current educational research.

1. When we come to introduce the course to the next cohort we intend to spend longer making sure that we explain our reasoning and approach behind the course.

2. We will also make sure that in the first few weeks we have some 'normal' lessons, those with which the students are most familiar, so that they become more readily acclimatised to the way the course works and can feel more secure.

3. We are also interested in the idea, stemming from work on 'desirable difficulties' (Bjork and Bjork, 2013), that building in interleaving could have benefits beyond developing the ability to recall, including the secondary skill of synthesising previous content within multiple Areas of Knowledge so helping students to understand the complexity of knowledge. This would be a simple adaptation to the course but clearly would need a good deal of explaining to the students. It is also important to be mindful of there being too many challenges for the students so that the danger that TOK becomes too foreign a style of learning is avoided. There are, as mentioned at the start of this chapter, significant differences between TOK and other DP subjects in terms of assessment and course content.

The changing role of the TOK teacher

The role of the teacher in TOK is in some ways different from that of other teachers on the DP. This springs from a certain level of autonomy in choosing the content of the course. Fundamentally, however, the role of a TOK teacher remains to find the best ways to help the students to learn. Our 'independent structure' course asks for teachers to take another step away from directly delivering the material and become part of the conversation of learning. The teachers become learners, too. Of course, they have somewhat of a head start in that they have had time to consider the material and have a breadth of knowledge upon which to draw, but they nevertheless remain closer to the role of learners than they do to that of instructors. This is partly because in TOK the students are ultimately in control of the wider content. TOK teachers also have to interact with content well outside their natural sphere of knowledge: some TOK teachers will not have studied Mathematics or sciences, for example, since their own formal education. If they teach another DP subject they will be more familiar with the content and the types of questions which arise than would be the case for TOK.

An essential ingredient is the attitude of the school's leadership team. It can be unsettling for a teacher to break from the norm – the worry of failure, complaints, poor results – they are all at play. It is a brave leader who gives the teacher scope to trial new ideas which may 'go wrong'. It is therefore important for the school's leaders to allow some innovation while, of course, making sure contingencies are in place.

Conclusion

In this chapter I have shared our experience of innovation within TOK. The aim was two-fold: to suggest that TOK offers a unique atmosphere in which innovation in learning and teaching can take place, and also to help encourage others to attempt innovative practice within their own schools and teaching. It is hoped that by sharing our developing experience it may help others to try some of these ideas in their own context. Teachers need the space to be able to innovate and school leaders need to allow new ideas to be tested. Things will not necessarily always go as expected the first time around, and although the learning of the students must never be risked at the expense of a fad or of our desire simply to experiment, TOK may be the space in which some of the risks may be reduced. It also provides the space for development of skills within the context of the content the pupils cover. It allows for the students to have ownership of their learning in a way not yet open in some subject areas that are very content heavy. Our project will continue to evolve, at times, no doubt, possibly quite dramatically, but this evolution will remain focused on keeping the students' learning at the centre of the programme.

References

Bjork E L & Bjork R A (2013) 'Making things hard on yourself, but in a good way: creating desirable difficulties to enhance learning', in *Psychology and the Real World: essays illustrating fundamental contributions to society.*

Clark R, Kirschner P A & Sweller J (2012) 'Putting students on the path to learning: the case for fully-guided instruction', *American Educator.*

Hendrick C & Macpherson R (2017), *What does this look like in the classroom?* Woodbridge: John Catt Educational Ltd.

IB (2013) *Diploma Programme: Theory of Knowledge Guide.* The Hague: International Baccalaureate.

Jesuit Institute (2018) The Rio Papers, accessed 10 March 2019 on http://jesuitinstitue. org?Pages/Rio2017.htm

Sherrington T (2017) *The Learning Rainforest: Great Teaching in Real Classrooms*, Woodbridge: John Catt Educational Ltd.

Chapter 10

The World Studies Extended Essay: Addressing Global Issues through an Interdisciplinary Lens

Robin Julian

The aim of the Diploma Programme (DP) Extended Essay (EE) is for students to engage in independent research with intellectual initiative and rigour, develop research, thinking, self-management and communication skills, and then reflect on what has been learned throughout the research and writing process. Essays written in specific disciplines such as biology, history, or social and cultural anthropology, allow students to fulfil these aims admirably, but the opportunity to research across two academic disciplines and focus on global issues through the lens of the IB's pivotal principle of international mindedness was boosted with the introduction of the interdisciplinary World Studies Extended Essay.

A World Studies variation on the traditional EE was first proposed by the UWC (United World College) Mahindra, India, in 2001 and was eventually set up as an EE pilot option in 2005. The development of the World Studies EE pilot was underpinned by extensive academic research. IB staff worked closely with teachers in the pilot schools and researchers from the Harvard Graduate School of Education, Project Zero Interdisciplinary Studies Project, to develop this exciting EE option. In this chapter I will describe the nature of the World Studies EE, examine how the research and writing of such an essay impacts students and their supervisors, and discuss the overall significance of interdisciplinarity in research and learning.

What is the World Studies EE?

The World Studies EE gives students the opportunity to undertake an interdisciplinary, issues-based investigation of a contemporary global issue. 'Interdisciplinary' in this context refers to research that draws on the methods, concepts and theories of two DP subjects. To encourage the most rigorous essays, it is strongly recommended that students are studying as part of their Diploma at least one of the subjects that they choose to frame their research and writing.

The World Studies EE must focus on a topic of global significance. This encourages the student to reflect on the contemporary world in relation to issues such as the global food crisis, climate change, terrorism, energy security, migration, global health, technology and cultural exchange. They must also develop a clear rationale for taking an interdisciplinary approach and make sure that they use the conceptual framework and vocabulary of the two DP subjects. To bring to the research a more tangible aspect, students must also explore how their chosen issue is evident in a local context using specific examples of small scale, local phenomena. In this way they are connecting the local to the global and enhancing their own views of their world by conducting research that is likely to have more meaning for them.

The process of researching and writing the World Studies EE connects the EE component of the DP directly with the IB philosophy that spawned it in 1968, in that it helps to develop international-mindedness and specifically to nurture global consciousness in students, a concept that encompasses three distinct strands:

- global sensitivity – a sensitivity to local phenomena and experiences as expressions of developments on the planet
- global understanding – the capacity to think in flexible and informed ways about issues of global significance
- global self – "a developing perception of self as a global actor and member of humanity, capable of making a positive contribution to the world" (Boix Mansilla and Gardner, 2007).

The IB's EE guide (IB, 2016) describes researching and writing a World Studies EE as providing students with the opportunity to:

- engage with a systematic, effective process of research informed by knowledge, concepts, theories, perspectives and methods from two chosen subjects
- develop communication skills, including the ability to convey ideas that both include and transcend different disciplines
- develop creative and critical thinking skills, particularly those concerned with integrating concepts, theories, perspectives, findings or examples from different subjects in order to develop new insights or understandings
- experience the excitement of intellectual discovery, especially the insights into how different subjects complement or challenge one another when addressing the same topic or issue.

To help students focus their thinking and planning, World Studies EEs are registered in one of six areas of study:

- Conflict, peace and security
- Culture, language and identity
- Environmental and/or economic sustainability
- Equality and inequality
- Health and development
- Science, technology and society.

Within these general areas students identify topics that derive from issues of global significance which are then best explored through a set of multifaceted, specific questions rather than broad, generalised ones. Examples put forward in the EE guide (IB, 2016, p371) to help students get an idea of the scope of World Studies research questions include:

Topic	DP subjects	Research question	Approach
Culture, language and identity: music as an expression of political dissent	Music History	To what extent can music be used as a method of political expression against oppressive regimes: a comparison of Shostakovich's work (1932–45) under Joseph Stalin's regime with Malek Jandali's work (2000–) under Bashar al-Assad's regime.	By analysing nine musical parameters of two composers as expressions of dissent under repressive regimes in different historical eras, and the contexts in which they were written and their reception, the student draws meaningful comparisons and contrasts using the skills of the historian and those of musical notation.
Health and development: multiple sclerosis and latitude	Biology Geography	To what extent do geographical factors play a role in the distribution of multiple sclerosis cases in Canada and Iran?	The essay challenges the suggested theory that MS is associated with high latitudes by looking at recent studies of Iran. Genetic factors and vitamin deficiency (biology), migration and environment (geography) are evaluated to enhance understanding.
Health and development: economic growth and obesity	Biology Geography Economics	How has globalization contributed to dietary changes and obesity in developed and developing countries?	The essay considers metabolic systems and the role of the endocrine system (biology) and recent qualitative and quantitative changes in diet in Liberia, Brazil and the USA to measure energy imbalance and a nutrition transition resulting from globalization (geography/economics).

Table 10.1: Examples of World Studies EE research questions

The impact of the World Studies EE

The World Studies EE framework as detailed in the IB's EE guide sets up students to tackle a significant research project, probably the biggest one they have attempted. If students develop research questions that investigate issues which really matter to them, then the act of research should also matter. But can research still be considered as something that really matters in an age

137

when search engines can respond in an instant, with increasingly credibility, to just about any question you can dream up? Is it possible to learn enough about significant global issues without the benefit of a World Studies EE framework? Perhaps it is best to distinguish between the simplistic exercise of browsing the internet, an auto-response by so many of us in our contemporary 'scroller society', and what is described as 'research' in the Oxford Living Dictionary, that is, "the systematic investigation into and study of materials and sources in order to establish facts and reach new conclusions".

Plainly the key ingredients of research as defined above imply digging deeper than just a quick question posed to Siri. Indeed this definition suggests an underlying thirst for new knowledge, and an enthusiasm to search for informed conclusions that can shape future decisions and actions. The EE, in particular the World Studies EE, can also be recognised as contributing to a person's capacity to discover for herself the answers to the enduring questions, big and small, encountered during her life. But what do DP students think of this claim? An IB 2018 survey of almost 400 IBDP alumni (IB community blog, 2018) revealed that most supported the EE as an important aspect of their Diploma studies, with more than 72% of respondents either 'agreeing' or 'strongly agreeing' that it was 'an academically significant part' of their DP experience. A further 19% were 'somewhat' in agreement. 68% either agreed or strongly agreed that their understanding of research had been enhanced through doing an EE, with another 20% 'somewhat' in agreement.

In terms of becoming competent in specific research skills, 71% of the DP alumni surveyed felt that they had acquired 'very good' or 'excellent' skills in citing sources and creating a reference list using a standard style (Harvard, MLA, APA, Chicago). 55% of respondents thought that they had developed a 'very good' or 'excellent' ability to construct a reasoned argument, with a further 31% regarding their argument skill as 'good'. The view of 87% of former students was that they had a 'good', 'very good' or 'excellent' capacity to draw conclusions from their research. These statistics affirm the perception of the EE as a very effective tool to help students to develop the self-regulated research and writing skills that they need to fulfil their aspirations at university.

The fact that 35% of alumni surveyed said they found formulating a research question 'too challenging' or 'far too challenging' emphasises the importance of good guidance and mentoring during this formative stage of the EE process. This is particularly pertinent for students doing the World Studies EE as this stage of the process includes decision-making about choice of DP subjects, areas of study, the global issue and local context. It is also at this stage that students need to be developing a clear understanding of what 'interdisciplinary' actually means.

Respondents' open-ended reflections on what they considered to be the most rewarding aspects of their EE experience provide personal context and enrich the statistics. The sense of trepidation experienced by some DP students as they faced the prospect of researching and writing a 4,000-word piece of academic writing was expressed in comments like "simply completing it was rewarding", but many respondents reflected on the enjoyment and benefits of independently researching a topic of their own choice, coming to an understanding of "what professional research looks like and the work required to do it". For some, the EE brought the "excitement of independent research", the "freedom of choice of topic", and "being able to research a topic about which I was passionate", while others enjoyed "working with a wonderful supervisor to learn about all the tools required for effective research".

As the alumni who responded to the survey have now also experienced college/university life, they were able to appreciate the value of the EE and the transferability of skills they had learned to the context of higher education. As universities are increasingly developing interdisciplinary study and research options, students with World Studies EE experience are well placed to take advantage of these. Some alumni were pleased to have the opportunity to learn and put into practice "proper, formal research skills that introduced me to college-level work", and appreciated that the EE gave them "a feel for what writing an academic paper is like". Others learned "how to commit to a long-lasting research project".

The long-lasting impact of the EE is captured in reflections such as "some years after leaving school, I still find myself citing my Extended Essay in conversations", and "the feeling of self-accomplishment remains to this day". For some the EE "sparked an ongoing passion for research", but perhaps the most poignant remark shared was one former student's reflection that researching and writing the EE had revealed "that I am capable of more than I had ever imagined".

Feedback from IBDP alumni affirms the view that the EE adds a remarkable piece of value to the overall Diploma experience. It seems that there is good reason to be feel confident that the World Studies EE in particular is doing its bit to bring a practical face to the IB mission to develop "inquiring, knowledgeable and caring young people who help to create a better and more peaceful world through intercultural understanding and respect".

Reflections of Extended Essay supervisors on the World Studies EE

In conjunction with the survey of alumni, EE supervisors were also invited by the IB to participate in an in-house survey investigating their experiences working with students. EE supervisors are appropriately qualified members of the school staff who guide students through the processes of research, writing and reflection. Supervisors who had experience with supervising World Studies essays reflected on that experience in a largely positive way. Some recognised that it is challenging to support students in a second discipline that is outside their own area of expertise, or that they found it more demanding to apply the IB assessment criteria to a World Studies context. They also expressed the view that students need quite specific guidance and advice to help them conceptualise and realise the interdisciplinary task of addressing the methods and approaches of two DP subjects while trying to maintain a focus on the issue that they are investigating.

While recognising that for some students the framework for a World Studies EE introduces a level of complexity that may impact their workload, supervisors also found much to praise. They appreciated that it links directly and specifically with the IB Learner Profile and the IB mission. As one supervisor commented, "it makes students think beyond curriculum and engage with international mindedness". Supervisors' views on the World Studies EE included these comments:

- "it's an enriching experience for both the student and the supervisor"
- "a great vehicle for authentic student engagement and approaching problem solving with nuance"
- "an interdisciplinary approach to solving problems is really effective"
- "demanding but so worthwhile and the best preparation for college"
- "it starts with the issue rather than the subject, so it's more organic than writing from a subject specific approach"
- "having the flexibility to allow students to explore these types of topics enhances individuality and engagement"
- "students show a significant level of personal growth during the process"
- "I enjoy the interdisciplinary collaboration with other supervisors in their disciplines"

In summary, an interdisciplinary approach to the EE is supportively endorsed by the supervisors responsible for mentoring students through the process. They believe it to be an enriching experience for students in that it 'lives' the IB mission and the Learner Profile and engages students with a range of perspectives and problem solving through different disciplinary lenses. With the World Studies EE students make connections across disciplines and between local and global contexts, under an umbrella of international mindedness.

The interdisciplinary nature of the World Studies EE

Underlying the World Studies EE is the understanding that sometimes the nature of an issue requires researchers to break out from the constraints of 'siloed', discipline-focused research methods and consider an interdisciplinary approach. But how do we explain this approach and why may it improve on a disciplinary research strategy?

First, it is necessary to distinguish the term 'interdisciplinary' from other related terms. Interdisciplinary research involves the researcher using the methodologies of more than one discipline to address an issue. In the World

Studies EE we are asking students to be 'interdisciplinary' as opposed to 'transdisciplinary', or 'multidisciplinary'. In the real world, the researcher would be proficient in both the disciplines being combined, whereas in the context of the DP it is recommended that students be studying 'at least one' of the two disciplines they are using for their World Studies EE. 'Transdisciplinary', it should be noted, is more concerned with the merging of two disciplines to form a new methodological approach, while 'multidisciplinary' implies a group approach to address an issue, with each member of the group bringing expertise from their particular discipline (Kroeze, 2013).

The norm for an EE, a disciplinary approach, teaches a person the acceptable methodology for that field. It 'disciplines' a person so that her/his work is acceptable to others in the discipline. Ken Robinson in criticising the 'western' model of education in schools and universities, wrote: "Public schools were not only created in the interests of industrialism—they were created in the image of industrialism. In many ways, they reflect the factory culture they were designed to support. This is especially true in high schools, where school systems base education on the principles of the assembly line and the efficient division of labour. Schools divide the curriculum into specialist segments: some teachers install math in the students, and others install history" (Robinson, 2009).

The World Studies EE provides students with a potential alternative to the disciplinary 'assembly line' and leads us to a discussion of the broader merits of an interdisciplinary approach not only to research but also to teaching and learning in general. The discourse in academic literature highlights the benefits, drawbacks and practicalities of interdisciplinary research.

In the course of my research for the IB's curriculum review of the EE I sampled about 20 academic/education journals in order to to understand the ongoing debate over the merits of an interdisciplinary approach to research. These articles, published between 2005 and 2018, were analysed to determine how the authors defined the term 'interdisciplinary', what they discerned as the positives and the challenges of interdisciplinary research, and their perception of the worth of interdisciplinarity in problem-solving.

Firstly, what is 'interdisciplinarity'? While Kroeze (2013) describes research that is interdisciplinary as using the methodologies of specific disciplines to address a problem, Boix Mansilla (2016) elevates this to a higher plane by referring to interdisciplinarity as being "capable of turning diffuse disciplinary insights into valuable understandings". Buizer et al (2015) point to the need for academics to engage in the "often difficult but essential debates about what is knowledge and how to work with, between, and among differing world views and methodologies", while Rawlings et al (2015) capture the desirable outcome of this endeavour, poetically expressed as "streams of thought, knowledge flows" leading to intellectual cohesion. North (2005) suggests that the world of interdisciplinarity may be inhabited by students who have the "flexibility to respond appropriately to different situations", looking beyond the knowledge and methods of a singular discipline for ideas and answers. Certainly, the integration of knowledge and methods from different disciplines may be viewed as a potentially fruitful research environment, one in which issues are investigated with a fresh approach, without the encumbrance of a singular lens.

Positive aspects of interdisciplinarity

The literature contains some compelling arguments in favour of taking an interdisciplinary approach to research. In general, interdisciplinarity may be described as systems thinking and practice, with all the benefits that come with that, i.e. "enhanced discussion, investigation, deliberation and development" (Ison, 2008). It is an approach that is capable of producing "different types of socially robust knowledge" (Polk, 2014). Interdisciplinarity introduces different ways of thinking to a research project. Requiring researchers to widen their academic horizons, it can be argued, is more cognitively engaging than otherwise (Applebee *et al*, 2007). Boix Mansilla (2016) develops this notion further by linking interdisciplinarity to "sophisticated conceptions of knowledge, learning and inquiry and heightened learner motivation".

Similarly, applying the methods and resources of more than one discipline encourages researchers to represent knowledge as both perspectival and factual (North, 2005), a philosophy that resonates with the thinking that IB students develop through the study of Theory of Knowledge (TOK) in their DP. Indeed, the cohesion of different ways of thinking can build an impressive knowledge flow, as ideas develop and are shaped by different perspectives (Rawlings *et al*, 2015). In TOK classes students develop critical thinking skills that allow them to consider issues and their associated knowledge questions from different perspectives, for example, asking why a scientist might approach the issue of global warming differently to an artist, an historian or an anthropologist. Indeed, how can we know if anything experts in their field say is reliable? Students are asked to critically evaluate the knowledge claims of different areas of knowledge, but also encouraged to regard their own voices as important and urged to put forward their informed, supported views with confidence.But how difficult might it be to determine an agreed position from the different perspectives of an interdisciplinary approach to research? For a researcher used to working within the confines of a particular discipline, the input from other disciplines may be challenging, confusing, or unexpected. Wittkower (2009) reassures us by suggesting that "it will not be rivalrous – there will always be a process of comparison and translation before obtaining any results which can validate or question any particular prior claim". Indeed, scientists would argue that the convergence of two or more 'scientific' disciplines can lead to a practical and theoretical integration of the disciplines involved, which would be unified. They point to biochemistry as an example of almost symmetrical integration and put forward Newton's work to show that unity of sciences works (Alvargonzález, 2011). The DP's own interdisciplinary subjects, Environmental Systems and Societies and Literature and Performance, similarly purport to symmetrically integrate disciplines.

Potential challenges associated with interdisciplinarity

Interdisciplinarity, however, is not a fail-proof approach to research. If we adopt the general perception that academic disciplines tend to exist in 'silos' and that this is in some way a bad thing, we put aside the notion that some issues are best suited to a disciplinary approach to research. To begin with, we should ask whether integration at the theoretical or methodological level is feasible or desirable when contemplating a particular issue (Ison, 2008). It may be that some disciplines resist infiltration by other disciplines because of the need to maintain their professional credentials, but this may also indicate that the thinking inherent to a discipline makes it difficult to accommodate different approaches (Kroeze, 2013). For example, researchers may find it challenging to let go of a disciplinary tendency to view knowledge as either absolute or constructed (North, 2005).

Interdisciplinarity in problem-solving, or problem-solving through interdisciplinarity?

The positives associated with an interdisciplinary approach to problem-solving can be tempered by the suggestion that researchers may "hold to and critique from their own disciplinary silos" (Beck, 2013), so making it challenging to reach a shared conclusion. However, problem-solving from interdisciplinary perspectives can also bring synthesis in our capacity to combine two concepts into a new unit of meaning (Boix Mansilla, 2016), a notion that lends credence to the World Studies EE as an option for DP students.

Generally speaking the literature speaks very positively about the capacity of interdisciplinarity to solve problems through research. Ison (2008) holds that it allows researchers to grasp the complexity of problems and consider the diversity of perceptions, while Koier and Horlings (2015) say that as many of today's societal problems are 'wicked' problems, i.e. difficult or impossible to solve due to there being insufficient, or contradictory knowledge, these require a new, integrated approach. Polk (2014) writes that interdisciplinarity encourages broader participation and balanced problem ownership, and Rawlings et al (2015) praise an interdisciplinary approach to research because its "creativity, discovery, and innovation often entail vibrant knowledge flows that circulate within and bridge a variety of problem areas".

At university level, Golding and Baik (2012) contend that interdisciplinary learning is important in the context of internationalising the curriculum: "The ability to synthesise and integrate diverse perspectives across a range of contexts is central to interdisciplinary thinking, and also promotes global engagement". Of course, the designers of the World Studies EE would endorse this view. Furthermore, it is encouraging to contemplate that DP graduates with experience in interdisciplinary research and writing will move on to universities, transfer their skills to a fresh context and make significant contributions to those new learning environments.

How popular are Extended Essay interdisciplinary options?

Given that interdisciplinarity is seen as fostering meaningful global interactions, a principle dear to the IB community, it is interesting to see the growth in student interest in taking up one of the interdisciplinary options within the EE.

Analysis of registration data for DP examination sessions from 2010 to 2018, shows that an interdisciplinary approach to research is growing in popularity. The proportion of interdisciplinary EEs submitted for the May examination session has increased from 1.48% in 2010 to 6.6% in 2018, and for the November examination session it has increased from 0.75% to 3.3% over the same time period.

Specifically, the number of World Studies EEs submitted for the May examination session increased from 73 to 4,184 between 2010 and 2018. World Studies EEs ranked as the 5th most popular option (of 98) at the May 2018 examination session (2010 – 42/100). The number of World Studies EEs submitted for the November examination session increased from 17 to 247 between 2013 and 2018, and World Studies EEs ranked as the 15th most popular option (of 48) at the November 2018 examination session (2013 - 30/47).

In addition, the number of Environmental Systems and Societies (ESS) EEs submitted for the May examination session have increased by 98.2% from 2010 to 2018. ESS EE's ranked as the 17th most popular option (of 98) at the May 2018 examination session, while the number of ESS EE's submitted for the November exam session have increased by 367.6% from 2010 to 2018. ESS EE's ranked as the 16th most popular option (of 48) at the November 2018 examination session (2010 - 19/49).

Connecting world issues with the student's own world

Finally, it is important to note that the World Studies EE does what any good educational task should do, that is it provides the student with a meaningful learning experience. The claim "what you learn is what you do" (Chua, 2017), encapsulates the inspirational context of the World Studies EE, an endeavour that encourages best research practice and stimulates students to dig deep into a contemporary global issue to which they can relate.

Supervisors play an important role supporting young researchers through the inquiry process, as they explore how viewing an issue through different lenses can provide important revelations and insights that lead to synthesis, potential problem solving and enhanced international mindedness. As Boix Mansilla *et al.* (2013) explain, interdisciplinarity requires deliberate instruction. Given the motivation that comes from having the freedom to design your own research project, clear guidelines, and good advice from EE supervisors, the World Studies EE can help students comprehend and analyse complexity and address the issue of fragmentation of knowledge among disciplines. It is worth noting that interdisciplinarity is being given an ever higher profile as an approach to research and learning at universities: "Today, interdisciplinary pronouncements are prominently featured in university mission statements – and capital campaigns – the world over" (Boix Mansilla, 2016). This is the world that DP graduates are entering, and the World Studies Extended Essay is helping them step into it with confidence.

References

Alvargonzález D (2011) 'Multidisciplinarity, interdisciplinarity, transdisciplinarity, and the sciences', *International Studies in the Philosophy of Science*, 25:4, 387–403.

Applebee A N, Adler M, & Flihan S (2007) 'Interdisciplinary curricula in middle and high school classrooms: case studies of approaches to curriculum and instruction', *American Educational Research Journal*, 44:4, 1002-1039.

Beck S J (2013) 'Moving beyond disciplinary differences in group research', *Small Group Research*, 44(2), 195–198.

Boix Mansilla V, Gardner H (2007) 'From teaching globalization to nurturing global consciousness', in Suarez-Orozco M M (ed). *Learning in the global era: International perspectives on globalization and education*. Berkeley, CA. The University of California Press.

Boix Mansilla V, Jackson A, Jacobs I H & Tree S (2013) 'Educating for Global Competence: Learning redefined for an interconnected world', in Hayes Jacobs H (ed) *Mastering Global Literacy* (5-27). New York: Solution Tree.

Boix Mansilla, V (2016) 'Interdisciplinary Learning: A cognitive-epistemological foundation', in *Oxford Handbook of Interdisciplinarity*. Second Edition, 1–16.

Buizer M, Ruthrof K, Moore S A, Veneklaas E J, Hardy G & Baudains C (2015). 'A critical evaluation of interventions to progress transdisciplinary research', *Society & Natural Resources*, 28:6, 670-681.

Chua F, Morrison K, Perkins D, Tishman S (2017) Portable Knowledge: A Visible Thinking Bundle to Foster Transfer of Content and 21st Century Skills. Available at www.pz.harvard.edu/resources/portable-knowledge, accessed 19 May 2018.

Golding C and Baik C (2012) 'Interdisciplinary Assessment', in Clouder L, Brougham C, Jewell S & Steventon G (eds.) *Improving Student engagement and Development through Assessment: Theory and Practice in Higher Education*. London: Routledge, pp.138-151.

International Baccalaureate Organisation (2016). Extended essay guide https://ibpublishing.ibo.org/extendedessay/apps/dpapp/index.html?doc=d_0_eeyyy_gui_1602_1_e&CFID=1110964&CFTOKEN=89176065&jsessionid=bc308386193706f7596f5a6172e777d5a404 accessed 22 June 2018.

IB Community Blog – https://blogs.ibo.org/blog/2018/09/03/what-did-the-extended-essay-do-for-you

Ison, R (2008) 'Methodological challenges of trans-disciplinary research: some systemic reflections', in *Natures Sciences Sociétés*, 16, 241-251.

Koier E & Horlings E (2015) 'How accurately does output reflect the nature and design of transdisciplinary research programmes?', in *Research Evaluation*, 24, 37–50.

Kroeze I (2013) 'Legal research methodology and the dream of interdisciplinarity', in *Potchefstroom Electronic Law Journal*, 16: 3

North, S (2005) 'Different values, different skills? A comparison of essay writing by students from arts and science backgrounds', in *Studies in Higher Education*, 30:5, 517-533.

Polk M (2014) 'Achieving the promise of transdisciplinarity: a critical exploration of the relationship between transdisciplinary research and societal problem solving', *Sustainability Science*, 9, 439–451.

Rawlings C M, McFarland D A, Dahlander L & Wang D (2015) 'Streams of thought: knowledge flows and intellectual cohesion in a multidisciplinary era', *Social Forces*, 93:4, 1687–1722. 7777

Robinson K. (2009) *The Element: How Finding Your Passion Changes Everything*. New York: Penguin.

Wittkower D E (2009) 'Method against method: swarm and interdisciplinary research methodology', *Social Identities*, 15:4, 477-493.

Chapter 11

The Extended Essay: Memorable, Challenging and Inspiring

Mary Donnellan

My first encounter with the Extended Essay involved acting as a supervisor to a brilliant 16-year-old, who went on to study PPE (Philosophy, Politics and Economics) at the University of Oxford. She wanted to write an essay in Philosophy, which the school did not offer as an International Baccalaureate (IB) Diploma Programme (DP) subject, and about which I knew nothing. Within Philosophy, she wanted to discuss the kalam argument for the existence of God, which I had never heard of. But, as the DP Coordinator in the first year of implementation in the school, and a teacher of GCSE Religion, it was decided I had all the qualifications necessary to be her supervisor! Thankfully, she was awarded a grade A – which was completely due to her brilliance and had nothing to do with my supervision.

Since then, I have supervised approximately 80 Extended Essays (EE), in History, World Religions, World Studies and Global Politics. As a History EE examiner, I have assessed 600+ essays, and as the moderator for the EE on the IB's PRC (Programme Resource Centre) I have viewed hundreds of queries – and answers to queries – about the EE. It is still the case, however, that my first encounter with the EE continues to colour my thinking about the task, the process, and the possibilities, which can be summarised using the three headings: Take the Risk, Could it be Otherwise?, and What Next?

Take the risk

In a commendable effort to assure good outcomes for their students in a programme which the IB refers to as involving 'high stakes' assessment (IB, 2010), many schools lay down rules about the subjects in which students can and cannot write their EEs. Such rules, in decreasing order of rigidity, might include:

1. Extended Essays can only be written in one of your three Higher Level (HL) subjects.

2. Extended Essays can only be written in one of the six subjects you are taking for your Diploma; this is one of the IB's suggestions (recommendations).

3. Extended Essays can only be written in DP subjects offered by the school.

4. Extended Essays can only be written in subjects which the DP teachers can supervise.

5. If written in a science, Extended Essays can only be written on an area in which we can provide the necessary laboratory equipment.

6. Even if you obey the above rules, and it's all going wrong, the above rules still apply!

Although limiting, these rules are understandable; they are student-centred and based on the wisdom consistently shared in the IB's EE Guide, and in IB EE reports, examples of which include:

Students who have not studied psychology formally should not undertake the EE, unless they can demonstrate that they have sufficient knowledge and understanding of the subject. Schools where psychology is not taught must be aware that students who submit an EE in psychology with no formal exposure to the subject may compromise their level of achievement (IB, 2016).

Social and cultural anthropology is not a 'residual' category for essays that do not fit into any other subject. Students should not attempt to prepare an EE in social and cultural anthropology if they have not studied the subject formally. Schools where it is not taught must be aware that students who submit EEs in the subject are risking being unable to meet the demands of the assessment criteria, and thus being awarded low marks (IB, 2016).

However, given what an amazing opportunity is provided by the EE for students to develop their passions, it seems a great shame to have the choice of subject hemmed in by constraints, however well–intentioned. This idea of the EE as a place where students can exercise creativity and 'intellectual initiative' in pursuit of their passions is clearly promoted in 'The Nature of the EE' (IB, 2016), where we read:

The extended essay is a unique opportunity for students to explore an academic area in which they have a personal interest. This takes the form of an independently written research paper that allows students to demonstrate their passion, enthusiasm, intellectual initiative and/or creative approach for their chosen topic. Such topics can range from focused, in-depth analyses of specific elements of a subject to critically evaluating responses to issues of global significance (IB, 2016).

It seems, therefore, somewhat contradictory to read in the same source:

The extended essay is an in-depth study of a focused topic chosen from the list of available Diploma Programme subjects for the session in question. This is normally one of the student's six chosen subjects for those taking the IB diploma ... It is intended to promote academic research and writing skills, providing students with an opportunity to engage in personal research in a topic of their own choice, under the guidance of a supervisor (an appropriately qualified member of staff within the school). This leads to a major piece of formally presented, structured writing, in which ideas and findings are communicated in a reasoned and coherent manner, appropriate to the subject chosen (IB, 2016).

This contrast in approach – from inspiring to constraining – is the contradiction faced by many schools when advising students about the subject discipline within which they should write their EE. If we are to honour the loftiest intentions of the IB, then perhaps we should be more willing to encourage students to become knowledgeable risk-takers, allowing them to follow their passions, once they are made aware of the risks inherent in this approach.

Why should students be constrained (or condemned) to only writing EEs in their six DP subjects? If we decide that risks can be taken, then here's my list of reasons why and when subjects beyond the six might be considered. This is in a world, of course, where supervisors are available – but never underestimate how willing teachers are to have a go at supervising a different subject!

1. Students taking sport at a high level: could they be allowed to write an EE in Sports, Exercise and Health Science (SEHS)? My (albeit limited) experience has shown that Physical Education teachers make excellent EE supervisors, and the students have access to many test subjects – their teammates or athletics club fellows. One of my favourite SEHS essays was written by a student who played badminton at national level and had noticed that many of his peers were left-handed. A lovely essay on the possible reasons for this phenomenon (noticeable in both badminton and tennis) was produced; the first SEHS essay to be supervised by a very proud PE teacher.

2. Should students who are not taking History as part of their six DP subjects be prevented from writing a History EE? Many students have studied History to the age of 16. One year away from the discipline does not mean they have forgotten everything about source evaluation! Occasionally, examining economic incidents cited within a History EE has the advantage of allowing those students who hanker after an EE in Economics to feel that they have been heard, even when no Economics supervisor is available.

3. Global Politics: While acknowledging the IB's advice that Global Politics is not a residual category for essays that do not fit into any other subject, this does seem to be a subject area in which students would benefit from being allowed to indulge their undoubted interest in the mechanics of the political world – precisely what it would seem the focus of a Global Politics EE should be: "In the Diploma Programme Global Politics course, a political issue is defined as: 'Any question that deals with how power is distributed and how it operates within social organization, and how people think about, and engage in, their communities and the wider

world on matters that affect their lives'." Perhaps, in an effort to ensure that IB students acquire an understanding of the world in which we hope they will be thoughtful leaders and active, reflective participants, we should make Global Politics essays a requirement? The emphasis of these essays, we are told, 'should be on current affairs'. Thus, supervisors need not have detailed, subject-specific knowledge, and although it is vital that students make use of 'key concepts, and theoretical foundations' in their essays, it is appropriate to assume that well-read, passionate, critical thinking, IB-educated young people should be able to acquire the theoretical knowledge they need to produce a focused piece of political analysis. To date, I have seen English and History teachers supervise Global Politics EEs in a school where the subject is not offered; the results of this risk have yet to be seen.

4. Mathematics Standard Level (SL) students: One wonders if there is an assumption that only students who are taking HL Mathematics can write EEs in Mathematics? This would seem to be supported by the IB's May 2017 statistics: only 2.3% of EEs were produced in Mathematics. What about the excellent mathematicians who have chosen to take their HLs in other subjects but are capable of achieving 6 and 7 in SL Mathematics? It would seem appropriate to allow/encourage such students to develop their passion for, and ability in, Mathematics by writing a Mathematics EE. I have rarely seen more excited, reflective supervisors than a Mathematics SL teacher who recently supervised her first Mathematics EE, by an able, interested student who was taking Mathematics at SL. Supported by a generous colleague who teaches HL Mathematics, and with constant reference to the EE Coordinator for presentation and practical matters, this proved to be a successful endeavour – for both student and supervisor. It will be interesting to see how the approach to writing EEs in Mathematics might change with developments in Mathematics from September 2019 onwards, when HL Mathematics is available in both analytical and applied Mathematics. One would expect to see more Mathematics EEs being produced: will the current Mathematics EE examiners be ready for this development, I wonder?

A useful advantage of the type of risk-taking suggested in these four examples is that, in schools where it is difficult to find enough EE supervisors, new possibilities start to unfold when a broader range of subjects can be supervised. And although I would take seriously the IB's advice that Social Anthropology and Psychology EEs should not be attempted by students or schools in which these subjects are not taught, I have allowed able, determined students to write Psychology EEs, under the supervision of supportive school counsellors. As long as the very clear requirement is followed that only secondary sources of information be used, the results of such an experiment can be successful – if somewhat more risky than even I would like.

One 'subject' within which this type of learned risk could be taken is the relatively new World Studies Extended Essay (WSEE). These essays are perhaps the most 'IB' of all assignments, aiming as they do to nurture "students' global consciousness" (IB, 2016). The specific focus of the WSEE – to consider a global issue at a local level – appeals to the idealism of young people, while having the great advantage that the subject discipline rules (the ten-year rule in History – that students cannot write about events from the ten years prior to the year of submission of their EE; the five-year rule in Economics – that topics should relate to economic information, policies, outcomes or events that are no more than approximately five years old) no longer apply, and so students can use events in a World Studies essay which would lose them marks in a single subject EE. Thus the constraints are removed, while the inspiration is retained. Given the many advantages of writing a WSEE, it continues to surprise me how very few of these essays are written each year. In the May 2017 examination session for instance, of the 79,635 EEs submitted for assessment, just 1,264 (1.58%) were in the interdisciplinary category. Given that there are three interdisciplinary categories (World Studies, Literature and Performance, and Environmental Systems and Societies), it would seem that only approximately 1% of EEs are World Studies (IB, 2017) – a great shame!

Some of the most interesting WSEEs I have seen include an examination of the viability of the Christmas tree market (Biology and Economics), a discussion of the way in which migration issues are presented in the media (Geography and English), an examination of 'tribes' in fashion (Social Anthropology and Visual Arts) and an investigation of the extent to which China's entry into the World Trade Organization led to job polarisation in Denmark from 2001 (History and Economics). In three of these essays, the student didn't start out with the idea of doing a WSEE – this was an organic development: sometimes because the essay didn't seem to be going well with just one subject, and sometimes because there wasn't a supervisor available for the student's original choice (Economics). In each case, the student and the supervisor took a risk – which paid off, both in the grade received and in allowing the student to follow through on an area of interest, despite it not being exactly what they originally wanted to investigate.

It may seem worrying to say that if an EE is turning into a bit of a disaster, students consider the World Studies option. You need a willing supervisor, a willing student, and a topic that lends itself to interdisciplinarity, but I would absolutely recommend taking the leap, and risking a WSEE. After all, according to Zahir Irani (2018), the university of the future will be interdisciplinary: "In a world where interdisciplinary research is of growing importance, dividing universities by academic department creates barriers, not benefits".

I continue to take risks with the EE – or, at least, to allow students to take risks. One of our May 2019 students presented a draft of an English EE which had very little to do with English, and a great deal to do with designing items with emotional appeal for children. Given the option of re-working it as an English essay or taking a huge risk and continuing with it under the Design Technology heading, the student chose to go down the Design Technology route. The risk is huge because we don't offer Design Technology as a DP subject, and in the school's history we have never submitted a DT Extended Essay. We have an IB Middle Years Programme (MYP) teacher who has said she will keep an eye on the Design element – but she has never supervised an Extended Essay. When I asked the student if she felt it was acceptable to allow her to take this huge risk, her answer was 'of course!' So, my risk-taking continues, 15 years on from my first encounter with the EE.

Could it be otherwise? The Extended Essay and inclusion

Inclusion is defined by the IB as "an ongoing process that aims to increase access and engagement in learning for all students by identifying and removing barriers" (IB, 2016). The EE, as we have seen earlier, is "an in-depth study of a focused topic … intended to promote academic research and writing skills, … which leads to a major piece of formally presented, structured writing, in which ideas and findings are communicated in a reasoned and coherent manner, appropriate to the subject chosen" (IB, 2016). These precise academic requirements of the EE can be (and in some schools, are) seen as creating a barrier to success within the DP for students who have been diagnosed with learning needs. In particular, the availability of only one format for the EE (a 4,000-word academic essay), even more than the academic rigour expected, can be seen as presenting some quite specific challenges for students who can access all other elements of the DP with the IB's inclusive access arrangements.

Of course, students with learning needs can be well-supported throughout the EE process. Deadlines can be extended, and the writing process is in any case scaffolded using a series of deadlines. Models are available for students to see best versions of EEs and, in those schools lucky enough to have learning support departments, expert support for students with needs linked to dyslexia, information processing challenges, ADHD and Asperger's can be provided. In many ways, it could be said that all students benefit from an EE process which is thoughtfully scaffolded through deadlines and a series of meetings with experienced, knowledgeable supervisors. We can legitimately ask which well-intentioned student would not do well when supervisors are available for one-on-one meetings, providing ongoing feedback on the research and writing processes? But there are students who find it enormously difficult to put this quantity of words on paper. Beyond this, they struggle to organise their thoughts into a coherent set of paragraphs though which a 'red thread' of argument runs. And while this will probably also be the case for the other written elements of the DP, on none of these individual pieces of work hangs the great fear: fail the Extended Essay, fail the Diploma.

Below is an extract from a first draft of a History EE from a student with learning needs – including original errors. His passion is football, and his working research question asks: To what extent did the creation of the premier league in the UK change the nature of English football?

'One of the major changes of the premier league was the tv coverage. typically all games in england were played at 3 o coll on a saturday and only a couple of matches a year were broadcasted on live tv. However new tv company sky partnered with the premier league to produce a whole new product that would change the money and commercial landscape of english football forever . As seen in this quote from the guardian "but in a shock move BSkyB, backed by Rupert Murdoch, tabled an incredible £304m bid for the five-year deal and blew their rivals away." this shows us that there was a huge amount of money brought into football that had never been seen before. It was also the first time tv rights had been sold to non governmental tv stations. The positives of this was it resulted in a lot more money being tickled down into the pockets of clubs and the premier league organisation. This gave the premier league clubs to have more money to buy players all over the world and therefore increase the quality of product on the pitch. The negatives are that due to the live tv broadcasting the kick off times had to be moved and evidence suggests that fans were unhappy'

The wonders of technology do not help such students as much as one might imagine: Google Docs doesn't show you where to use capital letters, and neither does it assist with correcting spellings which it already deems to be correct! Ethically, despite the author's learning needs, his supervisor may not edit the work, but can only suggest that the student looks again at his use of capital letters and spelling: not likely to achieve a successful outcome, as had the student known where to use capitals, he would have done so, for the most part at least, in the first place. More worryingly, of course, is that the rest of the draft followed a similar pattern – a series of paragraphs detailing what the student had heard from family, friends and pundits about the topic, with occasional links made to some source material, and with very little evidence that this was a piece of History writing, which required not just dates and setting in context, but also working within a conceptual framework of cause, course and consequence.

Now, imagine the same paragraph, but this time, being read in the background while a series of visuals plays out on a screen, much in the manner of a documentary. What a much more accessible piece of work that would be: both for the student, and for an audience. Capital letters no longer matter, while the writing becomes much more compelling when spoken rather than read. Of course, this is no easy fix – historicity is still missing, and there's no guarantee that the argument would be more coherent than when written. A key consideration here is the level of familiarity a student has with the assignment he is producing. After all, which of our learning needs students read 4,000-word academic essays? But, how many of our students watch documentaries, become absorbed in panel discussions on television, watch 'How to' YouTube channels, and/or subscribe to a range of real-life focused podcasts? If the format of the EE could be more flexible, could be similar to those just listed, it would be interesting to see whether students with specific learning needs might not find it a more accessible task.

It is therefore interesting to note that the Personal Project, which is the culminating piece of work at the end of the MYP (just as the Extended Essay is the culminating piece of work at the end of the Diploma Programme) can be presented in a variety of formats, "depending on the resources available and the interests of the students, ... taking into consideration learning preferences, personal strengths and the available resources" (IB, 2018). While not a specific mention of inclusion, the reference to 'learning preferences and personal strengths' can certainly be read as such. In addition, the MYP Projects Guide provides several helpful tables, outlining the types of format allowed, and how the written word can be converted into spoken word expectations which can be seen in Table 11.1 and Table 11.2 (both from IB, 2018).

Format	English, French, Spanish and Arabic
Written	1,500 – 3,500 words
Electronic (website, blog, slideshow)	1,500 – 3,500 words
Oral (podcast, radio broadcast, recorded)	13 – 15 minutes
Visual (film)	13 – 15 minutes

Table 11.1: Personal Projects Report Format (IB, 2018)

Time (audio or audio-visual recording)		Word limit
3 minutes	and	1,200 – 2,800 words 2,688 – 3,360 characters 2,400 – 5,600 kana/kanji
6 minutes	and	900 – 2,100 words 2,016 – 2,520 characters 1,800 – 4,200 kana/kanji
9 minutes	and	600 – 1,400 words 1,344 – 1,680 characters 1,200 – 2,800 kana/kanji
12 minutes	and	300 – 700 words 672 – 840 characters 600 – 1,400 kana/kanji

Table 11.2: Length requirements for multimedia reports (IB, 2018)

Wouldn't it be fantastic if DP students had the option of creating a film, or producing a podcast, in place of writing 4,000 words? When we consider what students are expected to do in the world of work, there are certainly places where writing lengthy essays will be required – but that won't be (or isn't) the norm. More often, young employees are expected to be able to gather, analyse and present data in a format accessible to a variety of audiences. Well-presented reports which are visually appealing and supported by comprehensive, interesting use of social media channels are the preferred means of communicating research in the current workplace. Is this the type of assignment we should be requiring our students to complete, necessitating the clever use of a range of audio-visual tools supporting tight use of text? Equally relevant assignment types might mimic the 'The Long Read' style articles in broadsheets, where case studies and investigative journalism are supported by arresting images and apt (comic) illustrations. In the realm of visual media, the construction of short, powerful news documentaries could be a replacement for the EE – which in the future might be replaced by the creation of virtual realities. These formats are much more typical of the world which our students inhabit, and into which they will transition. Equally, these are formats which, while likely to be more attractive to students, will be specifically of interest to those with certain learning needs, as they would seem to offer greater accessibility than that afforded by the production of written work.

Being inclusive need not mean reducing rigour; it could be argued that the type of assignments suggested here have the potential to be more demanding to produce at a high level than is the case with the current EE format. Of course, there would undoubtedly be complications in terms of there being overlaps in format with DP subjects which have similar assessment requirements – particularly film. New EE formats would also require a new approach to the uploading of work, more time would be needed for examiners to complete assessment and, perhaps most challenging of all, examiners would need considerable up-skilling to ensure they possess the ability to grade this style of assignment. But if it can be done in the MYP then, in time, why not also in the DP?

What next?

The Extended Essay is entering its curriculum review stage, with a new IB EE guide expected for first teaching in 2023 and first assessment in 2025. The format of the EE has remained almost exactly the same since its first introduction to the DP in 1970. Fifty years on, is it time for a radical change? Is interdisciplinarity the way forward? At one time, rumours abounded that all EEs would have to be World Studies essays. However, the need for students to demonstrate to universities an ability to conduct in-depth academic research in a narrow, subject-specific discipline left us with the choice of either single discipline or interdisciplinary essays. Perhaps, as discussed earlier, the time has come to remove this disciplinary option. Interdisciplinarity, after all, according to Darbellay (2012), "represents a new thought style and a promising future for education and research". Even in the supposedly specialised sciences, practitioners are beginning to be recognised for their breadth of knowledge; Venkatraman Ramakrishnan won a Nobel Prize in Chemistry, while studying A-level Biology and having completed his PhD in Physics. Perhaps we could require students producing their EE within a single subject discipline to make links to global contexts in an interdisciplinary fashion for at least one-third of their essay?

Could the EE be a collaborative task? Assessing individual contributions to a collaboratively produced externally moderated assignment is notoriously difficult. And, although the IB notes that collaborative tasks are "an important aspect that candidates will encounter in their future work place, but which are often neglected in academic assessment, ... given the individual nature of the way that IB results are used to make selection decisions, in general we do not think this is a fair approach to take and so generally try to avoid group assessments where individual candidate achievement cannot be measured". And, while acknowledging that "this approach can create cultural bias as the idea of individualism is traditionally a western European ideology", the IB recognises this issue but sets it in the context "that even in alternative cultures the assessment outcomes are often used to determine individual selection decisions" (IB, 2018). It is of interest therefore to note that the assessment of individual contributions to collaborative work is an area the IB is proposing to tackle in the upcoming iteration of the DP Group 4 (Sciences) subject guides. While I suspect that the EE will remain an individual task for some time to come, the work being done in the sciences may yet have an impact on how the EE can be undertaken and assessed. If we think about the way in which academic papers are authored, perhaps this offers a possible mechanism: with a lead author, and additional researchers. Maybe students could choose different levels of responsibility for their contribution to the essay/research, and be assessed accordingly?

This idea of undertaking part rather than the whole of an EE leads to another suggestion: perhaps in the future, we will see the EE as an optional part of the DP, rather than being required as it is at present. Those who choose to undertake the task might be awarded an 'Extended Diploma', in recognition of the additional challenge they had undertaken. Of course, one could question why it would be necessary to change what is the norm at present into something elitist in the future. But, just as the English educational establishment has had to find ways to reward the most able students with A* grades at A Level, or Grade 9 in GCSEs, perhaps it's time for the IB to recognise that there could be levels of differentiation even within the award of a Diploma. Rather like the Duke of Edinburgh's Award, perhaps we should consider awarding Bronze, Silver and Gold Diplomas, with the Gold Diploma being the one where the most demanding version of an extended research task has been successfully executed.

Elaborating on the earlier discussion regarding the possibility of offering the EE in different formats, perhaps we should reconsider the use of the written word when it comes to the creative arts. For DP Group 6 (Arts) subjects, wouldn't it be interesting to require the completion of a 'masterpiece', in the sense of the final product created at the end of an apprenticeship? I can envisage complications here in terms of overlap between this and other subject-specific assessment tasks, and there might be considerable challenges in terms of precisely how to validly and reliably assess hundreds of such pieces of work from across the globe. But medieval guilds managed it, so perhaps too can the IB!

Can we learn from the IB's newest programme, the Career-related Programme (CP)? The Reflective Project in the CP "focuses on an ethical dilemma of an issue directly linked to the student's career-related study" (IB, 2015). One wonders why ethical dilemmas should be available only to CP students, particularly given that forthcoming IB guides in TOK and Economics are likely to have ethics embedded across the subject, rather than as a discrete area of study. 'Ethics' is not a subject discipline for DP students, and while EEs discussing ethics could perhaps be written within subjects such as World Religions, Global Politics, Business Management, or Philosophy, this lacks the immediacy provided by an investigation of a current, 'world-of-work/current affairs' ethical dilemma. Could DP students be provided with the choice of producing either an EE in one (or more) subjects, or the CP's Reflective Project? Rather usefully, considering the earlier discussion, the Reflective Project can be produced in a range of formats: a short film, a storyboard, an interview, a spoken presentation or a play, alongside a written component of 1,500–2,000 words. While DP students would need to be carefully prepared to produce a rigorous examination of a current ethical dilemma, the synthesis of the DP and CP that a shared research assignment could offer certainly seems worth pursuing.

The Extended Essay forms one part of the DP core, with the remainder composed of Theory of Knowledge and CAS (Creativity, Activity, Service). Why can these three elements not be combined into one assessment? Could students be required to choose one or more strands of CAS, undertake a challenging (Service, Creativity) experience, conduct a critical examination of previous such experiences (academic and experiential), consider the ethical dimensions involved, and produce a report in one or more formats which describes, evaluates and assesses the outcomes achieved? This encapsulation of the elements of the DP core in one holistic, challenging task could certainly be an exciting replacement for the current rather one-dimensional Extended Essay.

Remaining memorable

When introducing the EE to students and parents, my impassioned speech (in common with many other Coordinators, I suspect) always contains the assertion that regardless of how many years pass, or what they choose to do in the future, students will always remember the topic on which their essay focused. This assertion was tested recently, when the first full DP graduate from the school in which I work was asked by a current student what his EE topic had been. The gentleman in question had graduated in 1972, 46 years previously. Without hesitation, he responded "I wrote about the Munich Crisis of 1938 – and I got a distinction". Point proven! It is this memorable nature of the Extended Essay process which we need to preserve, regardless of the changes we might make to format, content or how it is rewarded. When the IB celebrates its 100th birthday in 2068, I doubt that students will be writing 4,000 words, but I very much hope that there will still be an extended task of some type, which will be a memorable, challenging and inspiring piece of work for all students – just as, for the most part, it is today.

References

Darbellay F (2012) 'The Circulation of Knowledge as an Interdisciplinary Process: Travelling Concepts, Analogies and Metaphors', *Issues in integrative studies*, 30, 1-18

International Baccalaureate (2015) *Overview of the Career-related Programme.* Geneva: International Baccalaureate.

International Baccalaureate (2016) Extended Essay Guide. https://ibpublishing.ibo.org/extendedessay/apps/dpapp/guide.html?doc=d_0_eeyyy_gui_1602_1_e&part=1I

International Baccalaureate (2016) *Learning diversity and inclusion in IB programmes.* Geneva: International Baccalaureate.

International Baccalaureate (2017) DP Statistical Bulletin, May 2017. www.ibo.org/contentassets/bc850970f4e54b87828f83c7976a4db6/dp-statistical-bulletin-may-2017-en.pdf (Accessed 28 October 2018).

International Baccalaureate (2018) *Middle Years Programme: Projects Guide.* Geneva: International Baccalaureate.

International Baccalaureate (2018) *Assessment Principles and Practices: Quality Assessments in a Digital Age.* Geneva: International Baccalaureate.

Irani Z (2018) 'The university of the future will be interdisciplinary', *The Guardian*. London, 24 January 2018.

Chapter 12

The Extended Essay: the central roles of the Library and the Librarian

John Royce

In many ways, the Extended Essay (EE) is a practical demonstration of what an IB education is all about, and especially what the IB Diploma Programme (DP) is all about: a personal expression of the IB mission statement in action. Although the EE is an exercise in academic writing, the writing is not an end in itself. It is a springboard towards engagement with the world.

The EE "is intended to promote academic research and writing skills, providing students with an opportunity to engage in personal research in a topic of their own choice ... (leading to) a major piece of formally presented, structured writing, in which ideas and findings are communicated in a reasoned and coherent manner, appropriate to the subject chosen" (IB, 2018). Students have the the opportunity to use the skills practised and honed by the DP's Approaches to Learning framework (research, thinking, communication, social and self-management skills) in a major inquiry which calls for demonstration of subject awareness, the use of the concepts, language, conventions and methodologies of the subject, a knowledge and use of the tools of data collection and analysis of the subject, to produce a paper which makes a meaningful contribution to the literature of the subject, albeit it at upper secondary school or college entry-level.

One of the key terms used many times throughout the IB guide is 'reasoned argument'. It is not enough for students to tell their readers what is already known. Students have to apply, use and transform what is already known with what has perhaps not yet been considered, to answer a genuine research question and produce new knowledge resulting in a different way of considering what is known and has been found out. The very term 'reasoned argument' suggests that there may be alternative views or interpretations of the data and facts and theories; students must show awareness of these alternatives and be able to argue them down, or at least accommodate them, within their own discussion and argument.

The EE is not just about finding information, it is about finding good quality, reliable and authoritative information which can support an argument. Sometimes that information does not exist and the student must engage in original research to find it. These too are skills with which students need to research and to write a successful EE.

The whole process of research and writing the EE calls for critical thinking and the tools of information literacy; it calls for the highest standards of academic integrity, not just the integrity of the student writer but the integrity of the discipline and the field of research too. Although there is a physical product at the end of the EE process – the essay itself, able students will learn and use transferable skills which will stand them in good stead in their jobs and careers and in their daily lives. These skills (and more) are very much the stock-in-trade, the expertise and the special skills of modern school librarians. Librarians have much to offer students and their supervisors to assist and support them in the EE journey. This chapter aims to illustrate this.

The library and the librarian

Everyone – almost everyone – knows what a teacher does but it often seems as if few people, other than school librarians, know what school librarians do. This could in large part be because no two school librarians are alike and no two school libraries are alike. In a paper presented to a librarians' conference, Anthony Tilke suggested that the library and librarian be thought of as an interacting, interdependent system, the library/-ian (Tilke, 2015). Tilke was a member of the 'Ideal Library Project' focus group, out of whose deliberations came the IB publication *Ideal libraries: a guide for schools* (IB, 2018). Here, the definition is offered that:

> Libraries are combinations of people, places, collections and services that aid and extend learning and teaching (p. 2).

Not to labour this point too much, but it is worth considering university libraries which typically employ a large number of personnel who specialise in particular functions of the library system such as:

reference

readers' advisory

circulation, shelving, housekeeping

management

purchase and processing

repairs

library and research skills teaching

information literacy teaching

subject specialisms

management/maintenance of technology

website maintenance

database management

cataloguing

display and exhibitions

periodicals

digital imaging

inter-library loans

archives and more, including peripheral administrative roles such as human resources and finances.

Schools on the other hand tend to employ just one or two librarians, sometimes but not always assisted by paraprofessional staff who deal with the more mundane and clerical aspects of library housekeeping. The school library staff, large or small, may be called on to do it all, a little of everything. Moreover, schools' needs differ, as does librarian expertise and interest. These factors also contribute to the differences between individual school libraries and librarians.

There are other constraints and considerations which compound this. Training and qualification varies from country to country; a teacher librarian in some schools and in some countries may have qualifications as both teacher and librarian, in other countries may have qualifications in educational librarianship, and in still more countries may be a classroom or subject teacher with a reduced timetable to enable them also to look after the school library.

In some countries, local laws limit appointment of librarians in school to nationals of those countries, even when librarianship training in the country is minimal and school librarianship is non-existent. This can particularly affect IB programmes in international schools and can be a consideration in schools in which the IB cohort co-exists alongside a national programme which is less inquiry-driven, and in which the need for an effective (in IB terms) school library/-ian is less appreciated. Then too, administrator and teacher experience and expectations of library/-ians can be very different, exacerbated in that few teacher-training and education courses offer modules dealing with the library and librarian and how teachers might interact with them.

The IB organisation itself is developing its understanding of what the library and librarian are, and the roles they can play. IB's *Programme Standards and Practices: For Use From January 2014* and other documents and practices placed great store on the library as a storehouse of resources. The much revised thinking behind *Programme Standards and Practices* (IB, 2018), to be implemented in 2020, accepts the definition as used in *Ideal Libraries*. It will be a requirement that:

> The school maintains a functioning and active library consisting of adequate combinations of people, places, collections and services that aid and extend learning and teaching. (0202-01-0600)

In short, there is no one-size-fits-all school library/-ian. So it is that, in many schools, even IB schools, the library/-ian is a very under-used resource. As noted, the IB has made attempts in recent years to raise the profile of libraries and librarians, not among librarians who already know what they can do, and in many cases are already doing, but raising awareness in the wider school community. The introduction in the latest *Extended Essay guide* (IB, 2018) of a section exploring the role of the librarian supports this notion; the first and for over a year the only video in the Videos section of the 'In practice' section of the Extended Essay website was the 'The role of the Librarian'.

This video, the 'The role of the librarian', is a key activator in one of the learning engagements in one of IB's online professional development workshops, 'The role of the supervisor in the extended essay'. It is common for a goodly number of participants in each iteration of the workshop to remark how little they knew of the role of their own school's librarian, that they wished they'd known this before, and that they will be sure to make more use of their library and librarian in the future.

The IB publication *Ideal libraries: a guide for schools* (IB, 2018) is just that: not a guide for librarians but guidance for schools. In the chapter 'Beyond the basics: Shaping the IB library/ian', *Ideal libraries* identifies six librarian archetypes:

the teacher librarian

the school (or district) librarian

the media specialist

the designer librarian

the student life librarian

the super-librarian.

There is a degree of overlap between these archetypes; these are not distinct job specifications. In passing, we should note that *Ideal libraries* includes the advice that 'super-librarian' is not necessarily the ideal archetype; the guide includes the caution against super-librarians "over-extending themselves to meet the needs of the community", trying to do too much with too little (p.18).

So it is that when we talk about the role of the librarian in a school, it is all about possibilities, about what might or could be, not necessarily what is. When we talk about the role of the library in a school, it is all about what might or could be, not necessarily what is. And when we talk about the role of the library/-ian in the EE, it is again what might or could be, not necessarily what is.

Possible roles for the library/-ian in the Extended Essay process

With all this in mind I will consider possible roles for the library/-ian in the EE process, roles which some librarians in some schools perform, but not necessarily all librarians in all schools.

Supporting students in deciding on their topic

Librarians are often involved in the EE from the earliest stages, before students have even decided on their subject or area of interest. A common ploy is to invite students to browse through a selection of magazines and newspapers in the library, prompting them to find stories and articles which interest them and about which they might want to find out more. Once they have found some interesting articles, the students might then be asked to consider questions that come to mind, and how they might be investigated further using the lenses of one of their six DP subjects.

In many schools, before they get too involved, students are required to submit one or more proposals for their EE justifying their interest. They may be required to produce a preliminary reading list, possibly annotated, suggesting the background reading they have already done and the direction in which they would like to go, the questions which come to mind and which ones might be refined into research questions; students could also be asked to indicate the approach they will take, the reading or the research they will need to do during the research phase of the process. Librarians can help at this stage, suggesting resources which could be useful. Many will conduct a reference interview which might help them suggest possibly useful resources, while also helping the student consider and home in on what they wish to investigate. Some students might be guided into rethinking their initial lines of inquiry and possible research questions at this stage, as they realise that the information they need just is not available or that the resources which are available are too advanced for their understanding.

Helping students identify and locate resources

The most common role of the library/-ian in the EE is in the provision of resources to enable students to perform the initial research and sometimes the actual research needed for their EE: the library collection. Resources might be print or digital; they might be housed in (or accessible from) the physical or digital school library; they might be outside the school library, held in other libraries or collections. Resources might be text but they might also be audio-visual materials; they could well be artefacts, they might even be people. Librarians will help students connect with the resources they need.

In the later stages of the EE process, once students have formulated their (potential or actual) research questions and are focussed on detailed research, rather than suggesting resources, librarians are more likely to be involved helping students access specific resources as requested by the student. Students can be helped to appreciate that bibliographies are not just something that they have to produce to meet the demands of the EE; librarians can help them appreciate that bibliographies are intended to help readers retrace the steps of the writers. Bibliographies can be used to extend the student's reading; they can be used to enable students to track the original source of secondary references in the text being read. Although students are no longer required to provide an abstract for their EE they can be helped to see that abstracts can be used to provide blurbs for academic texts and that they can be used to decide if papers might be useful and worth following up, and that the notion of 'worth' can be significant if the paper is hidden behind a pay-wall on a journal website.

Many subject teachers claim that they do not have the time to teach their students academic writing in their subjects, or they expect students already to have the skills by the time they enter the DP – even if those skills are not taught lower down the school. One of the key features of the EE is that it is presented as a formal piece of sustained academic writing and yet, apart from their textbooks which are not necessarily good examples of academic writing, students may never have seen an academic paper. Even if they have, they may not be meta-cognitively aware of the conventions of academic writing, the structures of academic papers in specific subjects, or the language used in those papers.

Librarians can help students find materials in academic databases and repositories, some open-access such as Plos One or arXiv, some closed behind a pay-wall. Some librarians are able to arrange reference facilities for their DP students at local universities – which may well be subscribers to those closed databases. In addition, librarians have their own networks which can sometimes help find articles and papers requested by students.

Enabling students to evaluate and appreciate resources

One task of the librarian is often to help students appreciate different levels of writing and of formality, from tweet to blog post, from newspaper report or op-ed to magazine article, from professional magazine to academic paper. It is not just students who may need the appreciation. Teachers themselves may be unaware of academic journals in their subject; often when asked to bring a paper from an academic journal to a workshop, teachers will ask what one means by academic journal, or will bring magazine articles which are hardly academic.

Then again, not all blogs are equal, not all newspapers are equal, and not all academic journals are equal. A blog written by a scientist on recent work has more authority than a blog written by an interested lay-person. A review of a book in a tabloid newspaper probably has less weight and authority than a review published in *The New York Review of Books*. Information is not all equal, and students often need training and practice in evaluating the worthiness and authority of what they find. The EE is not about finding information – it is about finding good quality authoritative information which can support an argument. Professor Sam Wineburg's paper on lateral reading (Wineburg and McGrew, 2017) illustrates the often-superficial evaluation skills of students (and teachers). Helping students appreciate the nuances of information and the people who provide it is one of the skills and one of the roles of many school librarians.

Sometimes that information does not exist, the student must engage in original research to find it, by means of experiment or observation, survey or interview or other means of data collection – founded in and bounded by the tools and methods of the subject.

Teaching students the importance and skills of citation

Citation and referencing are not just hoops we make students jump through in writing their EEs. This is not always appreciated, especially when the lesson which students learn is that their main use is to 'avoid plagiarism'. It is not. We come back to this thought later. Here it is noted that librarians may show students how to use the 'Cited by ...' feature of Google Scholar to find other papers on the subject, not least because they will be produced later than the article they are looking up, so they might produce more recent information or thinking. Librarians can help students appreciate that scholarship is a conversation, with different people adding different things to what is known, that alternative views may be expressed or exceptions found in what has been said or thought before, and that in many cases there are no final answers.

This again is an aspect of the EE as a reasoned argument. With the possible exception of Mathematics (which tends to deal with truths), most of our knowledge can be considered as theory, as fact or law (or interpretation of fact or law), 'true' until we find exceptions and can show otherwise. It is not poor research to conclude an essay pointing out issues and problems and unanswered questions (as students sometimes think); just the opposite.

Daniel Levitin makes the point that "an anomalous, unexplained result is most interesting to scientists because it means their model and understanding was at best incomplete, and at worst completely wrong – presenting a great opportunity for new learning" (Levitin, 2016, p 249). Not just in science but in many other disciplines too, knowledge is built on knowledge, and it is vital to know the paths taken to attain that knowledge. This too ties in with notions of integrity and academic integrity; we do not have time or means or ability to check everything for ourselves, we need to be able to trust others and build on their work.

Teaching information literacy

Many school librarians are involved in teaching information literacy, helping students appreciate that information is not all equal. As suggested earlier, librarians might demonstrate, for instance, how the same piece of information can be seen as more authoritative depending on the context in which it is found: a sensational report in a tabloid newspaper might not be as authoritative (or accurate or complete) as a report in a broadsheet newspaper; a report in a weekly news magazine is not as weighty as a report in a magazine which specialises in whatever subject the information comes under; a blog-post by the author of a scientific study is not as authoritative as the original paper as published in a peer-reviewed journal. There are degrees of authority

– and the authors themselves may need to be investigated: might they have bias? Do the organisations which sponsor a project themselves have bias or political objectives? Such considerations are especially necessary when there are different and opposing views on certain topics.

Source evaluation is an important part of the research process, and making one's thought processes clear among the available information and sources can be an important indication of critical thinking; it can be demonstrated in the EE itself and will impress examiners – (use of) authority bestows authority. In the terms of the Association of College and Research Libraries (ACRL) framework for information literacy, "Authority is constructed and contextual" (ACRL, 2015), and links can be made with the Theory of Knowledge course which all students are required to take, along with the EE to qualify for the IB Diploma. In particular, Theory of Knowledge deals with knowledge, with how I, as an individual, know, and how we, as society, know; how we find out and build, make new knowledge and discard old knowledge. Knowledge is not absolute.

An understanding of this can be critical in our world today. Notions of reasoned argument, of alternative views and interpretations and theories brings to mind the phrase 'alternative facts', a phrase which President Trump's senior adviser Kellyanne Conway used to defend Sean Spicer's suggestion that the audience at Trump's inauguration in 2017 was much bigger than had attended President Obama's inauguration eight years earlier – despite all the evidence, including aerial photographs, that showed that the crowd was much smaller. 'Alternative facts' and 'fake news' have become buzzwords in this 'post-truth' world. These are not new notions; they are redolent of George Orwell's 'Newspeak' (1984) which is used to manipulate minds to our way of thinking – so often promulgated as the only way of thinking. There lies the difference between liberal thinking and fundamentalist thinking: in the terms of the IB's mission statement, the liberal thinker "understand(s) that other people, with their differences, can also be right"; fundamentalists hold that only they are right.

Fake news appeals to the emotions. Facts are based on evidence. We use other people's work to support our thinking, as evidence for our thinking. Knowing where the evidence comes from and enabling others to verify it is critical, as is our own thinking. Vital areas which librarians are able to support.

Promoting academic integrity

The ACRL has presented a model of information literacy based on six key areas or frames:

Authority Is Constructed and Contextual

Information Creation as a Process

Information Has Value

Research as Inquiry

Scholarship as Conversation

Searching as Strategic Exploration

The ACRL framework is intended for those working in information literacy in universities and colleges and some of these frames may be too abstract or advanced for secondary school students fully to grasp. Nevertheless, there is much which is within DP students' understanding.

I have already mentioned another of these information literacy frames, the notion of 'Scholarship as conversation'. While this overlaps the frame on authority (all six frames overlap to an extent), it can be a useful tool for introducing students to or expanding on their awareness of the conventions of academic honesty. The IB's *Extended Essay guide* tends to consider academic honesty mainly in terms of avoiding plagiarism through careful citation, referencing and the compilation of bibliographies. Certainly librarians can be of great support to students (and their teachers) in teaching the main points of whatever referencing styles the school supports or which students wish to use.

However, many librarians will go further, demonstrating how citation and referencing support academic writing and thus promote the authority and credibility of the student author, enhance the writing and exemplify a professional approach, thus demonstrating 'worthiness' to join the academic conversation. Academic integrity includes so much more than academic honesty, including the integrity of the writer as writer, the integrity of the research, the integrity of the subject and the discipline. What is more, teaching documentation in the light of academic writing brings home to students that the chores of citation and referencing are not just something that they are made to do in school, it is something that adds weight and merit to the essay. Furthermore, citing one's sources will ideally lead to consideration of them, of the authority and value of the sources chosen. Students are not looking for just any information, they are looking for solid, authoritative reliable information. Persevering students will make the effort to go to the original source and use that. Good academic practice!

Librarians are not permitted to correct students' references (EE supervisors cannot do this either), but they can show students how to reference. When students have specific referencing questions, librarians can show them how to reference similar types of source and leave it for the student to apply the pattern to their own work.

Teaching generic skills

Much of the time, the librarian will be teaching generic strategies and skills to DP students in groups or as classes. Ideally, librarians will be involved from early in the EE process, teaching or advising on search skills, find skills (including selection and rejection) and source evaluation, note-making skills, citation and referencing, uses of reference generators, note-making and mind-mapping applications, perhaps even the finer details of word processing and other organisation and presentation software and applications. Even more ideally, much of this training will have started well before the student ever embarks on the DP, in middle school and perhaps even in primary school. Students who come to the DP years without any experience in inquiry-driven projects and other research activities, or who have no experience in citation and referencing, are greatly disadvantaged; students who have never used a periodical database or perhaps even a print library will have little idea of what is available or how to find it and how to use it.

Students who have had this background, who have had opportunity to practise and learn, have a good start. Many schools teach just one style of citation and referencing in the middle years, getting students to understand why they cite and reference and how their citing and referencing helps the reader. Understanding the mechanics of documentation and appreciating the elements which go into building a full and helpful reference, such students may be in good position to learn different referencing styles, styles which might be considered more typical of a particular discipline and again enhance the student's awareness of the academic conventions used in the subject. The differences between the major referencing styles is relatively minor; the punctuation may be different or the order of the elements may be different. It is a matter of learning and patient checking. The patience pays off. It takes time to check and polish to ensure consistency in a reference list, but it is that final polish which sets the work off, which demonstrates care and craftsmanship. While examiners do their best to be completely unbiased, impressions of scholarship do count and presentation is one of the five criteria by which EEs are assessed.

There are schools in which teachers are free to impose their preferred referencing style on students who are just learning to cite and reference their work – students may have to learn three or four different styles all at once before they even know why they cite, never mind how to format a reference in the preferred style. This can lead to confusion, apathy and even antipathy. It is a practice to be avoided. Librarians are often the first to make the case for a single style, certainly while students are learning.

It is important that students recognise the elements that make up a bibliographical reference. While many teachers recommend the use of school-level reference generators such as Noodletools or EasyBib, it should be recognised that the quality of these tools varies. While a few are excellent, most are inaccurate and inconsistent or do not cover the full range of sources likely to be used. Students who do not recognise the elements of a bibliographical citation will not know if elements are missing or are presented wrongly or inconsistently. Similarly, references generated by databases and the suggested references provided on academic papers may be wrong; certainly they may be inconsistent with the style used by the student in the rest of the essay. Mistakes and inconsistencies in the formatting of bibliographical references are not academically dishonest in themselves, but they may cost marks in Criterion D (Presentation) of the EE. This, again, is an area of librarian expertise: helping students learn and get it right.

While much of the work librarians perform is with classes and is therefore generic, librarians also work with small groups and one-on-one. Work with small groups may also be generic, but it will be tailored for the group. Not every student writing an EE needs to know how to conduct an interview or how to pilot-test a survey; the librarian, perhaps alongside a subject specialist or two, may work only with the students who intend to conduct interviews or to carry out surveys. Such research methodologies are not confined to single DP subjects; they might be suitable research methods in a variety of DP subjects.

The greatest part of the librarian's work is often one-on-one with DP students, responding to individual student questions and needs. Here might be one of the great differences between a librarian and a school- or a teacher-librarian: the librarian will give the student the answer; the teacher-librarian will often think aloud, role-modelling the process and articulating the thought process, the whys as well as the hows. Students – possibly everyone – learn better this way, helped to find solutions by someone else thinking aloud as they show how it's done and then trying for themselves. The needs are real and the learning strongest.

Accessing and developing library guides (libguides)

Lessons are often imperfectly remembered or soon forgotten – especially those generic lessons which may have no immediate application and perhaps without immediate practice, reinforcement or feedback. Librarians often digitally curate their lessons or aspects of them, and sometimes write original content so that advice for the community is available 24 hours a day.

The Libguides platform (published by Springshare) is a popular vehicle for such curation, while many schools use their own intranets and library sites on which to mount guides and advice. Although Libguides provides a common platform, there is nothing uniform about the guides produced, as evidenced by the EE libguides at the Canadian International School (Singapore), the American School of Doha or the International School of Prague. Many other examples are publicly available; the LibGuides Community pages provide a set of filters through which one can search for publicly available libguides, while a simple search for [libguides 'extended essay'] can target school library sites which have pages devoted to the EE.

Libguides (and other school library websites) are not all equal. Much depends on the audience, the school, the librarian's expertise. They take time to build, so older libguides are likely to have more content than newer libguides. They take time to maintain. Changes in the IB's EE guide are made according to the DP curriculum review cycle, so major change will take place only every seven or eight years – but when those changes come, the need to update libguide or web-site pages can be huge.

Teachers can be and often are asked to provide content for these guides; it is not just the librarian's role to provide guidance. The subject specialist will provide tailored insight which may be beyond the librarian's ken. Librarians and EE coordinators frequently work together, planning and producing the content for these sites. Publishing the guides in just one place makes it easy for students to know where to turn for the guidance they need, when they need it. Content is often a mix of librarian- or teacher-produced materials, supplemented by embedded video-clips and links to other sites and services. Links to the school's subscription databases and other materials will often feature high on libguides and library sites.

The librarian as Extended Essay coordinator

Many librarians have taken on the role of EE coordinators at their schools. The role is not to every librarian's taste and, depending on staffing levels in the library, may detract from the time they spend on the library itself. For those who can manage the dual role, this can be an ideal fit: most librarians have the organisational skills for the role, they probably have a wider overview of the curriculum than any subject teacher (with the possible exception of the DP coordinator), they almost certainly have more exposure across disciplines than do single subject teachers, enhancing wide multi-disciplinary research and writing awareness, they see and know more students than do subject teachers – and the students know them too, they may feel more comfortable approaching librarians they have grown up with than the teachers of their subjects.

EE coordinators are responsible for more than administrative and organisational matters; their responsibilities include the supervising of the EE supervisors, which may include training supervisors and also ensuring that supervisors are aware of the IB documentation pertaining to their roles, and especially of changes in the documentation. In the role of EE coordinator, the librarian can ensure that students have opportunities to learn the skills they will need to complete the EE process; they can also ensure that supervisors have opportunities to learn what students are learning, the better to look out for and provide feedback on their process skills – not only in the EE but in their subject teaching too. They can provide students with opportunities to practise their skills.

The skills of research and of writing are not matters only for the the EE; this point cannot be stressed too strongly. The *Extended Essay guide* section on 'The role of the Librarian' includes much of the advice in this chapter. But the advice given, the skills suggested and other skills needed in the research and the writing of the EE, are not relevant for the EE alone. They are matters for everyday work. Many DP subject reports from the IB comment, for instance, on the amount of student work which shows lack of care in or awareness of citation and referencing practices, which demonstrates poor organisation, which lacks basic presentation awareness such as page numbering or consistent use of fonts. Librarian EE coordinators may be better placed than non-librarian EE coordinators to work with DP coordinators, ensuring that all DP teachers, not just the EE supervisors, have the knowledge and skills needed to enable students to succeed.

Providing support to teachers and students

Even if not appointed to the role of EE coordinator, the librarian can still be of great service and support, working closely with the coordinators and teachers in the DP to ensure that students have the skills they need, not just for the EE but in all their work. And it is not just DP teachers who need to know. As noted earlier, the sooner the start is made, the more the skills of inquiry, research, writing and more can be introduced and developed in student learning. Schools with an IB Middle Years Programme are at an advantage, as the IB's Approaches to Teaching and Learning should be embedded in the pedagogy during those years. Students who have not experienced the MYP may be disadvantaged if there is nothing in the school structure or curriculum to develop the necessary skills. Once again, the librarian, with support, can work with teachers to seek ways to develop these skills, even within a non-IB curriculum.

Impact studies such as those of or inspired by Keith Curry Lance, Ross Todd (2016) and others have provided quantitative and/or qualitative assessments of the impact that effective library/-ian systems can make in boosting student development and achievement. We return to the conundrum posed at the beginning of this chapter: it often seems as if few people, other than school librarians, know what school librarians do, the library/-ian is often a very under-used resource. This chapter may open eyes and make for opportunities. In terms of the EE and all-round academic success, the library/-ian can play a vital role in enhancing student understanding and learning and, ultimately, their achievement and success.

References

ACRL. Feb. 2015. Framework for literacy in higher education. American Library Association. Available at www.ala.org/acrl/standards/ilframework

International Baccalaureate. October 2018. Extended essay. Available at https://ibpublishing.ibo.org/extendedessay/apps/dpapp/guide.html?doc=d_0_eeyyy_gui_1602_1_e&part=1&chapter=1

International Baccalaureate. June 2018. *Ideal libraries: a guide for schools.* Available at https://resources.ibo.org/ib/resource/11162-47982/data/g_0_iboxx_amo_1806_1_e.pdf

Levitin D (2016): *A field guide to lies and statistics: A neuroscientist on how to make sense of a complex world*. London: Viking.

Libguides: Curate Resources, Share Knowledge, Publish Content. Springshare. Available at www.springshare.com/libguides/

Libguides Community. Available at https://community.libguides.com/

Tilke A (2015) 'IB school libraries as international-minded learning spaces and environments', in Das, L, Brand-Gruwel, S, Kok, K & Walhout, J (eds.), *The school library rocks: Living it, learning it, loving it*, vol. 1. Professional Papers presented at the 44th International Association of School Librarianship International Conference, Maastricht, June 2015, pp. 397-408.

Todd R (2016) Ross J. Todd's research while affiliated with Rutgers, The State University of New Jersey and other places. Available at www.researchgate.net/scientific-contributions/2041171431_Ross_J_Todd

Wineburg S and McGrew S (2017): Lateral reading: Reading less and learning more when evaluating digital information. Stanford History Education Group Working Paper No. 2017-A1. Available at http://dx.doi.org/10.2139/ssrn.3048994.

Extended Essay Libguides (examples):

American School of Doha : http://asd.qa.libguides.com/extendedessay

Canadian International School (Singapore) : http://cis.libguides.com/EE

International School of Prague : http://isp-cz.libguides.com/ee

Chapter 13

Making CAS meaningful for all

Christian Chiarenza

Good ideas often originate from problems. The problem I was facing was particularly striking because I found it existed equally in schools I had worked at in Asia and South America. My task, as the coordinator for the IB Diploma Programme (DP), was to oversee the successful integration of the elements of the Diploma Programme core into the DP as a whole. I had led Diploma Programmes in public, private, and for-profit IB World Schools and in a variety of cultural and socio-economic settings. It seemed that regardless of the culture or the economy the same problem persisted: many students seemed to be missing the whole point of Creativity, Activity, Service (CAS), while others were graduating from the DP citing it as the most memorable and meaningful part of their experience. How could I make CAS more meaningful for all DP students?

Like many, I was very pleased when, in 2010, the IB shifted the focus of CAS from counting hours of activity to the process of doing that activity and completing CAS requirements successfully. However, for a large portion of students, counting those hours offered comfort in a component of the DP in which they simply were not sure what they should be doing. Too many of them looked towards the shortest path such as joining a club, playing a sport, attending a service trip, or other such pre-packaged CAS experiences. What resulted was a CAS programme that worked for some, but not all, and frequently, not for those who needed it most. Students, and parents, still wanted to know "How much CAS do we have to do?" and "When are we finished?". Something more was needed to ensure that CAS lived up to its important role in the core of the DP, so that not only would students enjoy and value the experience, but they would also be able to capitalise on the connection that CAS has to their IB subjects. My idea was to reduce CAS to its essential properties so that it could be easily communicated to the school community, understood by students and advisors, and experienced by students in a meaningful way that allowed them to generalise the experience to a better Diploma and, ultimately, a better life.

The purpose of CAS

Firstly it is important to clarify how I have interpreted the purpose of CAS in the context of the DP. The IB's 2010 CAS guide stated that, "for student development to occur, CAS should involve real, purposeful activities, with significant outcomes". The 2017 CAS guide (IB, 2017) lists amongst its aims that students "purposefully reflect upon their experiences". The link between purpose and reflection was made explicit for the first time. It is easy to understand how the critical thinking skills of Theory of Knowledge (TOK) and the research skills of the Extended Essay are applied to students' other subjects, but what about CAS? There are two ways in which curricular enrichment can occur in CAS. The first is straightforward: it helps students make connections between the real world and what they study in class. For example, when a student immerses themselves as part of a CAS experience in a community from a distinctly different socio-economic group than their own, that experience will likely influence the way they will understand the theories they study in Economics or History, or the way they will understand and appreciate the novel they read in their literature studies.

However, there is a more profound way that CAS connects to DP subjects and it is this that I would like to focus on. This connection is based on the fundamental assumption of how students learn and is best understood by reference to the learning cycle. There are various forms of the learning cycle, but the one I use to communicate with my community is my own adaptation, as in Figure 13.1.

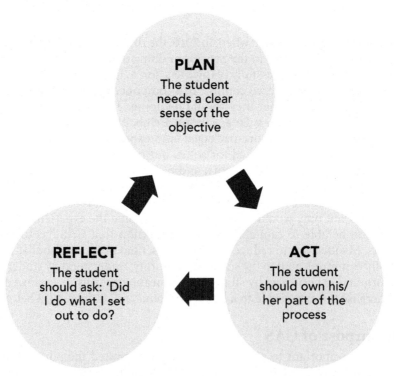

Figure 13.1: A version of the learning cycle

This diagram focuses on a process by which students set out an objective and develop a plan to meet that objective. They execute that plan, and then reflect upon the success of the plan, with reference to the objective. They then take the fruit of this reflection and apply it to the next task.

So often, a student's work is driven not by a clear objective of what they want to do, but by a desire to produce what the teacher or the examiner wants. This makes reflecting on the objective very different, as the question of 'how well did I meet my objective?' becomes better answered by the teacher than the student. In order for the learning cycle to work, students need to be clear about their objective, and it has to be their own objective. This is where CAS comes in. If I am building a house for a family in need, or trying to learn to play an instrument, I know exactly what my objective is. I am able to reflect meaningfully on how well my strategy worked. I do not need a teacher to tell me if this is good enough. CAS experiences are generally experiences that are not shrouded in the mystery of solving assessment criteria. As they are real world tasks, the success criteria are not only clearer, but self-determined. The student owns the objective. This is why the learning cycle can be applied in its pure form in CAS reflections, and why the key value of CAS as part of the DP core is to teach students how to navigate the learning cycle well and apply it appropriately.

Ensuring meaning in CAS: overarching core objectives

It is with this in mind that I came up with a solution for how to ensure the CAS experience is meaningful for students. I would reduce CAS to two clear and overarching core objectives that would be relevant to all students, and would allow them to get excited about their experience and to reflect upon it in a meaningful way. The objectives are:

- To make the world a better place
- To make myself a better person

It should be noted that 'the world' is interpreted in a general way here. It could refer to the planet, or it could refer to the students' school, their community, or country. It involves tasks that are both local and global in their nature. These two questions are then used to set the specific objective that gets the learning cycle rolling. For example, "I look at the trash bin in my school and see that it is full of items that could be recycled. So I decide that I will make the world a better place by creating a recycling programme in my school". Or, "I would love to express myself musically, I wish I could play an instrument, so I will make myself a better person by learning to play the guitar". With clear objectives in mind, the cycle begins. We act on this objective, we do things, and, at appropriate times, we reflect on the success of our actions. The goal is clear so that the student can keep their focus on how well they have achieved it, what is working well and should continue, and what is not and needs to be modified. Changes are then included in the reflection, and the CAS experience continues with those reflections applied to the continuing experience and experiences to come.

But what about the seven learning outcomes of CAS as specified by the IB?

1. Identify own strengths and develop areas for growth
2. Demonstrate that challenges have been undertaken, developing new skills in the process
3. Demonstrate how to initiate and plan a CAS experience
4. Show commitment to and perseverance in CAS experiences
5. Demonstrate the skills and recognise the benefits of working collaborative
6. Demonstrate engagement with issues of global significance
7. Recognise and consider the ethics of choices and actions (IB, 2017, p11)

A school is responsible for ensuring these outcomes are met, but is there not a risk in adopting the simple learning cycle approach that I have outlined that some of these learning outcomes will not be met? I strongly believe that through this process, all requirements of CAS will be met and more effectively than if they were focused on specifically, one by one. This is because the learning outcomes will be used in a more organic way to help stimulate thought through reflection, so becoming tools rather than requirements, with the student remaining in charge and connected to their objective.

For example, one learning outcome of CAS is that students 'demonstrate engagement with issues of global significance'. If a student tries to demonstrate this outcome specifically they are likely to look for one experience that can count as 'globally significant' perhaps joining an environmental awareness club, for example. They can now check that box and move to the next outcome. However, if they are looking to make the world a better place, as in my two core objectives, they may see that the school needs to stop throwing away so much food; and in their reflection they may realise how easy it would be for other schools to reduce waste in the same way. They have thus demonstrated engagement with an issue of global significance but in a much more purposeful and meaningful way. Additionally, the language the students are likely to use in their reflections on the second approach would be such that there is little doubt as to why the students made the connections they did. This approach conforms seamlessly with the students' intuitions about what is worthwhile, ensuring greater commitment to CAS and fewer cases of students feeling isolated and lost in the requirements of CAS.

The rest of this chapter will focus on how this approach works by looking at examples of how to introduce CAS to the school community, student CAS experiences, and the final CAS interview. My hope is that this is an approach that can not only improve the intrinsic quality of the CAS experience and the students' ability to generalise what they learn in CAS to their Diploma, but also, in a small way, help to make the world a better place.

Communicating CAS to the school community

As a DP Coordinator, part of my role is to ensure that the school community has a clear understanding of CAS and the expectations placed on students. While there are always many questions about the DP as a whole, there seems to be more mystery about the role of the DP core. TOK and the Extended Essay are generally new to everyone, but CAS is associated with service to the community, and thus parents and students come to information evenings with a belief they already understand CAS, hence questions are centred around 'how much CAS?', 'when can I begin?', and 'specifically what counts as CAS?'. Questioners also want to know how much of each element of CAS – Creativity, Activity, and Service – is required to complete CAS. This presents a challenge as the goal is not just to educate the community about CAS, but to change their minds about what they believe the purpose of CAS to be.

Another of my objectives is to move the community's understanding of CAS away from the belief that each of the three elements of the DP core is distinct and separate, by providing a means to reflect on how they interrelate and on the multiple ways in which student development is taking place, much in the same way that a person's weight and height develop together. Dispelling the preconceptions about CAS is why the use of two clear overarching core objectives is particularly useful. By starting with a slide (Figure 13.2) that sets out a simple, clear agreement about CAS, the rest of the discussion will be shaped accordingly, clarifying the role of the Advisors, Supervisors, the CAS Coordinator, and even the parents themselves. It also emphasises the personal growth that is an essential part of CAS, thereby sharing the spotlight with service as the purpose of CAS. Note that the use of 'your world' as opposed to 'the world' allows for a reflection on the various ways that 'the world' can be interpreted, and allows for a more personal connection to service. Both will make achieving an in-depth understanding of CAS more attainable.

CAS Core Objectives

All CAS Experiences should satisfy one or both of the following objectives. These objectives are the basis of all of your CAS reflections during your time as an IBDP Candidate:

- **To make your <u>world</u> a better place**
- **To make yourself a better person**

Figure 13.2: Opening slide for CAS segment of my 'Introduction to the DP' presentation.

It is likely that these two objectives will not cause much controversy, and the presentation can then move into how students are supported through planning and reflection. This approach is particularly valuable because it shows how the process of CAS translates to success in DP subjects. While in the past I would not have attempted to explain such an abstract connection at the beginning of the DP, this approach has allowed me to do so in a seamless way. The progression of the presentation goes as follows: once the two core objectives are established, it is emphasised that for this to work the planning (objective setting) and reflection parts of the learning cycle need to be prioritised. Students need to be clear about what they are trying to achieve. How are they meeting one or both of the core objectives? What are they hoping will get better, and how will they know? That is their objective: in the process of logging CAS experiences, rather than reminiscing about what they did, they are focused on how well they met their objective. This is done by the student following three lines of inquiry in their reflection:

- To what extent is the world a better place as a result of your actions?
- What was it about your actions that made a difference?
- How would acting differently have made a difference?

These questions are the characteristics of focused reflection, not a mere memory of the experience.

Having clarified the importance of setting the objective and explaining reflection, I refer back to the learning cycle, pointing out how much easier it is to follow this cycle when you are clear about your objective. CAS thus trains students to know what learning feels like, so they can aim for that in their other DP subjects. By now, hopefully, the community has shifted from thinking only about service to what CAS means within the whole DP experience; and it has been made clear, hopefully non-contentiously, how it all connects to students' success in the DP in general.

However, the presentation does not end there. I can now move on to the logistics of CAS, using the two core objectives and the connection to the whole DP. A discussion about the role of CAS advisors is now more relevant as we have, as teachers and advisors, clarified our core objectives. Conversations around expectations of quantity and quality of reflections are now more of a dialogue as to how best to reflect rather than, as was often the case in the past, a community of parents and students being told how much they had to do. Commitment to the core objectives of CAS is vital in having students construct a meaningful CAS experience, rather than react to a series of expectations copy and pasted from a guide that was written primarily for teachers. However, selling the idea to the community is just the first step. The true test of this approach is in the experiences themselves.

The experience of CAS

I will focus on students' experiences in two parts of the CAS process. The first is the process of choosing a CAS experience or project. The overarching core objectives will be shown to contribute towards helping students check the appropriateness of their ideas as well as helping them refine them. The second is the reflection. Reflections that are focused on the core objectives will be able to show the supervisor the progress the student is making in CAS; a lack of focus on the objectives will signal a need for intervention. I will look at two case studies to demonstrate how this works in real life. One of these involves a very typical task, joining the school softball team; the other is an ambitious project of making a film to raise awareness of women's issues in a local community.

Choosing CAS experiences

'Does this count as CAS?' is a question that every CAS Coordinator encounters. Students are usually happy with a yes or no answer, but this tends to prolong the problem of a lack of understanding of what CAS is. To that end, I have developed a sequence of questions to help students answer the question, either by themselves or via a conversation with their supervisor or CAS Coordinator. This sequence is intended to assist students in clarifying ideas, but is not itself a requirement. It works as a formative tool that helps students to answer the original question, and helps to facilitate in students a deeper understanding of CAS. The questions run as follows:

Question 1: What is my objective?

- If the student can articulate an objective, go to question 2
- If no objective can be articulated, NOT CAS.

Question 2: Does meeting my objective make the world a better place and/or make me a better person?

- If yes, go to question 3
- If no, NOT CAS

Question 3: By doing this, am I being Active, performing a Service, and/or being Creative?

- If no, NOT CAS
- If yes, congratulations, this is CAS! Go on to question 4

Question 4: Do I need to collaborate with someone in this experience?

- If no, NOT a project
- If yes, go on to question 5

Question 5: Is there a final product that I am working towards (this product could be abstract)?

- If no, NOT a project
- If yes, go on to question 6

Question 6: Is the experience BIG enough (evidenced by multiple steps and long term planning)?

- If no, NOT a CAS project
- If yes, congratulations, you have a CAS project!

The conversation that results from this sequence is streamlined and helps to clear up any doubts the supervisor may have about the experience or project as they work through it. Furthermore, it can easily be conducted by students and parents at home, encouraging families to have directed and purposeful conversations about CAS. When I work through the sequence with students, I work through the questions quite loosely, making notes on each question. To take the student who is joining the softball team, here is an example of how that conversation might have unfolded:

CAS advisor: Tell me about your proposed activity.

Student: I am going to join the softball team.

Advisor: Great! What is your objective in doing this?

Student: I want to be a better player. I want to develop my skills.

Advisor: Any specific skills you want to work on?

Student: Yes, I want to work on my batting skills. My fielding is pretty good, but I have poor technique at the plate. (*Now we have an objective that can easily be reflected upon, and a clear idea of how the student will become a better person*)

Advisor: OK. So, I see how you will improve by doing this. Will anyone else benefit?

Student: Well, I hope my team will, but actually there is another reason I want to do this. Almost nobody at the school watches these games. I want to also try and increase the interest in softball, and hopefully increase school spirit (*Now I have my second concrete objective*).

Advisor: OK, so as I see it, your objectives here are to improve your hitting and raise school spirit. Does that sound right? Is there anything you would like to add? (*Be careful here not to put words in their mouth*)

Student: That sounds right.

Advisor: OK, this sounds like a good CAS experience. Make sure you record the objectives we talked about. If you find they change over time, you can add to them.

The important outcome of this conversation is an agreement on which objectives will be reflected upon. However, in the case of the student making the film, that conversation continues:

Advisor: Who will you be collaborating with on this film?

Student: I am working with a crew, some friends who are helping with editing and acting. I am also working with a local NGO to help refine the content. My goal is to get this visible to the community, so I am working with the marketing team at the school to find ways to do that.

Advisor: So, is the final product the film or the showing of the film?

Student: Definitely the showing. I will not be finished until the film is out there. (*Here we have established that the film is not the last step*)

Advisor: When do you hope to finish? (*I do not ask how long it will take, as their guess is as good as mine. What I want is for the student to have a timeline, even if unrealistic. It can be altered in the reflections, if necessary*)

Student: I hope to show it by the end of the term, but that might be a little ambitious.

Advisor: What are the steps you need to take?

Student: I have to develop a storyboard for the film, which will involve… (*this goes on, but shows that the student is aware that they will not just grab the camera and film. This is enough to show that the experience is meeting the criteria of a project*)

Advisor: Great, we have a project. Make sure you record your objectives and put together a timeline. Remember that the end is the showing of the film. Good luck!

One key outcome from this initial conversation is to have objectives to reflect upon. As we monitor student reflections it is important to come back to these initial objectives.

Of course, in these examples, the conversation runs smoothly, but this method has also proven helpful when the process is not so smooth. For example, I had a student who wanted his daily gym routine to be part of CAS. We spent a lot of time on the first two questions. Simply saying 'to get fit' would not satisfy the requirements of an objective based on being a better person. He was easily able to clarify an objective of reducing body fat, gaining muscle mass, but struggled to answer how this would make him a better person. Eventually, we agreed that confidence was an issue for him and feeling like he was in control of his body would help him feel in control of his life. We also added that the routine would only be successful if it helped him balance his Diploma by allowing him not only to get a break from studying, but also to create a more energetic version of himself. He wanted to use exercise as a means of gaining energy and being more productive in his life. So now he had something specific to reflect on. His subsequent reflections referred back to these points. If his reflections simply described his gym routine, it would give me a reason to call him in and discuss his progress so that the reflections would be more focused on the original objectives. It is not possible to say if going to the gym, *per se*, is or is not CAS, but this sequence of questions provides a mechanism to understand, in this student's case, whether or not it was an appropriate and meaningful CAS activity. Additional benefits of the sequence of questions are that it clarified that it would be a good idea for him to collaborate with a trainer, and gave him an understanding of why the experience could not be a CAS project.

As a further illustration, Table 13.1 illustrates how the two previously mentioned students would navigate the flowchart:

	If answer is yes	If answer is no	Example of 'yes': Student 1	Example of 'yes': Student 2	If answer is yes
Can I clearly articulate my objective?	Go to next question	Not CAS	I want to be a successful part of the school softball team.	I want to create a film that raises public awareness of sexual assault.	
Does meeting my objective make the world a better place and, or, make me a better person?	Go to next question	Not CAS	By improving my skills I will become a better person, and the world will become a better place through the growth of school spirit.	While I want to learn about making a film, the main objective is to make a difference in this issue. Hopefully, if one assault gets detected before it can continue, it will be worth it.	
By doing this, am I being Active, performing a Service, or being Creative?	This is CAS! Go on to the next question	Not CAS	Activity	I think this counts for all of them, doesn't it?	For both students, this is now accepted as a CAS experience
Do I need to collaborate with someone in this experience?	Go to next question	Not a Project	Yes	Yes, there are agencies that work with women's issues, and my crew, as well as the school marketing team who will help me get it published.	
Is there a final product that I am working towards (This product could be abstract)	Go to next question	Not a Project	Not really. Maybe a league championship	A screening of my film.	For Student 1, this is not ruled out as a project
Is the experience BIG enough? (Evidenced by multiple steps and long term planning)	This is a CAS project			Yes, this should take a few months at least to make.	This is a clear example of a good CAS Project

Table 13.1: Flowchart of questions to support the choosing of a CAS experience

Writing CAS reflections

The quality of CAS experiences and projects are best evidenced in the quality of a student's reflections. It is in the reflections that, as supervisors and coordinators, we not only get a list of activities, but an idea of the impact those activities have had on the students and what other actions they might have led to. We also can see the extent to which objectives were met and, crucially, how students responded to failure. As mentioned at the outset, when the student is clear on their objective, these reflections have the potential to be highly meaningful. However, when seen simply as a requirement, they can be reduced to a series of vague memories about the experience and generic comments about how the experience was beneficial. With the procedure used for choosing a CAS experience, there is no reason that the reflection should not be as purposeful. The key is that students are clear about what a good reflection looks like, and are reminded that it is part of a bigger process. To help clarify what is expected in the reflection, I ask students to ensure that there are three key features of every reflection.

Reflections should:

1. Relate back to the objective
2. Evaluate the effectiveness of the specific actions
3. Suggest a way forward.

Focusing on these three key features is usually enough to help ensure students are reflecting effectively. However, in cases where this is not happening, once again it gives a clear indication of how best to intervene. It is not uncommon for strong CAS experiences to result in weak reflections. Consider these reflections from the student who joined the softball team:

> Today's game was rough. We played one of the best teams in the league, and we were outmatched from the start....

The reflection goes on to describe the game, and includes a promise to work harder to get a better result for the next time. This is a case where I intervened. I asked the student to talk about the game and discuss her reflection, and I asked questions related to her objectives. How many students came to watch? How did you do personally? Did you get a hit? What was the pitcher doing that kept you from getting a hit? Had you practised for that? What could you have done differently and what will you do next time? I asked her to make sure she added to her reflection by incorporating the issues we had discussed. The reflection that resulted from our conversation read as follow:

> Good news and bad news today. We lost, but there were more people at the game than any other game this season. I had asked some friends to come, which they did, but I also put an ad in the daily bulletin and there were kids I didn't even know there. I will have to write a follow up, hyping up the next game, so they don't get discouraged from one bad game. I was also

frustrated in my hitting. I tried to keep my weight forward and control my swing, but almost every time I hit the ball on the ground. I thought I was just swinging early, but then when I tried to adjust, I hit a shallow pop up. My coach pointed out that this pitcher had a higher arch in her pitch, so the ball was coming down much more sharply than I was used to. I am going to try visualisation strategies to help me time that type of pitching better…

Here we have all the elements of a good reflection: first, in starting with the objective, she has focused on improving hitting and increasing school spirit; secondly, in evaluating specific actions, she talks about advertising in the bulletin as well as trying to keep her weight forward as evidence of what she tried to do; finally, she suggests ways in which she can improve for next time (visualisation techniques for hitting) or improve on her progress to encourage more interest from the school in softball (write a follow up in the bulletin).

In the case of the student making the film, there was one line that caught my attention in her reflection: "I am getting frustrated that my friends are not coming to meetings prepared, and I feel like I am doing all the work". While the reflection was generally strong, this line was just left as a statement of fact. I asked to talk to the student and probe further. Here was an opportunity to reshape the objective based on her reflections. I started with a simple question, 'How can we make this work better?' This question is powerful because it uses the fact that the student owns the objective to generate critical thought as to how to solve a problem: it is her objective, her problem, and her solution. What she came up with was a new objective centred on how to be a better leader. The need to improve as a leader was a means to the end of creating the film. My role in this conversation was that of a facilitator. I used the key features of reflection to structure my conversation and as a means of sharing a common language with the student. However, I never told her what to do. I asked her to think of ways she could solve this problem and then add her ideas to her reflection. This is what resulted:

I have learned that I have the habit of doing everything myself, rather than trying to get other people to do their share of the work. It is hard for me to trust someone else with something I feel is important. I think this makes them anxious and this might be why they are happy for me to do everything. I talked to my dad and he suggested giving people shared responsibility, instead of me being the boss. I am going to have people work in pairs from now on, instead of on their own, so they can have more support and have a specific task to get done.

The student goes on to outline the various tasks that each member of her team will take responsibility for. What was added to an already strong reflection was sincere introspection designed to help solve a problem that was keeping her from being successful. In both these reflections, an intervention using the three key features of reflection allowed the students to get back in touch with their objectives.

Each element of the CAS learning cycle is connected in these examples:

- Plan – the two overarching core objectives: to make the world a better place and to make myself a better person, helped each student decide on an objective they could genuinely own.

- Act – the process of selecting the experience allowed the student to further define and operationalise that objective.

- Reflect – genuine, detailed reflection helped the students improve on their objectives, and made it more likely that they would be successful in meeting their objectives.

This process also can, of course, be applied to student work in other DP subjects. If a student is able to reflect in the same way on, for example, the quality of an essay they have written in any of the DP disciplines, then it should also help the student be successful in improving that essay, but such a reflection is only possible when the student is clear on the objective of the task. This is how CAS can best support DP courses.

The final CAS interview

The IB requires three documented interviews over the two years of the CAS programme for each student. These interviews offer an opportunity for students to reflect more holistically on their experiences in CAS. The two overarching core objectives, because of their general nature, can prompt fruitful and meaningful semi-structured interviews. By the time a student arrives at the moment of the final CAS interview, it really becomes a celebration of all that has been achieved.

I like to conduct this final interview in a largely unstructured way, using the two overarching core objectives as my only prescribed questions. This offers students an opportunity to think about the impact they have had over the last two years, both on themselves and their community. My interview might begin, after a brief exchange of congratulations, with the question: 'So, are you a better person now than you were two years ago?'. This leads to probing follow-up questions and discussion about their experiences and eventually leads to the questions: 'How have you been able to make your world a better place? What is now better than it was two years ago because of something you did?'. These questions often lead to further searching questions and revealing answers. The culmination of the interview is a recognition of the impact that CAS has had on the student, with perhaps a follow up conversation as to what this might look like in the next stage of their life. My goal is for the student to walk away from the interview with a sense of pride in what they have achieved, and a feeling of being empowered to make a difference that they will take with them when they leave the school. This is why we say that CAS never ends.

While there will be great variety in the range and quality of students' CAS experiences, I have found that encouraging them to reflect on two years of intensive work is a genuinely eye-opening experience for students. It is the first opportunity they have had to get a sense of just how much they have achieved. For many it is the first time they are really recognising that they have grown as an individual through their experiences.

The final interview is a celebration not an evaluation, and success for me rests in the student walking away from it excited to share the ideas we have discussed. I walk away from it also with an evaluation of my own success in helping these students grow through CAS. While there is always room to improve, and students whom I wish I could have helped more, by focusing CAS on the two overarching core objectives of 'making the world a better place' and 'making myself a better person' I find that I am seeing fewer students who felt disconnected from their CAS experiences, and seeing more students who have not only enjoyed their CAS, but also recognise that it has become a significant part of their lives, a part that hopefully will lead them to continue trying to make the world a better place.

References

International Baccalaureate (2010) *Guide to CAS*. The Hague: International Baccalaureate.

International Baccalaureate (2017) *Guide to CAS*. The Hague: International Baccalaureate.

Chapter 14

CAS: making connections with Diploma Programme subjects

Tom Brodie

Why do students study your subject – and why did you become a teacher?

I would conjecture that students mostly choose their academic subjects because they have, or think they will have, an affinity to it. They are interested in what the teacher's subject has to offer them in terms of knowledge and understanding. They may want to connect the subject to the world around them; they may have questions to which they seek answers. They may have studied the subject before and found it interesting, or they may be new to it and expect to find it interesting. However, after just one semester this can all too often be forgotten, with the goal having changed: from the search for understanding and enlightenment to the search for the highest grade. Understanding is exchanged for short cuts. In-depth study is exchanged for learning what the examiner wants. Likewise, if you are a faculty member, why did you become a teacher of your subject? I know that personally it was through an affinity for young people; a love of my subject and a desire to help youngsters understand, as best they could, the world around them. I never once thought when choosing this career that my main focus would be on improving exam grades – which all too often seems to be my professional focus. Making connections between the academic and the broader educational context is important for us all, student and teacher alike. This chapter will provide examples of how one busy Economics and Business department attempts to make those connections through utilising the opportunities that CAS provides.

Why is it important to connect academic subjects and CAS?

CAS is the embodiment of 'doing' in the IBDP. It is the action that students can take, outside of their demanding academic programmes, to apply their knowledge and understanding to the real world. Having CAS activities that support connecting academic subjects is, in my mind, vital to allow students to apply their understanding in the real world. This raises engagement in their subjects, leads to improved understanding, analysis and evaluation, gives students real-life examples to draw upon and, notwithstanding my first paragraph, will lead to improved results! So perhaps it is something of value for teachers to consider encouraging within their own context.

CAS Portfolios and Basic Rules

As many readers will know, for their CAS engagement students need to develop a portfolio of *experiences* that cover the three CAS strands (Creativity, Activity, Service), and one extended project. They are not assessed formally, but assess their own progress towards seven learning outcomes that will be explored below. Not everything can be counted for CAS: activities that are part of their academic programme, and paid work, are excluded. Otherwise, almost any activity that students undertake outside of their academic study *could* count as a CAS *experience* as long as it is agreed by the school's CAS Coordinator. The most challenging question to arise (as referenced by the CAS Coordinators forum) is "Is it CAS?". My answer is always "It could be!". Due to the nature of a *portfolio*, a student should strive to include several varied CAS experiences. In the following sections of this chapter I will describe CAS activities we have run in my, Economics and Business, department and link these to possible CAS learning outcomes. If a student only had one CAS experience from those shown I would not consider them to be meeting their CAS learning outcomes and responsibilities. However, if they were undertaking one of these along with others that perhaps had a greater focus on Activity, Service or Creativity then I would consider them a more than valid addition to the student's portfolio of activities. Students need to engage in what they are interested in and what helps them. As a CAS Coordinator I have always encouraged students to add a variety of experiences to their portfolio and to worry later about whether they are C, A or S – and what learning outcomes they may contribute towards. The experiences below certainly did that for some of the students I have taught, and have inspired them to become more interested in Economics and Business.

The CAS Learning Outcomes

In CAS, there are seven learning outcomes (LO): see Table 14.1

LO 1	**Identify own strengths and develop areas for growth**
Descriptor	Students are able to see themselves as individuals with various abilities and skills, of which some are more developed than others.
LO 2	**Demonstrate that challenges have been undertaken, developing new skills in the process**
Descriptor	A new challenge may be an unfamiliar experience or an extension of an existing one. The newly acquired or developed skills may be shown through experiences that the student has not previously undertaken or through increased expertise in an established area.
LO 3	**Demonstrate how to initiate and plan a CAS experience**
Descriptor	Students can articulate the stages from conceiving an idea to executing a plan for a CAS experience or series of CAS experiences. This may be accomplished in collaboration with other participants. Students may show their knowledge and awareness by building on a previous experience, or by launching a new idea or process.

LO 4	Show commitment to and perseverance in CAS experiences
Descriptor	Students demonstrate regular involvement and active engagement in CAS.
LO 5	Demonstrate the skills and recognize the benefits of working collaboratively
Descriptor	Students are able to identify, demonstrate and critically discuss the benefits and challenges of collaboration gained through CAS experiences.
LO 6	Demonstrate engagement with issues of global significance
Descriptor	Students are able to identify and demonstrate their understanding of global issues, make responsible decisions, and take appropriate action in response to the issue either locally, nationally or internationally.
LO 7	Recognize and consider the ethics of choices and actions
Descriptor	Students show awareness of the consequences of choices and actions in planning and carrying out CAS experiences.

Table 14.1: CAS Learning Outcomes (IB, 2015, pp 10-11)

Our Department

Before introducing the experiences, some context is necessary. We are a busy Economics and Business department. We offer six examinable courses: IGCSE Business, IGCSE Economics, A-Level Business, A-level Economics, BTEC Business and IB Diploma Economics. We teach around 160 students aged 14-18, in a busy boarding school that has 50% boarders. We have five staff members and are lucky to have financial support available if we need it. Our school offers an Enrichment timetable and most of these activities fall under that heading. It is recognised that not everyone is so lucky.

The experiences

The following are CAS experiences we have run in the department, or supervised student-run experiences, over the past three years.

BASE Business Competition

BASE is ICAEW's National Business and Accounting competition for students in school or college aged 16-17. A unique and exciting experience, students are able to engage in business challenges that enable them to develop key employability skills and understand what it's like to be an ICAEW Chartered Accountant. (icaew.com).

Every country I have worked in has had some variant on the young people business competition. BASE used to be run as a day experience when we travelled to a local university to undertake business challenges as a group. This meant that we were limited to taking one team a year. In its latest iteration it is entirely online until the final, so we are able to enter as many teams as we wish.

189

Challenges involve "Apprentice"-style activities such as designing a marketing campaign and making recommendations on what choices a business should take.

The learning experience here was focussed around students being set challenges, new and unique to the individuals, that they must work to overcome as a team. Although the staff member presented the opportunity to the students, students were then responsible for the entire activity. The process involved forming teams, signing up online and then undertaking the activities together. The first was an online task considering various scenarios and deciding on appropriate responses, while the second was a more creative marketing task.

Possible Learning Outcomes:
1. Identify own strengths and develop areas for growth
2. Demonstrate that challenges have been undertaken, developing new skills in the process
3. Demonstrate how to initiate and plan a CAS experience
4. Show commitment to and perseverance in CAS experiences
5. Demonstrate the skills and recognise the benefits of working collaboratively
6. Demonstrate engagement with issues of global significance
7. Recognise and consider the ethics of choices and actions

Schools can register for BASE (UK only) via https://careers.icaew.com/campaigns/base-competition

Share Club

There are many possible share simulations to be found on the internet that allow students to 'virtually' run their own portfolios and learn about the pros and cons of investing in the stock market. This year we went a step further and joined the Shares4Schools competition. This is *real money* investing. Students had to buy in to the club, £40 each. This money was then matched by the competition, meaning that we had £2,000 of real money to invest. The competition runs from October to May and the school with the highest returns wins as a prize a trip to the City of London. None of our students had ever invested in the stock market before, so the process involved students firstly learning about stocks and shares, what they are and how they work, then working together to investigate possible investment strategies, and present them to others in the club. Votes are held, stock is tracked, ethics considered and much discussion ensues. The club appointed a chair and a finance officer to keep track of payments and trades. Due to the nature of the decision-making, it was vital that everyone was present at all votes. One of the more interesting early discussions regarded whether we should follow an investment strategy that was broadly considered ethical; staying away from firms that follow environmentally damaging activities such as fossil fuel extraction and mining.

The group are currently following a fairly high-risk strategy that is focussed on emerging biotechnology companies, in the hope that we can support firms that both make profit and find solutions to humanities challenges. This is very much a student-led activity giving some students the opportunity to meet Learning Outcome 3. Staff have to supervise it, as legally it is staff who have to make the trades. So far, we haven't lost too much money!

Possible Learning Outcomes:

1. Identify own strengths and develop areas for growth

2. Demonstrate that challenges have been undertaken, developing new skills in the process

3. Demonstrate how to initiate and plan a CAS experience

4. Show commitment to and perseverance in CAS experiences

5. Demonstrate the skills and recognize the benefits of working collaboratively

6. Demonstrate engagement with issues of global significance

7. Recognize and consider the ethics of choices and actions

Shares4Schools may be accessed via www.shares4schools.co.uk/

[See also Student Investor: www.studentinvestor.org/]

ReThinking (Stretch) Economics

This student-led, staff-helped society meets once every two weeks to examine an extension or off-syllabus area of Economics. It uses for its structure the ReThinking Economics website and support – an organisation set up by students who felt that university teaching was not answering their questions regarding the challenges and errors of our current economic systems. A different pair of students in each weekly meeting introduce a topic and provide activities to engage the other members of the society. Topics have included Pluralism, Feminist Economics, Behavioural Economics, Marxism, and "The Death of Homo Economist". These meetings allow a small group to undertake in-depth study into an area of the subject that they would not normally meet – on their own terms and sharing it with other, like-minded, students. As such it goes above and beyond the syllabus in Economics, and also stretches the students to question their own understanding. It benefits all who attend, whether those aiming for the top grade or those who are heading towards a pass grade, as it provides an opportunity to develop understanding, examples and evaluation.

Possible Learning Outcomes:

1. Identify own strengths and develop areas for growth

2. Demonstrate that challenges have been undertaken, developing new skills in the process

3. Demonstrate how to initiate and plan a CAS experience

4. Show commitment to and perseverance in CAS experiences

5. Demonstrate the skills and recognize the benefits of working collaboratively

6. Demonstrate engagement with issues of global significance

7. Recognize and consider the ethics of choices and actions

Rethinking Economics: www.rethinkeconomics.org/

Young Enterprise

This is actually the jewel in the crown of our extra-curricular activities. Each year it is over-subscribed and students compete to form the final team. The team then needs to undertake activities to raise funding and launch a firm that produces a service or product. They then market and sell the good, before being judged and given feedback on their ideas, business and presentations. There are several rounds in the UK and it progresses from local to regional to national competition.

Last year our school team undertook a social enterprise called 'SoxBox': see Figure 14.1. They sold a box that contained a random pair of socks for the buyer to keep or give as a gift. For each pair of socks purchased another pair of thermal socks was donated to our local homeless charity in response to a genuine need in our town for socks for homeless people – socks are seldom donated to homeless charities. In all, the team donated over 500 pair of socks to the homeless charity.

Figure 14.1: SoxBox 2017/18

This year the group sourced and sold ethical tea, with the message that one way to combat mental health issues is to move away from social media and have a cup of tea and a chat with friends: see Figure 14.2.

Figure 14.2: Go-Sip 2018/19

Possible Learning Outcomes:

1. Identify own strengths and develop areas for growth

2. Demonstrate that challenges have been undertaken, developing new skills in the process

3. Demonstrate how to initiate and plan a CAS experience

4. Show commitment to and perseverance in CAS experiences

5. Demonstrate the skills and recognize the benefits of working collaboratively

6. Demonstrate engagement with issues of global significance

7. Recognize and consider the ethics of choices and actions

Young Enterprise is available worldwide, and in the UK at www.young-enterprise.org.uk/. Its slight disadvantage is that it is quite costly to join, although that cost covers a support network and competition element that adds significant value for the students.

Another similar option is Peter Jones Tycoon Enterprise: www.peterjonesfoundation.org/foundation-for-enterprise/encourage-tycoon-enterprise-competition/

Corridor Display

This CAS activity came about from a group of students who were struggling to meet their CAS project requirement. I quite selfishly identified a need I had – to lighten up and engage students in the corridor of what was a quite boring building – and gave them that challenge to meet. They were encouraged to use the CAS Stages Framework (Figure 14.3), and Table 14.2 shows how they mapped on their activity to that framework.

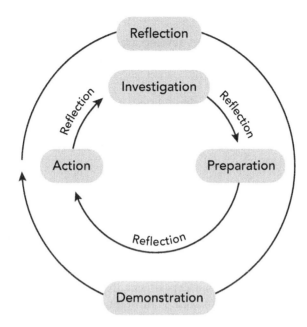

Figure 14.3: CAS Stages (IB, 2013)

Investigation	Measuring wall Coming up with ideas Getting approval for ideas
Preparation	Considering materials and methods of production Getting permissions, coordinating with other adults and agencies
Action	Mocking up the wall
Preparation	Making adjustments Clarifying materials Considering health and safety
Action	Building the display and installing it
Demonstration	Finished interactive wall display
Reflection	Via blog and reflective journal

Table 14.2: Corridor display mapped on to CAS Stages framework

The three students involved were studying Design Technology so used their skills from that academic subject in order to plan, design and build the display. At the time of writing, we have not quite completed it, but I have high hopes for an interactive display that brings to life Economic History for all the students who use the corridor for many future months.

Possible Learning Outcomes:

1. Identify own strengths and develop areas for growth
2. Demonstrate that challenges have been undertaken, developing new skills in the process
3. Demonstrate how to initiate and plan a CAS experience
4. Show commitment to and perseverance in CAS experiences
5. Demonstrate the skills and recognize the benefits of working collaboratively

Writing a Journal

Our school promotes student-edited and student-run academic 'journals'. Students form an editing and peer review committee, generate submissions, review them and publish them. We have started this process several times and have got as far as producing a magazine and webpage. The goal for our journal is to explain items in the news to the wider school community in a manner that they can understand. It aims to reach students within our department, those who are considering joining it and those with just a wider interest. A further benefit is that it can build on the work of the IBDP Economics Portfolio of Commentaries, and the best – or most interesting – examples can be included in the journal so that IBDP Economists have further examples to draw upon. Such a journal could be published in-house or a professional printer could be employed.

Possible Learning Outcomes:

1. Identify own strengths and develop areas for growth
2. Demonstrate that challenges have been undertaken, developing new skills in the process
3. Demonstrate how to initiate and plan a CAS experience
4. Show commitment to and perseverance in CAS experiences
5. Demonstrate the skills and recognize the benefits of working collaboratively
6. Demonstrate engagement with issues of global significance

Essay Competitions

As a department, we promote national and international essay competitions that students can choose to enter if they wish. We are happy to provide any support they request, but generally all I do as Head of Department is promote the competitions and let students enter them. Examples include the Royal Economic Society's Young Economist of the Year essay competition (https://www.res.org.uk/education/young-economist-of-the-year.html) and CORE Schools Economics Challenge (www.core-econ.org/core-schools-economics-challenge-2018-2/). Most subjects have some sort of academic essay competition in the UK and USA, and in Scandinavia it is possible to enter the Youth Nobel Prizes.

Possible Learning Outcomes:
1. Identify own strengths and develop areas for growth
2. Demonstrate that challenges have been undertaken, developing new skills in the process
3. Demonstrate how to initiate and plan a CAS experience
4. Show commitment to and perseverance in CAS experiences
5. Demonstrate the skills and recognize the benefits of working collaboratively
6. Demonstrate engagement with issues of global significance
7. Recognise and consider the ethics of choices and actions

Run an Economics Forum or TedX event

Our school has run both of these activities, and the key to making them CAS experiences is focussing on the student-led aspect. For our Economics forum, we had a keynote speaker, after which break-out groups discuss and analyse the impact of the expected economic change on different industries. These groups were student-led, requiring preparation, leadership and reporting back. The activity was twinned with a careers fair for Business, Law and Finance, and students from other schools also took part.

We have similarly led a TedX event (www.ted.com/participate/organize-a-local-tedx-event), and have also participated in events run by local universities. Last month we went to *Discover Economics* in Bristol, and although this was more participatory than requiring leadership skills, the students still developed skills and had a worthwhile *experience* connecting their studies to the real world. In the afternoon they had to create proposed solutions to closing the gender pay gap.

Possible Learning Outcomes:
1. Identify own strengths and develop areas for growth
2. Demonstrate that challenges have been undertaken, developing new skills in the process
3. Demonstrate how to initiate and plan a CAS experience
4. Show commitment to and perseverance in CAS experiences
5. Demonstrate the skills and recognise the benefits of working collaboratively
6. Demonstrate engagement with issues of global significance
7. Recognise and consider the ethics of choices and actions

Enterprise Club for the Lower School

To promote the department in the lower school we have run a club to engage younger students. This entails playing simulations and games that allow the youngsters to begin to understand what Economics and Business actually are. Older, CAS, students can begin by helping to support a staff member and then move on to planning and initiating their own activities, with staff support, once they understand what is needed. This is a creative activity that requires some bravery and commitment!

The club meets every week to play economics- or business-themed games. The aim is for younger students to learn without realising, while having fun and engaging with issues of a business and economics type. Some of their favourites include a lobster fishing simulation, and the term concludes with the £10 challenge where teams of younger students gain investment of £10 and compete to make the most profit. If a CAS group really takes the lead in this, then they can meet many learning outcomes.

Possible Learning Outcomes:
1. Identify own strengths and develop areas for growth
2. Demonstrate that challenges have been undertaken, developing new skills in the process
3. Demonstrate how to initiate and plan a CAS experience
4. Show commitment to and perseverance in CAS experiences
5. Demonstrate the skills and recognise the benefits of working collaboratively
6. Demonstrate engagement with issues of global significance
7. Recognise and consider the ethics of choices and actions

Tutoring Activities

As the age range in our department is from 14 to 18 there is often an opportunity for older students, or more accomplished students, to help with tutoring younger or weaker students. This is mutually beneficial; the younger student receives support and, hopefully, encouragement, while the older student gets to review and check their understanding, since they will not be able to teach something if they do not fully understand it.

Possible Learning Outcomes:
1. Identify own strengths and develop areas for growth
2. Demonstrate that challenges have been undertaken, developing new skills in the process
3. Demonstrate how to initiate and plan a CAS experience
4. Show commitment to and perseverance in CAS experiences

5. Demonstrate the skills and recognise the benefits of working collaboratively

6. Demonstrate engagement with issues of global significance

7. Recognise and consider the ethics of choices and actions

In conclusion

To conclude, there are many opportunities available for academic departments to increase engagement and to develop academic understanding and application in the real world. As a CAS Coordinator, don't get hung up on sports, service and arts activities; students can meet these strands in many different situations as sometimes they don't know how until they start. CAS is also the students' chance to apply their knowledge, or stretch themselves or find some other sort of challenge. None of these activities singularly will make up a successful CAS portfolio, but they could contribute to a successful portfolio along with some other key experiences or projects.

If you are not a Business or Economics teacher or student, don't worry; more ideas may be accessed via this Google Doc, where they are recorded by subject area: https://docs.google.com/document/d/1MFLK8grJ3e5gAs0e3bpM6H05 lKoqsUKJNZMo2X_-A3I/edit?usp=sharing. Please feel free to visit and add ideas of your own, or to gain inspiration for CAS experiences that allow you to integrate your own academic subjects.

Starting a CAS experience in an academic department can seem like an extra burden on students and staff with already busy work and study lives, but the rewards are worth it. Start small and build up with one or two activities, and inspire the students to engage. While you provide the initial push, they should provide the momentum to run the activity on an ongoing basis.

Table 14.3 provides a summary of the learning outcomes met by the various examples provided above.

Experience/ LO	1	2	3	4	5	6	7
BASE	X	X	X	X	X	X	X
Share Club	X	X	X	X	X	X	X
ReThinking Economics Stretch Club	X	X	X	X	X	X	X
Young Enterprise	X	X	X	X	X	X	X
Corridor Display	X	X	X	X	X		
Journal	X	X	X	X	X	X	
Essay Competitions	X	X	X	X	X	X	X
Run an Event	X	X	X	X	X	X	X
Run a Club for Younger Students	X	X	X	X	X	X	X
Tutoring	X	X	X	X	X	X	X

Table 14.3: Possible Learning Outcomes Met by Given Examples

Reference

International Baccalaureate (2015) *CAS Guide*. Cardiff: International Baccalaureate.

Chapter 15

Teaching the DP core: developing Students as internationally minded Thinkers, Researchers and Community Leaders

Heather Michael

I have a love/hate relationship with the core of the IB Diploma Programme (DP) and it all has to do with how it is taught (or not taught) in schools. The DP core has the potential to foster the circumstances necessary to inspire critical thinking in students, to cultivate in them a love for research and to inspire them to leadership. It can also do the opposite. It comes down to whether the core is taught or tasked. If it is taught with enthusiasm about what it means to inquire into personal interests, to turn those interests into inquiry, and to turn that inquiry into academic research and/or community engagement, then it can be a lasting, even life-changing, experience. If it is tasked, that is if deadlines are the whole focus and students are only expected to meet the deadlines without meaningful teaching about what happens along the way, it can be tedious and meaningless. The DP core needs to be well taught. When this happens, it becomes about the identities of students: who they are as thinkers, researchers and community leaders, and this self-exploration can drive the rest of the DP, creating a language and a framework that allows for connections between personal interests and academic development across the whole programme. To that end, this chapter is intended to promote the teaching of the DP core. I will argue that its purpose is to foster students as internationally minded thinkers (Theory of Knowledge), researchers (Extended Essay) and community leaders (Creativity, Activity, Service) through engagement with the teaching and the opportunities presented by this unique part of the DP.

What follows is designed to explain my rethinking of the purpose of the core, and to provide tangible steps for coordinators and school leaders to engage with staff and to work with students in a way that will drive the core as being primarily about developing students' sense of themselves and their identities as internationally minded thinkers, researchers and community leaders. It is divided into four parts. Part One explores what it means to think about the DP core as being about student identities. Part Two outlines the importance of establishing a vision for the DP core with teachers, before working with students. Part Three looks at grounding the core in student reflection that can then serve as the foundation for work across the core. Part Four looks at specific examples of ways to connect the core elements. This chapter presents one way to turn theory into practice.

Part One: Who am I? The purpose of the core

Like many IB educators, my thinking about international mindedness and the core has shifted and changed throughout my career. My first role in an IB school was as a coordinator for the Extended Essay (EE) and, like many EE coordinators, I was preoccupied with making sure that the teacher advisors and the students were clear on timelines, expectations and deadlines. I generated due dates and passed out assessment rubrics. I told students to find topics that they were interested in without giving them strategies to do so, and most of my energy went towards managing a process. In leading IB workshops about the EE I have come across many others who do the same thing: they unknowingly manage a process rather than cultivate a love of research which is the bedrock of the EE.

One can argue the same thing is true about Theory of Knowledge (TOK) and Creativity, Activity, Service (CAS). Many TOK teachers, for example, are rightly concerned that their students do well on assessments, so they assign extensive readings and many writing assignments, losing sight of the idea that perhaps the course is more about the ways in which we can become internationally minded critical thinkers who recognise that "others with their differences can also be right" (IB Mission statement, 2019), and that this can happen with a different approach to teaching TOK. Likewise in the implementation of CAS, many students miss the goal of meeting the IB's seven aspirational outcomes which include identifying their own strengths and developing areas for growth; demonstrating that challenges have been undertaken and developing new skills in the process; showing commitment and perseverance; working collaboratively; engaging with issues of global significance and considering the ethics of choices and actions (IB, 2015), and instead focus on making sure they log their reflections on time!

Between 2015 – 2018, I conducted a research study in four IB Diploma Programme schools in North America that focused on the experiences of 16 adolescents and their experiences with the core. In almost every case, when asked to 'talk about your experiences with CAS', students first talked about writing reflections and documenting their experiences online or in a journal. It was not until prompted to do so that they connected CAS to the actual experiences that they had had in the school and community. This is not to discount the value of reflection – I discuss the value of meaningful reflection later in this chapter – however it is to say that in many schools, there are teachers with good intentions reducing the core to a series of tasks, rather than using it as an opportunity to foster a strong sense of self in the adolescents they work with.

The intention here is not to disregard or minimise the assessment that is connected to the core, but if we put the assessment first, we have tasked the core, leaving little room for joy, personal growth, and connection to other fundamental aspects of the DP including the mission statement, international mindedness and the IB Learner Profile. Instead, I am suggesting that if we put the big questions first: 'Who am I as an internationally minded thinker, researcher, and community leader?', then there is greater potential for authentic, personal engagement with each element of the core and between all elements of the core and, more broadly, engagement with the philosophy of the IB. The remainder of this chapter explores how to make this shift.

Part Two: Working with teachers to establish a vision

Before we can ask our students to consider themselves as leaders, it is important to ask question of the programmes we run, and of the teachers who work with our students. In the speed of the school year, it is easy to forget the purpose of the work that we do, the vision of our school, our goals and why it is that we believe in the educational philosophy of the IB. It is important to give time to ask these key questions so that what we do in the classroom every day has meaning.

As IB educators we hopefully all subscribe to the idea that internationally minded education matters for a reason; that using the DP's approaches to teaching and learning is important for the growth of both students and teachers; that the IB Learner Profile is more than a list of attributes, and that the IB Mission statement, including the idea that "others with their differences can also be right", is of importance to the work that we do each day with students. However, it is easy to forget these big goals in the day-to-day realities of schedules and the assessment pressures that are tied to the DP. Moreover, without tangible ways of making sense of the theoretical framing of the DP, it is also easier to focus on the mechanics of the classroom and assessment. It is the responsibility of school leaders in a DP school to lead this work with teachers so that similar work can be done with students.

Step One: Decide what you believe by spending time, as adults, reflecting on purpose.

In order to convince students that the DP core provides the opportunity to think about their identities, it is necessary to have adults believe it. To do that, they too need time to sit together and ask and answer questions about the purpose of their teaching, the goals of the DP, and their vision for their students. To that end, step one in this process is about creating time for adults to reflect together. This kind of reflection will look different in each school context; perhaps it will happen at a staff meeting, in departments, or through professional development. Maybe it will be shared, maybe it will be personal. What is important is that we ask teachers and school leaders to be part of the process of articulating the purpose of the DP, and teaching the core in a way that reflects an understanding of that purpose.

There are many questions that can be asked, some might include:

Questions about the purpose of the DP at the school:

- What is the purpose of being an IB educator?
- What is the goal that we have for our students when they are with us in our classrooms, and when they leave us as graduates?
- What does international mindedness mean to us?
- How do our students reflect and embody international mindedness in their thinking and actions?
- Why do we value the DP and the educational philosophy of the IB, and what do we want our students believing when they leave?

Questions about being a DP teacher:

- What do I value about teaching the DP?
- What is it that I hope to impart to my students?
- What are the skills that I value in my classroom?

Questions about the core:

- How can we use the core to teach students about international mindedness?
- What skills do I want to teach my students as they relate to research, leadership and internationally minded thinking?
- How can we drive our school's vision through the way we implement the core with our students?

Step Two: Make commitments to time, language and value when it comes to the core.

There are three practical commitments on which school leaders and teachers need to agree in order to drive the whole of the DP from the elements of the DP core: a commitment to give the core sufficient time, a commitment to adopt a language that is about student identities and not assessments, and a commitment to prioritise the core in relation to the other subjects that are in the DP.

One of the most valuable currencies in schools is time; students recognise that what is important for the school is given time, and teachers understand that school leaders will free them up for things that are priorities. In order to make the core a priority, and to cultivate student identities, time needs to be built into the week/month for students to talk about and reflect on elements of the core that are connected to their identities and experiences in and out of school. There are many ways that schools find time to make this work: some schools' schedule a Core Block, others borrow time from classes, others have regular (weekly, bi-weekly or monthly) periods or days devoted to engaging with the core. Regardless of how it is scheduled, it is necessary for students to see the core valued like other subjects, by being given time in the school day.

Otherwise, the core remains an 'extra' outside of the day, and, subsequently, an 'extra' in terms of the DP experience.

Another way that the core becomes important is in the language used to talk about it. If each time a component of the core is discussed it is in relation to assessment, then the core is perceived as simply a series of tasks, regardless of what we believe. If, for example, at each parent meeting and student presentation the focus on CAS is only about how the outcomes are documented, then the language, and the reality of CAS becomes about record-keeping, not identity building. Instead, teachers need to commit to asking questions about identity as it relates to the core. This can be as simple as the following questions that can be given to teachers, posted in the school, and presented to students:

- Tell me about how you are becoming a community leader through CAS?
- Tell me about how you are becoming a researcher through your EE?
- How are you learning to be a better critical thinker in TOK?

We can inform how the purpose of the core is to be understood, simply by how we agree to talk about it.

The final commitment that needs to be made is that the assessment of the core matters as much as the assessment of any of the other DP subjects. This connects to giving the core time, and to how we talk about the core, but it also has to do with what we prioritise when it comes to the daily realities of the IB experience. Does the core receive the same consideration when creating the school calendar? Are there opportunities in place to celebrate student achievements in the DP core? Do subject teachers have conversations with students about their core experiences?

To drive the whole Diploma from the core so that there is an agreed focus on the identities of students, the adults in the building need to first spend time reflecting on and naming the purpose of the work that they do, and it needs to go beyond the assessment and students' final grades. From there, they need to agree to give time, consider language use, and make the core an equal part of the DP experience. With these agreements in place, what follows is possible.

Part Three: Making the core matter to students

In our own ways, we are all seeking meaning in the world. The core has the potential to cultivate this for our students. In my research into the experiences of the core by DP students, I met one student who had worked this out for himself. A lover of video games and computers, he managed to do his EE, CAS and TOK work, along with his internal assessment tasks for other DP subjects, centred on this hobby. While some might take issue with this, I would argue it is smart, efficient and identity building. When he realised that he could take his talent for reconstructing computers and volunteer at the local library to help assemble desktops out of donated parts, he went from having a hobby to being a community leader. When he realised that he could research vector use in video games, he went from player to researcher. And, when he was able to talk about what constitutes creativity through his TOK presentation, relating creativity to video games, he came to realise that his way of understanding his hobby was important, relevant and academic.

Stories like this cannot be the exception to how students engage with the DP core. We all teach athletes who could become role models, simply by turning their passion for sport into talent as coaches. We all teach students who naturally delve into their hobbies, whether they be dance moves, historical battles or top recipes, and never correlate these activities to academic research. We all teach students whose abilities to think critically, and to apply that thinking to the world around them, are enhanced when they link personal interests to big ideas. The challenge is to find a way to make this happen purposefully and joyfully in the classroom.

One way to achieve what is being proposed in this chapter is through a planned extended reflection process that drives the facilitation of the core. I am suggesting that this can happen through a series of personal engagement activities that help to build up knowledge of the interests and talents of students. These reflections can serve as the foundation to the work done in all core elements. Students can be encouraged to go back to these activities and use them as the starting place for their work across the DP.

This reflection can take a variety of forms, depending on contexts and interests. What follows are four Teaching Ideas.

The first Teaching Idea is a sequence of reflective activities that could be used with students in a TOK class or in a grade level meeting.

Teaching Idea 1: Thinking about identity in five steps

Engage students in the following five activities, in sequence, using the questions at the end as a way to debrief and connect to bigger aspects of an IB education and to the core elements.

1. Give students white paper and ask them to: "Draw how you think". Encourage them to use symbols, key words, drawings etc...

2. On another piece of paper, ask them to: "Map your world". They can choose how to interpret the direction and scale.

    Ask students to put these two artefacts side by side: What do they say about you? Compare your illustrations with someone else. What do you learn by listening to someone talk about how they think and understand their world? Could this be one way of engaging in international mindedness?

3. Ask students to write down five statements they are prepared to defend (inspired by Margaret Heffernan's TED Talk: Dare to Disagree (2012), which can also be watched as part of this lesson). Specifically, ask them to:

    Write down 'five things I'm prepared to defend'. These can be literal, abstract, personal or global. (You may want to stipulate that they won't have to share all of them). With a partner, choose one or two of the statements (that you are prepared to share) and explain the assumptions that underpin your statements. How do you construct this belief? How would someone counter your stance?

4. Guide students to look across the first three artefacts (the maps and the list of statements and the statements). As they do, ask them to:

    a. Think of three ideas, concepts, beliefs, values that are foundational to who you are and/or how you act that emerge when you look across these artefacts.

    b. Write them on three different post-its.

    c. Use these post-its to create a tower.

    d. Draw yourself atop of the tower. (A stick person is fine)

    With a partner, talk about how these big ideas might drive your decision-making. What are the implications of understanding the assumptions that we stand on? What are the implications of understanding the assumptions that others stand on? Where might conflict lie?

5. Ask students to reflect on all three artefacts (the maps, the list, the tower). On your own, in a journal, with a partner (depending on the context), consider:

    What does this say about you?

    What does it reveal about how you think?

    What does it say about how you compile knowledge?

    Debriefing: Making connections to the core, the IB Learner Profile and international mindedness:

    •   What attributes of the Learner Profile do you see in yourself as you look across these artefacts? Which attributes do you need to work on?

    •   When you think about how you make decisions, particularly in relation to others in the class, can you make any connections to the line in the IB Mission statement that "others with their differences can also be right"? Does this connect to the idea of international mindedness, in your opinion?

- When you consider how you think and make sense of the world, what connections do you see in how you engage as a community leader?...as a researcher?...as an internationally minded thinker?

While the first Teaching Idea encourages students to think about their philosophical understandings of the world, what follows is a Teaching Idea that encourages them to mine their own lives for practical examples of things they are interested in. This could be done in sequence with the lesson above, or as a launch into CAS or EE work.

Teaching Idea 2: Mine your life for interests and talents

Make a list or draw a map of...

- Five things you're interested in spending time doing outside of school
- Five things you've searched up on your phone, online, or in a book recently
- Five ideas you find yourself thinking about
- Three people who you admire
- Three songs/movies/books that you love
- Three things you've done in your life that you are proud of
- Three things you've always wanted to try and have never made time to do

Use this list to prompt questioning about CAS, EE and/or TOK conversations. For example:

- Circle 3–5 things on this list that you love to do. Look at the outcomes for CAS. How could you turn this love into a CAS experience or Project? Now, look at these same 3–5 things...what is a question you could ask about one or all of them that could become research? Try asking questions in at least two of the IB subjects that you take.
- Finally, look at these things and make connections to the Ways of Knowing in TOK. What Ways of Knowing do you draw on naturally? What Ways of Knowing don't tend to come up in your daily life?

The next two Teaching Ideas are further examples of how to create a foundation of interests, ideas and definitions of international mindedness for students to later draw upon.

Teaching Idea 3: Defining the big ideals of an IB education

In establishing a foundation for students to draw on that centres on the big ideas of an IB education, there is value in being explicit about exploring the attributes of the Learner Profile and the concept of international mindedness; there is also value in having students establish working definitions of these key ideas and concepts so that they can be used to make connections between their work in all components of the core.

One way to ground this conversation is to ask students to think about their own working definitions of international mindedness. This conversation can happen in a TOK class, at a grade level assembly, or in some other context where students are all together. From there, students can be encouraged to draw on, refine, change and adapt their definition depending on their experiences. It is important to remind students that there is no one definition of what it means to engage in an internationally minded way.

After students have arrived at their own definition, ask them to work in pairs to:

- Compare their definitions

Discuss:

- What is similar?
- What is different?
- What are the ethical assumptions that underpin these definitions? What does international mindedness look like in action in: Mathematics? Visual arts? History? etc…

Revisit the Learner Profile. How does the Learner Profile connect to your definition of international mindedness? Are there certain attributes that connect to your understanding of what it means to be internationally minded?

Teaching Idea 4: Reflection journal

Encourage students to carry a reflection journal (either electronic or on paper) throughout the two years of their DP experience where they jot down ideas they think about, moments of interest in their classroom experiences, things they research outside of school, questions they want to explore later etc. This journal can then become a holding place for authentic ideas that can be mined, not only for the core, but also for internal assessments that students do in other DP subjects.

At each meeting, make it a requirement that students pull out their journals and discuss what they have added, making connections between their interests, international mindedness, the Learner Profile and their CAS, EE, TOK (and classroom) progress. It can serve not only as an ideas journal, but also as a reminder to everyone to make bigger connections across the programme.

These Teaching Ideas are not so different from strategies that many teachers are already using. To that end, think about teaching strategies that are already being used, and repurpose favourite activities in the form of reflective foundations for connecting the components of the core.

Part Four: Bringing it all together

If a shared foundation for meaningful reflection about student identity is created through activities such as the four Teaching Ideas, when it comes time to ask students to connect to big ideas, including international mindedness, the Learner Profile and Approaches to Learning, the question of 'why' when it comes to finding purpose for assessment is much easier. From there, exploring each core element and its potential to build student identities also becomes easier. What follows are some suggestions to get educators started in this process.

Theory of Knowledge

Conversations about international mindedness, the complexity of decision making, and how it connects to CAS and EE experiences can be part of the daily fabric of student life. Students will often bring in examples from their lives that can become part of the TOK classroom. If teachers across disciplines begin using reflective journals, or if students are encouraged to mine their lives for interests and talents, the TOK classroom can naturally be a place where they authentically explore varying perspectives on issues of personal relevance, allowing them to analyse their assumptions and to better understand themselves as internationally minded thinkers.

In my research, one of my participants when reflecting on her TOK experiences said, "When I started TOK, I considered myself to be open minded, but looking back, I don't really think that I was. I had one line of thinking, and sort of almost looked down on other lines of thinking. I've noticed that this year, I've stopped doing that and thoroughly think about each new opinion that I come across". Our goal as TOK teachers should surely be to create the conditions where this kind of personal growth is available to all of our students.

Creativity, Activity, Service

CAS presents a unique opportunity to demonstrate what it means to be internationally minded in action. In addition to wanting students to derive their CAS experiences and projects from their personal and authentic interests, having them reflect on and build their understanding of what it means to engage in a way that embodies international mindedness is one way to elicit authenticity. Reflection in CAS, like everything else, should start from a place of mining personal interests and working out ways to choose experiences and projects that are both meaningful and authentic. This may come from the aforementioned teaching ideas, or might come from other existing practices in your school. Regardless, it is important that students start from where they are, and build towards turning what they are interested in into how they become community leaders.

Reflection in CAS can unintentionally become a regurgitation of a daily agenda, summarising activities that have occurred without connecting them to a bigger and meaningful goal. This is where a personal definition of international mindedness, commitments to the Learner Profile, or conversations about ethics in TOK can help to connect reflections about particular activities to bigger ideas about the meaning of leadership and community engagement. Some questions that can help with this are:

In the beginning.....

- How do your proposed CAS experiences connect to your personal interests?
- How does your CAS project connect to your vision of who you are as a community leader?
- Look at your definition of international mindedness; how does it connect to your decision making about what to take on for CAS?

In the middle.....

- What have you learned about yourself as a leader so far in your CAS experiences?
- When you think about your CAS experiences, what are the Ways of Knowing you find yourself drawing on?
- Discuss a moment of conflict that you have experienced while engaged in CAS. How can you explain what happened, using your definition of international mindedness?
- Consider your research so far in your Extended Essay. How could you share that knowledge through your CAS engagements?

Towards the end....

- How have you become a community leader through your CAS experiences/project?
- If you were to name three Ways of Knowing that you used in both CAS and your EE, which would they be and why did you use them?
- Talk about a moment in your CAS life in which you felt like you embodied your own definition of international mindedness.

The result of front-loading connections, and building towards bigger ideas of leadership in CAS, is also better final reflections that are more meaningful and genuinely interesting to read.

Extended Essay

The EE should be an assessment that students love as it should be an opportunity for them to take something that is of genuine interest to them and to become an expert on it through the research process. To achieve this, it is important to ground the generating of the idea in personal interests, and to really slow down the beginning of the process. Give students small steps and guidance to come up with a topic that they are sure they will love. For example, at the beginning of the process, you might ask students to mine their interests list and their CAS experiences to come up with three possible topics that could form the basis of research. Then, ask them to do some simple investigations in order to be able to write a paragraph for each of the three topics to determine which one actually holds the most promising potential. Multiple false starts at the beginning will help students to find a topic that will hold their interest.

One place where students get into trouble when writing the EE is that they become invested in something they are interested in without taking the research method into consideration. Once students have a topic, ask them to go through the IB's EE guide (IB, 2016) and explain why the method they have selected matches the topic. This could happen with an EE guide or in a TOK class: explaining how, for example, a topic is best suited to being formulated as a history essay is not so different from asking a student to think of history as an Area of Knowledge in TOK and to explain how knowledge is constructed in that discipline. Slowing down the beginning and making these connections will, arguably, lead to better essays as students will understand the research decisions they are making. This is how the EE can go from being a task to being an opportunity for students to see and understand themselves as researchers.

If the core turns into an opportunity to build student identities, bridging personal interests with international mindedness and the Learner Profile, it shifts the growth that can happen for students. One way to see this is to celebrate it as a school. Many schools celebrate the completion of elements of the core: a CAS fair, an EE showcase, public presentations of the TOK essay or oral presentations. One final suggestion is to connect these together, asking students to demonstrate how they have become internationally minded thinkers, researchers and community leaders across their experiences with TOK, EE and CAS. Invite your IB community to come, particularly younger students who can learn from the older ones.

Conclusion

I began this chapter by saying that I have a love/hate relationship with the DP core and it all has to do with how it is delivered in a school. The core has the potential to be the most meaningful part of the DP, developing skills, attitudes and behaviours in our students that cultivate their sense of themselves as internationally minded thinkers, researchers and community leaders. For this to happen, the school has to decide that the core matters. It has to support teachers in building their own knowledge and understanding of an IB education and all the components of the core, and it needs to find time for students to engage in careful and sustained reflection. When all of this happens, the possibilities for students are certainly greater than the sum of the parts of each element of the core. And it's way more fun!

Perhaps what it comes down to is thinking about the risk of tasking the core as opposed to teaching it. The risk of tasking the core is that students complete a series of school tasks and move on with their lives. The risk of teaching the core is that students' lives can be shaped as researchers, leaders, and thinkers and, in turn, they may be able to shape the lives of those in the communities where they live and work.

References

Heffernan M (2012). Dare to Disagree. Retrieved from: www.ted.com/talks/margaret_heffernan_dare_to_disagree?language=en

IB (2015) *Creativity, Activity, Service guide*. The Hague: International Baccalaureate.

IB (2016) *Extended Essay guide*. The Hague: International Baccalaureate .

IB (2019) *IB Mission Statement*. www.ibo.org. Accessed, February 25, 2019.

Chapter 16

A coherent Diploma Programme Core Curriculum: a team approach to developing a holistic curriculum

Ann Lautrette

Anyone who participates in any sport or fitness endeavour knows that 'core work' is tough. Sit-up after sit-up, five-minute planks and boat poses can all cause pain in parts of the body that would be otherwise undiscovered. But with every episode of muscle soreness the core becomes stronger and better equipped to support the rest of the body and to protect against injury. Like the human body, the IB Diploma model is held together by its core, and the 'muscles' of CAS, the Extended Essay and Theory of Knowledge (TOK) must be regularly flexed in order to strengthen a student's understanding of the six other subject areas, of themselves as learners and of the key skills needed for success in the Diploma Programme (DP) and beyond. Holding the muscles together from the inside are the Approaches To Learning (ATL), which must be explicitly developed in students if we are to improve their capacity to apply their learning during their time at school and throughout their lives. To strengthen the core of the DP is to support the student's performance in every aspect of the Diploma and to prepare the student for challenges in developing the skills to learn, the ability to reflect and the capacity to give back.

Despite the importance of the core however, it is frequently not given its rightful place at the heart of the Diploma. In many schools the individual elements are found in isolation, with little connection between them and limited links to the subject areas. The core can be seen by students as something 'to get through' and an addendum to the six Diploma subjects rather than as a vital aspect of their learning and their becoming learners. Against that backdrop, this chapter explores how to give the core its central role as the abdominal muscles of the Diploma through coherently integrating CAS, the Extended Essay, TOK and the ATL, along with elements of a non-DP Personal, Social and Health Education (PSHE) course, into a holistic programme with its own curriculum guide. In this chapter I describe the process by which a team of teachers conceived of, created and implemented the 'Core Curriculum' as a subject structured as a series of units and supported by self-assessment.

The principles of the core curriculum

As a team working to develop a new curriculum we started by trying to articulate the philosophy behind the course of study we envisioned. This ultimately led us to agree on four key principles:

1. Students need to understand the connections between the elements of the DP core, and between the core and the DP subject areas.

2. Students need to develop Approaches To Learning skills, which can and should be explicitly taught.

3. The IB Diploma Programme is challenging and students need support.

4. Students need the space and time to develop the ability to reflect.

These fundamental principles were our articulation of a philosophy that the DP core is vital to success, and that the core elements do not exist in isolation. To exemplify how we turned these principles into practice we will consider each one in further detail, as follows:

Principle 1: Students need to understand the connections between the elements of the DP core, and between the core and the DP subject areas.

Every DP core guide refers to 'coherence in the core' and every DP subject guide refers to integration of the core. But if the reality in a school is that the subjects and the core operate in relative isolation, then it is difficult to see how students are to understand subject interdependence and interdisciplinary application. To address this issue, the team built the Core Curriculum units in layers (see Figure 16.1). In each unit the first layer is the conceptual understanding we hope to develop in TOK. The second layer is the explicit ATL skill to be focused on in the unit. Layer three is the connected PSHE content to be explored with students, while layer four is the link to the CAS learning outcomes.

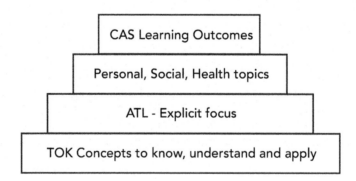

Figure 16.1: a layered curriculum

To exemplify how this model works in practice, the first unit we designed is called 'Defining and Generating Knowledge'. As the first unit in year one of the two- year DP, the intention is to introduce the big TOK questions of what knowledge is, and where it comes from. In this unit we want to introduce the Ways of Knowing, Areas of Knowledge, Personal and Shared Knowledge, and the Knowledge Framework. At the start of the first year we want to focus on affective self-management as an ATL skill in order to support the (often difficult) transition to the DP, and this is tied to the TOK questions: Where does knowledge about ourselves come from? Why do we think the way we do? Where does emotion come from and how does it affect us? This takes us neatly into PSHE by looking at how we can better manage our self-talk and inner voice. How are we motivated? What are we passionate about? What do we hope to achieve in the Diploma and beyond, and how do we achieve it? And, finally, asking how we begin to plan a personal CAS programme based on our interests, our needs, and the needs of the community we will serve. (Learning outcome 1: 'I identify my strengths. I identify areas for growth'). Figure 16.2 shows how the model in Figure 16.1 becomes an initial unit plan for Unit 1: *Defining and Generating Knowledge*.

CAS: LO1 'I identify my strengths. I identify areas for growth.'

PSHE: *How can we better manage our self-talk and inner voice? What motivates us? What's our passion? What do we want out of IB and life? How do we get there?*

ATL: Affective self-management skills: *Where does knowledge about ourselves come from? Why do we think the way we do? Where does emotion come from and how does it affect us?*

TOK: *What is knowledge and where does it come from?* Ways of Knowing, Areas of Knowledge, Personal and Shared Knowledge, the Knowledge Framework

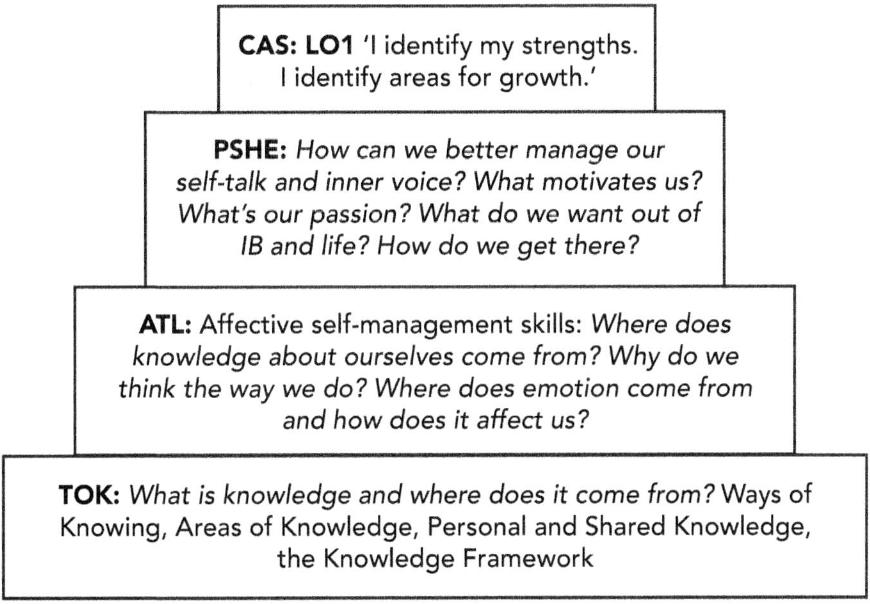

Figure 16.2: Unit 1 in layers

This layered model then serves as the basis for each of the units which weave fluidly through the connected elements of the core, strengthening the links between elements of the core, as well as the students' ability to apply the skills they develop both in their subject areas and to life as a DP student. Figure 16.3 provides an overview of the units which form the curriculum of the two-year course.

Unit Title	Key Focus
Unit 1: Defining and Generating Knowledge	TOK: Key concepts ATL: Affective self-management skills PSHE: Self-talk and inner voice CAS: LO1 – 'I identify my strengths. I identify areas for growth'
Unit 2: Validating Knowledge	TOK: Reason as a Way of Knowing (WOK) and a means to validate knowledge; defining 'evidence' ATL: Research PSHE: What's 'reason-based' decision making? CAS: Validating success through the CAS learning outcomes
Unit 3: Communicating Knowledge	TOK: Shared and Personal Knowledge. Language as a WOK ATL: Communication PSHE: Sexual relationships: empowerment through communication CAS: LO5 – Demonstrate the (communication) skills and recognise the benefits of working collaboratively.
Unit 4: Applying Knowledge	TOK: How do we apply knowledge in different ways in the Areas of Knowledge (AOK)? ATL: Social Skills – working together to apply knowledge PSHE: Discrimination and tolerance of different perspectives CAS: LO7 – Recognise and consider the ethics of choices and actions.
Unit 5: Storing Knowledge	TOK: Memory as a Way of Knowing and its role in the AOKs ATL: Self-management – organisation PSHE: Managing stress CAS: How to record CAS project information for sustainability
Unit 6: Expanding Knowledge	TOK: Can multiple systems of knowledge co-exist? ATL: Thinking PSHE: Preparing for the world beyond school CAS: LO6 – Demonstrate engagement with elements of Global Significance

Figure 16.3: Core Curriculum Overview

Principle 2: Students need to develop Approaches To Learning skills and these can and should be explicitly taught

As seen in Figure 16.3, each unit was designed to include the development of one specific ATL skill. However, in planning classroom activities all skills were taken into account and explicitly planned for. As an example, when focussing on 'communication' as an ATL skill in unit 3 we explicitly taught presentation skills and effective use of visual aids, with a focus on limiting text on slides and effective use of image. We explored email etiquette through email templates for communicating with CAS partners and advisors. When applied to the sexual relationships PSHE topic, we looked at affirmative consent and communicating needs and desires in a relationship. Within TOK, the focus on communication allowed us to explore language, metaphor and its advantages and pitfalls, and consider the way in which the different AOKs communicate their knowledge.

To improve thinking skills, we focused on introducing visible thinking routines as a way to explicitly organise thinking, with the 'claim, support, question' routine from Harvard University's Project Zero serving particularly well during the writing of the TOK essay. Thinking routines are also very useful for helping students to structure effective CAS reflections. It is often a challenge to move students away from describing what they did during a CAS activity, and so a routine such as 'I used to think ... Now I think ...' is a way of keeping the reflections focused on the learning and growth from a CAS experience.

Building research skills into unit 2 was a strategic attempt to introduce the skills needed for the Extended Essay while simultaneously considering how the AOKs validate the knowledge that is generated. This focus on methodology from two different angles allows students to see how their Extended Essay research fits into a larger body of knowledge within an AOK and how they are required to operate as a 'knowledge producer' through the Extended Essay process. We explicitly planned to teach online and offline research skills, from formulating good research questions to experimental design and referencing. Students need particular support with accessing, recording and interpreting academic sources, and space needs to be created in the curriculum for the development of these complex skills.

On the surface, social skills appear to be difficult to actively teach to this age group; however, CAS presents a unique opportunity to teach students how to work together in small 'project management' groups. We taught students how to identify individual and team strengths, how to delegate and assign roles, how to run meetings (including taking and sharing minutes), as well as how to interact with CAS partners external to the school. We also explored cultural, social and linguistic differences and how they affect interactions both at school and in the workplace.

Teachers generally agree that Diploma students need to develop their self-management skills. However, students are often expected to meet deadlines and organise their time without any explicit instruction in how to do this. We taught our students how to meet deadlines starting with to-do lists, moving on to scheduling, backwards planning, calendar use and prioritisation tools. We also explored research-backed effective study techniques and the affective aspect of self-management through managing emotions with positive self-talk, mindfulness and reflection.

Figure 16.4 summarises the Approaches To Learning and how they can be linked to units in a Core Curriculum.

ATL	FOCUS	WHERE?
Communication	Presentation skills, effective use of visual aids, writing for different audiences	Unit 3: Communicating knowledge – Language as a WOK, key concepts and language in the knowledge framework
Thinking	Visible thinking techniques – 'claim, support, question', 'I used to think…, now I think …', 'connect, extend, challenge', fallacies and critical thinking	Unit 2: Validating knowledge – Reason as a WOK, Methodology in the knowledge framework
Research	From formulating research questions to referencing	Unit 2: Validating knowledge – skills for the Extended Essay, methodology from the knowledge framework
Social	How to run and participate in an effective meeting. Role allocation. Agenda setting, minute taking and action planning. Persuasion, argument and perspectives.	Unit 1: Defining and generating knowledge Unit 6: Expanding Knowledge – understanding different knowledge systems (Religious Knowledge Systems and Indigenous Knowledge Systems)
Self-Management	How to meet deadlines through backwards planning. Using to-do lists, calendars and prioritisation tools. Effective study methods and avoiding procrastination. Managing emotions through positive self-talk and reflection.	Unit 1: Defining and generating knowledge Unit 5: Storing knowledge: Emotion as a WOK, memory as a WOK

Figure 16.4: The Approaches To Learning in the Core Curriculum

One of the challenges in developing ATL skills in students is to engage them in activities which they find meaningful without a grade attached. In order to provide an authentic leadership opportunity for students, to allow them to practise the skills they have learned, and to challenge them to see the need for the skills in action, we held a student-led ATL conference. The basic premise was that first year DP students would plan and lead workshops connected to the ATL skills for the younger students in the school. Each group of grade 11 (first year DP) students was given two of the ATL skills to focus on and they were expected to plan and resource two 50-minute workshops that they would lead on the day, with the intention of developing the specific ATL skills in the younger students. We used a scheduling website called Sched (https://sched.com/) to create an authentic workshop schedule where the younger students could sign up for specific workshops, and we had an opening keynote speech on ATL which was delivered by a grade 11 student after an application and selection process.

The images in Figures 16.5 and 16.6 illustrate the range of workshops students offered and the sort of imaginative activity the students designed.

Figure 16.5: The range of communication workshops from sched.com

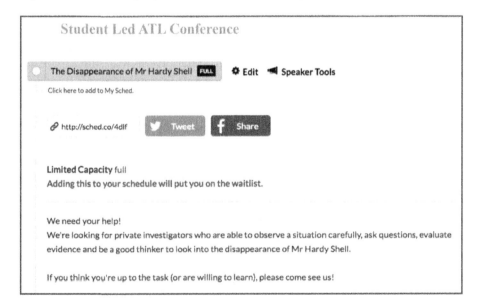

Figure 16.6: Description of one of the 'thinking' workshops from sched.com

To prepare for the planning and presentation of the workshops we gave the students lesson planning templates and talked through the fundamental principles of lesson design. As a by-product of the experience, students gained a better understanding of the work their teachers have to engage in to plan meaningful and engaging lessons!

Principle 3: The IB Diploma Programme is challenging and students need support

The DP is designed to be rigorous preparation for the next stage of a student's academic career, and so by its very nature it is demanding. The content of the Core Curriculum is intended to offer support to students through the development of skills which help students to learn, through preparation for the challenge of the Extended Essay and through creating a greater understanding of the connectedness of their subjects to each other and to TOK. The PSHE content (which is a school-based course and not an official part of the IB DP) is included to support students in their well-being and in making healthy choices as they transition to adulthood.

However, despite all of the positive intentions of teachers, students are frequently overwhelmed by the amount of work and the demands coming simultaneously from six DP subjects and the core, as well as the preparation that goes into applying to university. For this reason, when looking to create more coherence in the core, we felt that the teaching structure needed reviewing along with the content. Students typically have six different teachers in their subject areas, as well as interacting with a TOK teacher, an Extended Essay supervisor, a CAS advisor and, depending on the school, a tutor or homeroom teacher. The number of people involved with one student can make it challenging for students to develop a relationship with one supportive person, even though coaching or mentoring can be a very powerful method of student support. For this reason, we wanted to restructure the schedule to ensure that each student had one Core Curriculum teacher who would cover all the elements of TOK, CAS, ATL and PSHE. This teacher has a holistic overview of a student's academic progress, and of their well-being. They are thus well placed to get to know the work habits of their students and support them with personal and academic development. In addition, because core lessons are collaboratively planned, reviewed and reflected upon as a team, teachers can discuss student concerns and provide support to one another. In terms of demonstrating to students that the elements of the DP core are inter-connected, having one teacher focus on all elements in a holistic way is powerful.

Principle 4: Students need the space and time to develop the ability to reflect.

The elements of the core are linked by reflection and, indeed, students in the DP are assessed on their ability to reflect well on their learning experiences. However, the ability to reflect is not necessarily innate and students left to their own devices have a tendency to describe what they did, rather than to articulate what they learned and how. Yet this reflection is a part of the thinking skill to be developed through ATL, so as Diploma teachers we must actively support students in reflecting well. Understanding how to reflect is only part of the challenge however. Students also have to learn to appreciate the importance of reflecting, beyond the 6 marks for Criterion H in the Extended Essay or having to complete CAS reflections. A starting point for achieving this understanding may be to keep reflections all in one place. A student blog can be an ideal place for a student not only to reflect on CAS, but also to keep their Researcher's Reflective Space for the Extended Essay, and reflect on their developing understanding in TOK. A blog also allows students to be creative with their style, supporting their communication skills and their Language A courses, and allowing them to build a positive digital footprint. Used as an exercise book for the Core Curriculum, a blog becomes a record of the student's academic and personal development as a thinker over the two years of the DP.

Figure 16.7 shows an example of the power of a blog as a CAS reflection journal.

Figure 16.7: CAS reflection journal (J Wells, 2017)

A challenge when teaching students how to reflect well is to develop the understanding that there is no one right way to reflect. Reflections may need to vary in length and style according to the activity. In order to encourage a flexible approach to reflection we asked them at times to do something different with their reflection. As an example (Figure 16.8), we asked students to create an Instagram-style reflection referencing two CAS learning outcomes and using three hashtags to capture the key points of learning from their project.

Figure 16.8: Instagram-style reflection (A Darmawan, 2017)

Not everything was done online however, with flexible reflection extending also to our CAS posters at the end of the projects, as seen in Figure 16.9.

Figure 16.9: End of CAS project reflective posters

The four principles explored in this chapter acted as drivers for all lesson and activity planning undertaken by the team when developing the Core Curriculum. They also underpinned the decisions made about assessment in the curriculum, though in this chapter I give assessment its own section in line with its importance in the DP.

Assessment in the Core Curriculum

Designing an assessment model for the Core Curriculum posed several challenges. The summative assessment for the TOK aspect of the curriculum is clear, and provided by the IB. PSHE is school-based, however, and is not assessed by the IB, while the question of how best to assess the development of ATL is one many schools have wrestled with. In principle we felt that the success of the Core Curriculum could largely be seen in the six DP subjects: increased attainment, and students better able to cope with the demands of the Diploma. For this reason, we decided to design self-assessment tools for the ATL skills. We felt that students were best placed to identify which skills they needed to improve upon, and through regular self-assessment they could set targets and personalise their learning. To do this we designed our assessments using Google Forms, and developed a series of questions which highlighted the key aspects of each ATL skill. Students were to rate themselves in terms of perceived competence with the particular skill. Once complete these assessments gave teachers the data they needed to be able to design the learning based on the needs of the group, as well as to help students to develop their own plans for improving their areas of difficulty. To use Self-Management (Organisation) as an example of one of these self-assessments, students were asked to rate themselves in response to the questions noted in Figure 16.10. Possible response options were 'Totally Me', 'Mostly Me' or 'Not Me'.

Self-Management (Organisation) Questions
I get to all classes on time
I plan short and long term assignments
I meet deadlines
I create plans to prepare for summative in-class assessments
I keep and use a weekly planner for assignments
I set goals that are challenging and realistic
I plan strategies and take action to achieve personal and academic goals
I bring necessary equipment and supplies to class
I keep an organised and logical system of files and notebooks
I use regular review of subject matter to improve retention
I select and use technology effectively and productively

Figure 16.10: Self-management (organisation) self-assessment questions

From an assessment tool such as this, core teachers were able to ascertain that planning for assignments and summative assessments (and planning in general) were the areas where our students felt they had the most learning to do. As core teachers this allowed us to use the introductory sessions for the Extended Essay and the requirements of the Extended Essay process to improve the students' planning skills. We taught the students how to develop a timeline for the Extended Essay process, providing a template and structured deadlines for supervisor meetings, the draft essay and the final essay. We also taught students how to action plan, again providing a template for the Extended Essay action plan which was reviewed by supervisors and students in every meeting. As we were developing these planning skills simultaneously in CAS through the teaching of project management skills, and through the ATL conference which required time-dependent planning, students increased their ability to schedule and prepare for assessments in a structured way.

The Core Curriculum: learning examples

To appreciate how the threads of TOK, CAS, PSHE and the ATL skills can be woven into one curriculum, it is helpful to consider what a lesson might look like when it draws on at least two of these aspects. Here, I describe a lesson entitled 'Tame Your Thoughts' where the focus is on a PSHE topic of exploring negative self-talk and its impact. In order to do this in connection with TOK, we ask the big question at the start of the lesson: 'What claims do you make about yourself?' Using the TOK terminology of 'claims' ensures connectedness to personal knowledge and enhances understanding of TOK's real life application. In this lesson we go on to suggest some negative claims that students may make about themselves, such as 'I'm no good at Maths', or 'People disagree with me because they don't like me'. We then go on to explore what kind of thinking leads to statements such as these and ask whether they are rational or irrational. This leads us into the introduction of Reason as a Way of Knowing, and as we explore inductive and deductive reasoning we begin to see that actually these thoughts are based on a rational process of either induction or deduction. This helps us to understand why these thoughts are so powerful, but once we introduce students to the problems associated with inductive and deductive reasoning, they begin to see that there may be flaws in this thinking and can hopefully begin to step back and analyse the validity of claims about themselves. Towards the end of the lesson we look at some of the real world consequences of inductive reasoning, such as 'stereotyping', 'catastrophising', 'leaps in logic' and 'black and white' thinking. Then finally, we use the 'true for who?' thinking routine from Harvard University's Project Zero to consider how we might explore the different perspectives on a claim, and why those different perspectives might arise.

In another lesson focused on memory as a Way of Knowing, but also on the implications that the flaws in memory have for study, we begin by playing some memory games such as 'I went to the market …' and remembering a series of numbers and images to demonstrate the challenges of memorisation. We then discuss how listening without taking notes is rather ineffective as a study habit. We ask students to practise active listening and note-taking while watching a video about how memory can be falsely created through suggestive techniques. This then leads into a discussion connecting the Human Sciences and Ethics as Areas of Knowledge about whether the knowledge gained about memory from an experiment involving suggesting painful memories to participants outweighs the negative impact of such a study.

These lesson examples demonstrate how the threads of TOK, PSHE and the ATL skills can be woven together into coherent lessons which connect abstract concepts to the real world and, significantly, to the student's experience. Many students do have difficulty with the concepts and the ways of thinking they are introduced to in TOK, and the more we can demonstrate the subject's concrete application, the more we can demystify it. Similarly, the more we can develop understanding of the importance of the ATL in students, the better they will be at engaging in the self-improvement process necessary to increase skill level.

Challenges to the implementation of a Core Curriculum

Conceiving of a curriculum, writing it and putting it into practice is not without its challenges, particularly in an international school that is wrestling with adapting to the changing needs of its students, the expectations of its stakeholders, and staying faithful to IB philosophy. The greatest barrier to success is the same as it is for all things in schools: time. School leaders need to provide collaborative planning time for teachers creating a Core Curriculum, and there needs to be commitment to carving out time in the school schedule for lessons to take place. A further challenge is to garner the support of all stakeholders in valuing the curriculum: relatively easy when it comes to teachers, who recognise that ATL skill development and interdisciplinary transference are vital for success in the DP. Parents, if fully informed of the content of the curriculum and the benefits to their children, typically support the implementation of skills development. The toughest to convince are students, who can struggle to see the value of anything that does not clearly have a grade attached to it, or is not mandated by IB. This is the value of integrating CAS, TOK and the Extended Essay into the Core Curriculum, rather than only developing a skills class. The team in this case study provided many opportunities for students to be part of building the curriculum by seeking frequent feedback through surveys and small group discussions. We asked students what they believed was working, what was useful and what needed adapting. The shared ownership of the new course, with some responsibility placed on students to improve it for the following cohort, helped gain their support for Core Curriculum as a class.

This chapter began with a metaphor likening the core of the DP to the abdominal muscles of our bodies and suggested that, like our abdominal muscles, if we want strong students in TOK, in the Extended Essay, in CAS and in their DP subjects, then we have to specifically train the core muscles of the ATL skills. Through the development of a holistic curriculum focused on connecting the core elements of the DP to each other and to the subjects, it is possible to strengthen student understanding of abstract concepts, to help them apply these concepts to real-life situations, and to prepare them for the next stage of their lives with the skills needed for lifelong success in learning.